Buffer States
in World Politics

About the Book and Editors

Buffer states—countries geographically and/or politically situated between two or more regional or global powers—function to maintain peace between the larger powers. Contributors to this book, the first devoted to the buffer state concept, analyze the geographical and political factors necessary for the establishment and maintenance of a buffer state and examine its role in helping to maintain world peace. The problems and prospects of buffer states and buffer zones and the multiple roles played by the buffer in international politics are also explored. Using information from a number of countries, including Lebanon, Afghanistan, Korea, and Uruguay, the contributors argue that the function of the buffer state has not diminished with the advance of modern technology, but that the prospects for a long life for any particular buffer state are tenuous. Nevertheless, they conclude that although the international benefits from any one buffer state tend to be short term, the continued existence of the system will be an important element in preventing armed conflict in many parts of the world.

John Chay is chairman and professor in the Department of History at Pembroke State University. **Thomas E. Ross** is professor of geography and chairman of the Department of Geology and Geography at Pembroke State University.

Buffer States
in World Politics

edited by John Chay
and Thomas E. Ross

Westview Press / Boulder and London

Westview Special Studies in International Relations

This Westview softcover edition was manufactured on our own premises using equipment and methods that allow us to keep even specialized books in stock. It is printed on acid-free paper and bound in softcovers that carry the highest rating of the National Association of State Textbook Administrators, in consultation with the Association of American Publishers and the Book Manufacturers' Institute.

Published in 1986 in the United States of America by Westview Press, Inc.; Frederick A. Praeger, Publisher; 5500 Central Avenue, Boulder, Colorado 80301

Library of Congress Cataloging-in-Publication Data
Buffer states in world politics.
  (Westview special studies in international relations)
  Includes index.
  1. Buffer states. 2. World Politics. I. Chay,
John.
II. Ross, Thomas (Thomas E.) III. Series.
JX1391.B84 1986   327.1′1   86-13318
ISBN 0-8133-7264-X

Printed and bound in the United States of America

∞ The paper used in this publication meets the requirements of the American National Standard for Permanence of Paper for Printed Library Materials Z39.48-1984.

6 5 4 3 2 1

For June and Cheryl

CONTENTS

TABLES AND FIGURES

Tables

Figures

PREFACE

Buffer states are countries geographically and/or politically situated between two or more large powers whose function is to maintain peace between the larger powers. This book is a study of the buffer state concept and its effect upon world political affairs and as such analyzes the geographical and political factors necessary for the establishment and maintenance of a buffer state and examines the importance of the buffer state in maintaining world peace.

A primary objective of this volume is to provide an examination of the conditions, problems, and prospects of buffer states and buffer zones. The major aspects of the study include a definition of the buffer system, an analysis of the structure and functions of the system, and studies of the roles played by the system. Accordingly, one important question to be raised is: what is the meaning of the buffer system and why are particular countries defined as buffers? Additionally, an effort will be made to clarify the nature, characteristics, structure, and operation of a buffer. The most important purpose of the book, however, is to provide a clear understanding of the multiple roles played by the system: hence, the roles of buffer states are studied in relation to specific regions and to the entire international political community. Both the negative and positive roles of the buffer will be explored and the future of the buffer concept will be evaluated.

The book grew out of two sessions of papers on buffer states presented at the 25th Annual Meeting of the International Studies Association in Atlanta, Georgia in March 1984. Chapters by John Chay, Joseph Maila, Joseph Tulchin, Sheridan Johns, and Thomas Ross were among the presentations in Atlanta that eventually were developed into chapters of this book. All the remaining chapters were written especially for this book and have not been published elsewhere. In compiling this volume we have attempted to collect articles that discuss aspects of the "buffer state concept" from several different scholarly points of view. Contributors come from various disciplines, including history, geography, and political science. The diversity of the material should enable many social scientists to find pertinent information relevant to their particular field of study and will be particularly beneficial in the study of geopolitics. To this end several case studies illustrating the role of and effectiveness of buffer states are presented.

We wish to express our appreciation to the authors of the chapters included and to colleagues and others who gave valuable suggestions and assistance. We thank Professor Elizabeth Kuo, of the Pembroke State University Department of Geology and Geography, for drafting a map used in this book. Other Pembroke State colleagues to whom we are grateful include Professors Thomas Leach of the Department of Communicative Arts and Barney Pauze of the Department of Sociology. Both read and made comments on one or more of the chapters in this book. Professor D. Gordon Bennett, of the Department of Geography, the University of North Carolina at Greensboro, is also acknowledged for his valuable comments on some of the works in this volume, as is Professor Emeritus Shannon McCune of the University of Florida. We are also indebted to Professor Mickey East of George Washington University. Shirley Deese, secretary in the History Department at Pembroke State University, is thanked and commended for all the typing and clerical assistance she provided. We appreciate the fine typesetting and layout work of Betty Evans, Alice Britt, and Roy Barnhill. We are grateful to editors Bruce Kellison and Barbara Ellington at Westview Press for their encouragement and assistance in this project. And finally, Cheryl Ross is thanked for proofreading assistance. The editors and contributors alone are responsible for errors, omissions, and interpretations presented in the book.

John Chay
Thomas E. Ross

Pembroke State University
Pembroke, North Carolina

INTRODUCTION

John Chay
Thomas E. Ross

All of the earth's surface has, with few exceptions such as Antarctica, been subdivided into political units referred to as *states.* Since the most important part of the state is land area (territory), mankind has developed many schemes to maintain or expand state territory. Usually, expansionistic activities involve armed conflict or the threat of force. Thus an everpresent risk of military confrontation exists between states, especially among those who share a common border. To reduce the risk some ancient powers created unpopulated "waste" zones between the two powers. Another buffer scheme, used by Rome, involved the establishment of zones called *march states* to keep unfriendly forces away from Roman territory. In more recent times, particularly in the late nineteenth and early twentieth centuries, the buffer state idea grew in popularity as a means to keep hostile neighbors from engaging in military activities against each other. In many instances, however, the buffer was not a permanent solution to the adversarial nature of neighboring states and many of the buffers were eventually absorbed by other states. The disappearance of the buffer condition in a country has in the past led to conflict, such as that in what is now North and South Korea and what was North and South Vietnam, both of which have recently served as buffers.

But what exactly is a buffer state or buffer system? The buffer state, as a concept, is not new, although the term *buffer state* is relatively recent, probably being first applied by the British in 1883 to refer to Afghanistan. The buffer concept, or "buffer effect," as used by Knudsen in this volume, is probably as old as mankind's endeavors to delimit territory based upon sovereignty of the earth's surface (see Ross' chapter in this volume). In a real sense, the buffer phenomenon is a universal one as humankind has been, in

1

all parts of the world, ingenious in creating all kinds of cushions of buffers to serve as protective mechanisms.

Before proceeding further, let us provide a clarification of the terms *buffer state* and *buffer system,* both used throughout this book. Although similar in several respects, each term possesses distinguishing characteristics. Most importantly, though, they are similar in that *buffer* refers to regions or zones situated between conflicting spheres of influence and whose primary function is to separate the conflicting sides and thus reduce the likelihood of physical (military) contact. The simplest defintion of a buffer state is that it is a small independent country located between two or more large rival powers. This definition can be elaborated as much as one wishes, but it contains the three crucial elements of the buffer state: (1) A small country, in area and population, (2) Two or more large, adjacent rival powers, and (3) the geographical location of the small state between the opposing large powers. In our interpretation a buffer state denotes a country in a buffer situation while the buffer system refers to any level of political organization, whether a portion of a single state, a group of countries, or a large regional area of continental proportions such as Eastern Europe or Middle America. The buffer state is thus more confined and definite while the buffer system is more broad and general.

Today many of the political trouble spots found on the earth once functioned as buffers between greater powers, but with the removal of buffer status internal, as well as external, factions were allowed to exert their dormant hostilities. Places such as Lebanon, Iran, and Iraq in the Middle East; Korea, Afghanistan, and Cambodia in Asia; Poland and other Soviet satellites in Eastern Europe; El Salvador, Nicaragua, and other countries in Middle America; and South Africa and her neighbors in southern Africa are among the most obvious areas of political and military conflict. What is disturbing about the unrest in these places is that it is not momentary, but appears to be, in most cases, a perennial political problem with the potential to grow into conflicts involving the superpowers. Thus political leaders and scholars must study and analyze the conditions in these trouble spots that are producing threats to world political stability and impacting upon international relations. They must also determine if buffer states are a useless relic on the international political landscape or do they continue to have important functions to perform in modern international relations.

Several questions emerge in an attempt to study the world's political "hot spots." First, does a system or method of analysis exist that would allow us to gain a better understanding of these places? Are common cultural, political, strategic, or economic factors present in all the troubled places? Or is there a similarity in relative (vicinal) location? Are the trouble spots about the same size in terms of population and land area? These and similar questions emerge in a study of international relations, especially in the context of the above mentioned "trouble spots."

We have in this volume attempted to develop an explanatory framework with emphasis on buffer states in order to provide a better understanding of how international relations are affected by areas of conflict such as those mentioned above. As a matter of fact, many of the "regional trouble spots" discussed during the November 1985 summit meeting of President Reagan and General Secretary Gorbachev are or have been buffer states.

Our hope for this volume is that it will provide a better understanding, through an examination of the buffer state concept, of the common problems experienced in politically troubled areas. The particular objectives of this volume are to explain the structure and operation of the buffer state, the roles of the buffer for international relations, and future prospects of the buffer concept. To enhance our understanding of the subject we must examine the nature, characteristics, and structure of the buffer state. To these ends we have included review and theoretical essays as well as case studies of several conspicuous buffer states/systems.

Absolute location (the actual geographic position according to longitude and latitude) is very important in the buffer concept; however, the most fundamental and basic component of the buffer state is vicinal location, which is more fully discussed in a following chapter. It is important to recognize that although modern transportation and military technology have greatly affected the value of geographical location (aircraft and missiles can fly over the buffer to reach the enemy), vicinal location has not been substantially altered. Even as the distance between opposing powers is being reduced by modern technology, the buffer remains as a moderating influence in regions of conflict and a potent peacekeeping force regardless of the ability of its neighbors to destroy it or each other. The buffer is in a precarious situation, then, and cannot remove itself from this position. But the situation is not just spatial; it can be conceptual. For example, the buffers between two major ideological camps - capitalism and communism - can be found anywhere on the globe and do not necessarily have to be geographically located between the two conflicting ideologies. However, such a conceptual buffer does not limit the importance of the locational factor.

In addition to the locational factor, a number of secondary elements are involved in the origin and maintenance of a buffer state/system and are more fully discussed in the following chapter. One is the topography of the state, including such elements as marshes, mountains, deserts, and other physical barriers. Another factor of considerable significance is the strategic value of the buffer region because of the existence of important transportation lines, natural resources, and other industrially and militarily strategic resources. If the physical barrier is an inhibiting or repelling factor, it is attractive in terms of the development of a buffer. The third secondary factor involves cultural and economic considerations. The buffer state is not just a highway for the "king's men and horses," but it becomes a highway for cultural and economic interaction between the various social groups living in the region. Chay's chapter on Korea focuses on this element. He points out that with a "new age" comes a new product; for example, the post-World War Two era produced a new element for the buffer system - one clearly involved with primarily ideological ramifications rather than competition for land or resources. He points out that wherever tyrannical communism and democracy come in contact, an invisible barrier is erected, and sometimes it is even more manifested in visible barriers such as the infamous Berlin wall. But if the barrier is invisible it is more difficult to deal with effectively and becomes extremely formidable.

Another important element relevant to the effectiveness of the buffer is the condition of power distribution among the political entities involved - usually the buffer state and its two neighboring powers. The buffer situation cannot evolve and exist even if the location factor and secondary factors are present unless the power distribution within the above mentioned three political entities is divided in a particular way. To clarify, there are at least three aspects of power distribution which must be considered. The first is that the buffer state should be smaller and weaker than the two neighboring big powers. The buffer state, however, does not necessarily have to be small; it could be a middle sized or even a large state but the key is that the buffer must be smaller and weaker than the two neighboring powers. If the state located between the two powers is stronger and larger than the powers it will become a "middle kindgom" rather than a buffer state. In other words, the two neighboring powers should be more powerful than the middle state. The second condition is that the middle state should have strength adequate to maintain self-determination. The buffer then must be strong enough to absorb shock exerted by the neighboring large powers yet remain independent. If the buffer is too weak it will either be destroyed or become incapable of executing its buffer role. History provides numerous instances in which expansionistic neighboring powers intervened in the affairs of buffer states because of the weakness of the buffer. The excuse provided by the powers was that since the buffer was so weak it could no longer function as a bufer and therefore threatened the power's security. The result of intervention usually was the demise of the buffer. The third condition is that the two big powers must maintain an approximate parity or balance of power. In addition to the balance of power, a balance of interests is vitally important because power without an interest will not exhibit any influence in international relations. One of the best illustrations of the need for a balance of power and a balance of interest is Korea. When the power balance there broke down twice near the turn of the century (in 1895 and 1905 at the end of the Sino-Japanese War and Russo-Japanese War, respectively) the buffer system disappeared and with it Korea's independence. Chay develops this concept more fully in his chapter on Korea.

In addition to the structural nature of the buffer system, an understanding of the operational characteristics, or foreign policy operations, is also important. The most important element in this category is neutrality. Unless a certain degree of neutrality is maintained by a state it cannot effectively operate as a buffer. There is, however, a large gray zone between the black and white of strict neutrality and close or overly friendly relationship with one of the two neighboring powers. Joseph Maila, in his chapter in this volume, differentiates neutrality into four categories: (1) sovereign neutrality, (2) neutralization or multilateral declaration of neutrality, (3) legal neutrality, and (4) pragmatic neutrality. Thus it may be hypothesized that a buffer state plays its buffer role to the limit or extent of its neutrality. Once it begins to deviate from its neutral position the buffer role is compromised and when or if it allies itself with one of its powerful neighbors its value as a buffer terminates. Leaning toward or establishing closer relations with one of the powers is a delicate game for the buffer state, but it does have advantages as well as risks.

Some buffer states have deviated from neutrality by turning to and forming an alliance with a third power located outside the immediate region. This ploy has its own set of risks. For example, it is not easy for the third power, especially if it is located a long distance from the buffer, to generate sufficient interest in a country, especially a country in a buffer situation; however, if the buffer is fortunate enough to secure a "third power" benefactor there always exists the danger that another "third power" may be brought in and the buffer state may find itself in an even more complicated predicament in which it must deal not with just two rival powers, but with two sets or four powers. For example, presently, wherever the Soviet Union becomes involved in the Third World - Africa, the Middle East, or Middle America - the United States finds it necessary to become involved in the same area and *vice versa.*

Many questions arise concerning the operational aspect of the buffer system. Perhaps most important is what is the role of the buffer system for modern world society? Is it positive or negative? Also, what is the role of the buffer effect for the buffer state and how does it affect the buffer?

As observed earlier, the fact that most of the world's trouble spots are or have been buffers seems to indicate that the buffer states are among the most unfortunate of all states. However, careful analysis reveals that the unfortunate situation comes mainly from the vicinal location factor and not from the act or function of being a buffer. Thus a state with the "bad luck" of being located between two warring powers is more likely to be involved because of its location than for any other reason. Actually, successful playing of the buffer role means neutrality, strength, and independence for the state and increases the likelihood that it will not become involved in disputes involving its powerful neighbors. A state in the buffer situation does not appear to have any meaningful choice; it has to do its best to play the assigned role of peacekeeper. Successful functioning of the buffer system also makes an important contribution to the system itself by lessening the probability of conflict between the two neighboring powers or groups of powers. If the buffer fails to function, it becomes a transport route for the invasion forces or a battleground for its strong neighbors. This is what happened to Belgium during two world wars. We must keep in mind, though, that if the two powers are determined to fight, the buffer system is not an effective deterrent. But, if the pressure or shock coming from either side is relatively small and manageable, the buffer state is capable of playing its role and making an important peacekeeping contribution to the region and hence the world. We conclude that the buffer system has a definite limit, in terms of its effectiveness, but within those limits it can and should play a positive role in international relations.

Few would deny that many buffer states and buffer systems have served well as peacekeepers, but the major question today is are buffers still a valid force in international relations in terms of preventing hostilities between major powers? Many of the following chapters focus on this important question. Here the key is on the role of modern and future technology for the operation of the system. An important fact is that technological impact has limits, and at least the locational factor will remain in the future much as it has been in the past. If the locational factor remains stable, the buffer system will also remain stable far into the future. future.

The book consists of an introduction section and twelve chapters, including a conclusions chapter. A geographic portrayal of buffer states, past and present, is the focus of Chapter 1. Definitions of states, territories, and buffer states and their functions are provided as a general review to the evolution and maintenance of buffer states. Chapter 2 continues the review, but is centered upon the political perspective of buffer state sovereignty. Seminal ideas related to buffers are presented in Chapter 3 in which a non-traditional concept, that all buffer states do not have to be located between other states to keep states apart but can be used to separate races of mankind, is presented by using the "homelands" of South Africa. This is followed by another provocative essay in which Middle America is defined as a buffer between the Soviet Union and the United States. Part Two is composed of essays on the historical and strategic roles of various regions and states as buffer zones. Emphasis is upon the particular historical and political factors relevant to the development and maintenance of the buffer condition in the areas studied.

NOTES

1. Michael G. Partem, "The Buffer System in International Relations," *The Journal of Conflict Resolution,* 27 (1983) : 13-16.

PART 1
REVIEW AND THEORY

CHAPTER 1
BUFFER STATES:
A GEOGRAPHER'S PERSPECTIVE

THOMAS E. ROSS

Many countries have served as buffer states since the evolution of the state concept early in mankind's recorded history. Where and why they came to be is, of course, clearly within the scope of the discipline of geography. Few geographers have, however, generated published works concerned specifically with buffer states. Most of the references in the geographic literature have been brief discussions within a broader topic, such as boundary or frontier studies.

The primary purpose of this chapter is to present one geographer's perception of buffer states. Identification of some past and present buffer states and factors important in their evolution will be discussed from that geographer's point of view.

THE STATE IDEA

Understanding of buffer states is predicated upon knowledge of the state concept itself. The following synopsis of the state idea is presented as a prelude to the buffer state discussion.

All states, buffer and nonbuffer, are creations of mankind and, as such, are depicted on maps as territory enclosed by boundary lines established by man. States are, to the geographer, however, much more than portions of the earth's surface in which human beings have established a way of life - a culture - that may or may not be similar to that of their neighbors. It is important to realize that the state is not just people, but is territory with a distinct homogeneous core and from this core extends into marginal areas of heterogeneity.[1]

Although many characteristics are ubiquitous to all countries, others are found in some but not in other states, a fact which helps make one unique and different from all others. The geographer, therefore, is concerned with the state as a whole, with the synthesis of physical and cultural phenomena that together constitute it, and with the characteristics that make it distinct from all the others. He is also interested in the location of the state and how this location affects its relations with other states.

Grounded upon the premise that all states include territory and population, geographers look at territory as more than merely a piece of real estate or an area of land inhabited by *homo sapiens sapiens.* Area by itself does not constitute territory, especially if territory is regarded as land which is inhabited "and to whose intrinsic value man has added an extrinsic value of his own."[2] Along this line of reasoning, Jean Gottmann defined territory as "a spatial notion establishing essential links between politics, people, and the natural setting" and he perceived territory "as the unit in the political organization of space that defines, at least for a time, the relationships between the community and its habitat on one hand, the community and its neighbors on the other. . . ."[3] Thus, the components of any state are territory and a human society which has organized an independent government to occupy and exercise sovereignty over the territory.

Hence, the state can be defined as a politico-geographical phenomenon whose relationships with other countries are based upon the sovereignty of its population over the territory.[4] More importantly, though, is the reality that the population must believe its state has a reason to exist. If that reason evolves from within the boundaries of the state territory, that is, has its roots among the state's populace, the state may be more likely to remain viable than if the reason for its existence is externally derived. The importance attached to internal forces of creation and the strength of conviction of the inhabitants to support the state was emphasized by Derwent Whittlesey when he wrote:[5]

> Because every infant is born into a state, mankind grows up with an unreasoned conviction that his country or people is immutable, a force inseparably linked to a specific portion of the earth's surface. This feeling transformed into argument underlies many of the attempts to make political geography to serve the purposes of this or that particular state ...
> The brutal, temporary dissection of territory incidental to warfare, and the more permanent and hardly less rude dismemberment produced by

dictated peace terms do not dislodge this faith that the state is inherently entitled to its proper space, to its 'place in the sun.' Even the stubborn fact that two different states may lay equal claim to the same border zone fails to undermine the devotion of the opposing nationals to their respective articles of faith.

Closely associated with the reason for existence is the idea that all the diverse territorial regions within the state must be unified into a single organized political unit if the state is to prevail. It is important to realize that regional differences in physiography, climate, or mineral deposits rarely are directly responsible for serious problems within a state. Neither are regional disparities in economic production a major barrier to unification. In fact, regional diversity in economic development may in some instances "stimulate interchange and so encourage interregional coherence. Marked differences in regional economic levels may lead to more serious difficulties, not as economic problems but rather as social problems - i.e., results of differences in human attitudes."[6] Within the state, racial or ethnic group differences are not problems unless the diverse groups hold negative attitudes in regard to the racial or ethnic differences present in the state. Also of considerable importance is the fact that the citizens of a state must possess or accept a common body of political attitudes - a political ideology that supercedes differences in languages and racial-ethnic background. Moreover, an independent state must be capable of operating as a unified unit in its external relations or "it may disintegrate and vanish from the map."[7] To ensure its existence, a state must have the resources and desire among its populace to implement and execute the purposes for which it was created. Therefore, each state must develop purposes which are based upon its own unique circumstances and which are acceptable to the great majority of its inhabitants. These purposes, "with which the citizens of the state can identify themselves, constitutes the state idea."[8] It is within this framework that all states, buffer and nonbuffer, must operate to remain as independent political entities.

THE BUFFER STATE CONCEPT

One of the most geographically significant factors in the study of buffer states is their location in reference to their neighbors, or vicinal location. In general, we can utilize three "methods of expressing the geographical location of a specified place or area:

(1) in terms of degree of latitude and longitude; (2) in terms of its relation to water bodies and land masses; and (3) in terms of its position with reference to its immediate neighbors (vicinal location)."⁹ The generally accepted notion is that buffer states owe their existence to the location of two or more politically or militarily powerful spheres of influence within close proximity to each other and that these opposing powers, in an effort to maintain peace, may cooperate in the establishment of an independent state to separate their interests. In other instances, secondary factors, not just simply location between two powers, usually were associated with creation of buffer states or buffer zones. Such factors would include: (1) hostile physical environments, such as deserts, marshlands, or rugged terrain; (2) the presence within their territory of strategically important transportation routes; and (3) the existence of zones of cultural transition.

In the first case, the country may have become a buffer state because the states which grew up around isolated and environmentally hostile territory chose to not absorb the undesirable area into their political territory, leaving it instead as a "no-man's land" until finally it came to be used as a buffer to separate its neighbors. A state could also evolve into a buffer in a region if strategic transportation routes passed through its territory; thus neighboring states unable, because of the strength of another neighboring power, to lay sole claim to the important routes would accept the presence of an independent buffer state with sovereignty over the plains, passes, and rivers connecting the opposing spheres of influence. Closely related to and influenced by the location of strategic transportation gateways is the multicultural character of many buffer states. The buffer area might be populated by and located between two distinctly different cultural spheres, in part because of its function as a strategic transportation route. Thus the buffer might possess linguistic, ethnic, and religious characteristics of both cultures and thus serve as a transition area not incorporated into the state area of either of its neighbors because neither state wishes to become entangled with the possibility of irredentist activities by the minority segment of its population; a minority that would result from the incorporation of the buffer zone in one of the existing states. Thus the multicultural aspect of many buffer states can be attributed to their location at continental or axial positions; buffer states not located thusly will most likely have a more homogeneous population than states located in zones of intense and frequent intercultural contact.

Regardless of the secondary factors, vicinal location is of utmost importance in the creation of buffer states. Thus geographers accept that a buffer state is a country located between two or more powerful states or spheres of influence and whose continued existence as an independent country is tolerated because it serves to spatially separate the powerful states.[10] According to Nicholas Spykman, "When . . . pressures are approximately equal, and it still proves difficult to arrive at a stable common frontier, a buffer state provides a certain degree of security for both sides by acting as a neutral zone, and functions as a keeper of the peace by affecting at least temporarily physical separation of the potential combatants."[11]

One example of how buffer states were established to maintain peace is the agreement between the British and Russians concerning India and Southwest Asia. The Anglo-Russian accords were developed because Russia was, in the nineteenth century, extending its influence into Central Asia and was thus exerting pressure upon the British controlled Indian frontier, which was at best weakly held by the British. According to Spykman, in his discussion of this agreement:[12]

> British and Russian influence clashed in Afghanistan, Persia, and Turkestan, where each power was trying to establish its own domination in order to check the advance of the other. Boundary agreements between 1887 and 1889 offered no final solution, and it was not until the Anglo-Russian agreement of 1907 that danger of a conflict was finally past. This agreement recognized Afghanistan as a British sphere of influence, and divided Persia into three zones, the northern to be a Russian sphere of influence, the southeastern a British sphere, and the third a neutral zone between the other two.

Although the British-Russian agreement prevented hostilities between the two powers, peace is not always achieved by the creation of a buffer state. In some cases, the buffer becomes a battleground between opposing forces, as for example, Poland, whose vicinal location unfortunately made it a zone of conflict between the countries situated on opposite sides of it. However, regardless of the importance of vicinal location, buffer states are not maintained simply because of their location. Some have, with the passage of time, outgrown buffer state status and remain independent because the will of the people to retain autonomy is firmly held by the general populace. Finland, for example, has remained free partly because of its fiercely independent-minded citizenry.[13]

Ideally, buffer states are not satellite or puppet states of either of their powerful neighbors, nor are they necessarily strictly neutral states. The concept of a buffer state:[14]

> in presupposing a free and effective organism in the region interposed, rules out partition or any form of breakup enforced by the great powers on either flank. Indeed, the small states most notable in history for contributing towards the successful maintenance of equilibrium between powerful neighbors are made up of an amalgam of the peoples, languages and traditions surrounding them.

Thus, many buffer states can be classed as zones of cultural transition and "as such partake of the cultural and ideological patterns on either side of them."[15] In short, buffer states absorb the shock exerted, whether it is cultural, political, or military, by the powers on its borders. It appears, however, that in terms of buffer states, vicinal location is the most significant factor in the states origin and continued existence and that the population of the state must work within this context in formulating their purposes and reasons for existence.

To acquire a geographic perspective on buffer states, it is important to take into account that we are dealing with human beings residing within a specific territory that must adjust to the powers surrounding them. Also, innumerable combinations of physical and cultural phenomena are possible that could affect the growth and wellbeing of the state. Thus knowledge of the physical and cultural environments present in buffer states is necessary in any geographical analysis of buffers.

EARLY BUFFER STATES

The term *buffer* was first applied to a political entity in 1876; *buffer state* was first used in 1883.[16] The buffer state concept, however, is not a nineteenth century development. Its roots reach back about 3500 years, to the fifteenth century B.C., when the Kingdom of Kadesh was established on the Orontes River of Syria by the king of Mitanni to keep the Egyptians away from his territory in the Euphrates River region (Fig. 1.1). Fifteen hundred years later, Pompey, in an attempt to secure a neutral zone between Rome and Persia, used Syria as a buffer.[17]

The world's earliest states, for security reasons utilized transition or border zones to spatially separate themselves. For the most part, these were sparsely populated or uninhabited areas that Spykman referred to as "waste border zones."[18] In time, because of

Fig. 1.1

The Middle East, circa 1400 A.D.

Source: Modified from R.R. Palmer, ed., *Atlas of World History* (New York: Rand McNally, 1957).

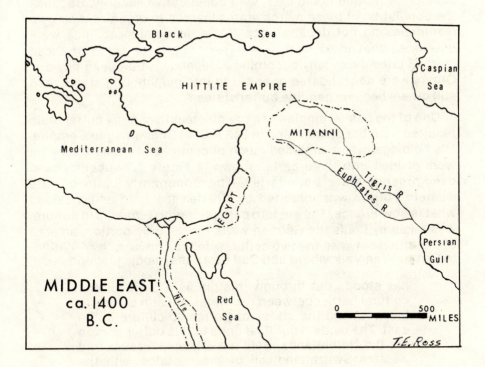

population pressure on and population growth in the natural waste zones, they became ineffective as buffers and were supplemented by artificially created waste zones. The Greek city-states probably created the first man-made waste zones. Rome followed suit when she "transformed twenty-three Volscian cities into the Pontine marshes and destroyed the towns of Latium in order to surround herself with waste territory."[19]

The Romans eventually used the wastelands concept to create *march* states, which were primarily military outposts with few civilians, whose prime responsibility and function was to guard the frontier of the Roman empire. The march states were expected to utilize their own resources to ensure that the built-up territory behind the frontier could exist with comparative security. Because the population of these march states learned to organize their own resources and not depend upon Rome, leadership abilities were developed that most likely were responsible for some of these march states eventually becoming independent European powers. Others were consolidated or annexed into neighboring states, and still others became genuine buffer states.[20]

One of the best examples of a pre-nineteenth century buffer state resulted from the dismantling in 843 A.D. of Charlemagne's empire. His holdings, which included much of central and western Europe, were divided into three parts, shown in Figure 1.2 superimposed over present state boundaries. The dominantly Latin culture western portion was inherited by Charles the Bald and included what is now France. The eastern part, primarily Germanic in culture, was taken by Louis the German while the "middle portion, an area of transition between the two cultures, fell to Lothair I."[21] According to Samuel Van Valkenburg and Carl Stotz, the middle kingdom:[22]

> has stood out through history as a physical and cultural barrier between the states of Latin culture in the west and the states of Germanic culture in the east. The modern political units in this buffer portion are the Netherlands, Belgium, Alsace-Lorraine, and western Switzerland; all of these states with the exception of Switzerland, have been the scenes of many wars. Except for Alsace-Lorraine, which is a part of France, all of them are still independent.

One note of clarification: western Switzerland did not evolve into a separate state but merged with other territories to form the present-day country of Switzerland.

Fig. 1.2
Partition of Charlemagne's Empire

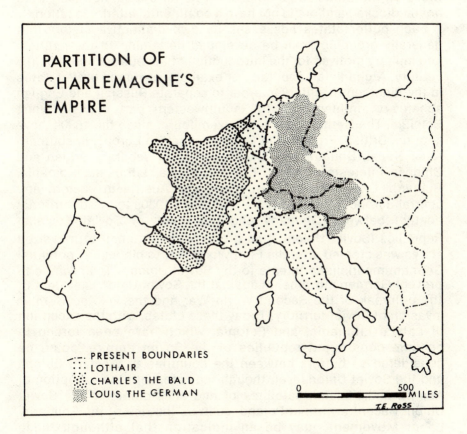

PARTITION OF
CHARLEMAGNE'S
EMPIRE

PRESENT BOUNDARIES
LOTHAIR
CHARLES THE BALD
LOUIS THE GERMAN

0   500
■■■■■■MILES

T.E. ROSS

TWENTIETH CENTURY BUFFER STATES

Of the 200 or so national political entities on the planet today, at least thirty-two have at some period during this century served as buffer states (Table 1.1). Most buffer states of the twentieth century can be characterized as possessing an interior location, especially those on the Eurasian landmass. All buffer states, however, were not landlocked and/or did not have a continental interior location.

Each buffer states possesses its own distinctive history, but generally groupings can be developed pertaining to the political and military motives for the introduction of the buffer condition in a country. Afghanistan and Iran, for example, assumed buffer status in the nineteenth century in order to separate Russian and English spheres of influence in the southwestern part of Asia while Belgium, The Netherlands, and Luxembourg, since the 1580s, have kept the British, French, and Germans apart in Europe. In southern Asia, Nepal, Bhutan, and Sikkim served to separate British and Chinese interests. Finland, Estonia, Latvia, Lithuania, Romania, Bulgaria, Czechoslovakia, Hungary, and Austria in eastern and central Europe were used in the 1920s and 1930s to avoid territorial contact between Germany and the Union of Soviet Socialist Republics (Soviet Union). This group of rather small to mid-sized states was created after the First World War to hinder any potential German imperialistic threats to the Soviet Union.[23] Their failure to prevent German movements against the Soviet Union is evident by the outbreak of the Second World War and the ill-fated German invasion of Soviet territory. Today these states, with the exception of Latvia, Lithuania, and Estonia, which have been forced to become constituent republics of the Soviet empire, could be considered as buffers between the countries of Western Europe and the Soviet Union, even though they are, with the exception of Austria and Finland, satellites of and subordinate to the Soviet Union. Recent events in Poland, such as the rise of the Solidarity Labor Movement, may be an indication that although these countries are under the control of the Soviet Union, they may not necessarily be counted as totally supportive of the imperialistic, expansionistic, and totalitarian objectives of the Soviet Union. Although Poland, Romania, Hungary, and Yugoslavia appear at times to be at odds with Soviet policies, the Soviets have shown that they still possess great control and influence over the countries of Eastern Europe. For example, in 1984 a scheduled meeting between the heads of state of East Germany and West Germany was abruptly cancelled by the East German leader,

TABLE 1.1

TWENTIETH CENTURY BUFFER STATES

Country	Buffer Between
Afghanistan	Russia (prior to 1917) - England
Albania	Austria-Hungary - Russia; Italy - Austria-Hungary; Italy - Greece; Yugoslavia - Soviet bloc;
Angola	Republic of South Africa - black states of Africa
Austria	Germany - Union of Soviet Socialist Republics (USSR)
Belgium	England and France - Germany
Bhutan	England - China
Bulgaria	Germany - USSR
Cambodia	England - France
Czechoslovakia	Germany - USSR
Estonia	Germany - USSR
Finland	Germany - USSR
Hungary	Germany - USSR
Iran	England - Russia (prior to 1917)
Korea	Japan - China; Japan - Russia; United States - USSR
Latvia	Germany - USSR
Lebanon	Israel - Arab states
Lithuania	Germany - USSR
Luxembourg	England, France - Germany
Mongolia	Japan - USSR
Mozambique	South Africa - black states of Africa
Nepal	England - China
Netherlands, The	England, France - Germany
Pakistan	USSR - India
Poland	Germany - USSR
Rhodesia (Zimbabwe)	South Africa - black states of Africa
Romania	Germany - USSR
Sikkim	England - China
Switzerland	Northern - Southern European countries
Thailand	England - France
Tibet	England - China
Uruguay	Brazil - Argentina
Yugoslavia	Germany - USSR

presumably at the insistence of the Soviet Union. To the Soviet way of thinking a divided Germany and continued control over the countries of Eastern Europe are necessary for Soviet security as these states serve as a buffer between the Soviet Union and the countries of Western Europe and their American ally.

In Southeast Asia, portions of Thailand (Siam) were used in the twentieth century by the British and French to separate their respective spheres of influence in that region of the world. In 1907, the British and French agreed to a plan to establish a buffer in Thailand. According to the agreement, the territory west of the Menam River and the Gulf of Siam would be in the British zone and all lands to the east would be in the French zone of influence. After the First World War both countries recognized Thailand's independence.

Korea has been used by at least three Eurasian countries (Russia, Japan, and China) as a buffer state. It initially served as a buffer between Japan and China, later between Japan and Russia, and in more recent times between the Soviet Union and the United States.

Japan perceived Korea as an ideal buffer between herself and China until the Japanese victory in the Sino-Japanese War of (1894-95) ended Chinese influence on the Korean Peninsula. Problems between Japan and her Asian neighbors did not cease with victory over China, however. The Russians began to cast covetous eyes toward Japanese territory and Japan reacted by deciding that Korea once again should serve as buffer between her interests and the Russians. The role of Korea as a buffer between Asian powers ended with the Japanese victory over Russia in 1905 and the subsequent absorption of Korea into the Japanese Empire. At the conclusion of the Second World War, Korea was divided into two countries, North and South Korea. Since that time South Korea especially has served as a buffer between American and Soviet spheres of influence in Eastern Asia although she is closely allied with the Americans.

Mongolia, for a few years in 1930s, separated Japanese and Soviet interests on the Asian mainland. Other buffer states of the twentieth-century include Uruguay, separating Brazil and Argentina; in Africa, Zimbabwe (Rhodesia), Angola, and Mozambique have been used as buffers. The latter three were used in the 1960s to control contact between the Republic of South Africa and the militant, nationalistic, and usually Soviet supported states of Black Africa.

BUFFER STATE PHYSIOGRAPHY

The concept of a physical barrier between two or more antagonistic states appears to have developed early in man's political history. Early civilizations used, as have more recent societies, swampy or marshy lowlands, deserts, mountains, and rugged hill or plateau country as buffer zones. In many instances, independent states without a buffer function grew out of the desert and mountainous regions that served earlier as buffers, for example, Iran and Afghanistan. Of the thirty-two twentieth century buffer states identified in this chapter, twenty-six possess considerable territory that is either desert or highlands (hills, dissected plateaus, or mountains); this is, however, not meant to imply that the buffer condition evolved solely because of physiographic characteristics. Although spatial interaction in these areas was not prevented because of rugged terrain, it was severely constrained; thus terrain served as a temporary barrier and usually slowed military activities, thus serving to keep the peace. In some cases, though, the rough terrain within a region resulted in localized areas, particularly those with mountain passes or gaps, becoming focal points and transport crossroads for the surrounding regions. Afghanistan, Austria, and Yugoslavia are three excellent examples of a "crossroads" situation resulting from the rugged topography within a region. This meeting place of diverse cultures and the subsequent tardiness by the crossroads region to develop a strong sense of nation is one causal factor for the region evolving into or being utilized as a buffer.

Examination of the landsurface forms of buffer states indicates that many of them are located in areas that might be described as waste zones, such as deserts, hill country, or mountainous land. Most buffer states, however, regardless of their topography and other physical attributes, have in common the presence of strategically important transportation routes. Hence, the buffer state should be considered important in terms of neutralizing the use of strategic routes by opposing forces. In some instances the location of these strategic routes was perhaps more important in the creation of the buffer state than was the idea of a simple physical barrier. Furthermore, several buffer states have been the target of numerous invaders and have been conquered many times, especially those in lowland plains, such as Poland. The powerful neighbors, in many cases not wishing to risk having the buffer area come under the control of an enemy state, agreed to the formation of an independent state to act as a barrier and at the same time neutralize the strategic routes through the buffer zones. Also important is the fact that since many of these buffer areas have been frequently invaded, the population is an amalgam of different peoples who may have been perceived by the powerful neighbors as unable, because of their diversity, to create a nation unified or strong enough to challenge either of the neighboring powers. Thus because of the cultural heterogeneity of the buffer area resulting, in many cases, from the region's physiography, the neighboring powers held a synoecious attitude toward the buffer area and thusly independence was, if not assured, greatly encouraged by the powers.

ETHNIC GROUPS, RELIGIONS, AND
LANGUAGES OF BUFFER STATES

It would be expected that because of the transitional and border character of buffer states and the numerous invasions to which many of them have been subjected that a diverse ethnic situation would prevail. Furthermore, it is assumed that the inhabitants would follow a variety of religions and possess a polyglot of languages. Many buffer states do indeed possess great diversity of ethnic groups, languages, and religions. Much of this diversity can be attributed to the fact of location - that these states are at strategic points of contact between two diverse cultures or astride historic trade and/or invasion routes: thus many cultures have been introduced to these areas. The numerous cultural differences also may have worked to ensure the development and maintenance of the states and their subsequent buffer status. Because of their complex cultural nature, areas that became buffer states were probably deemed no threat to the adjacent states since it was thought by the powers that such an amalgam of cultures could never unite and form a viable nation unified enough to challenge the neighboring powers.

The development of buffer status in several states, namely Austria, Belgium, Bhutan, Iran, Nepal, The Netherlands, Poland, Romania, Switzerland, and Yugoslavia, owes much to their location as invasion routes or points of contact between differing peoples. Because these states were in strategic locations, the more powerful countries in the region agreed to or accepted the idea of an independent country located between the competing states. The continued existence of these states as independent entities rests upon their relations with their neighbors; relations which must not favor one or the other of the neighbors. The powers must view the buffer state as serving a useful purpose in keeping peace and ensuring that their interests are not compromised. If one of the powerful states separated by the buffer perceive an advantage in destroying the buffer there is little the buffer can do to prevent it. Sometimes when war occurs between the two powers, the buffer, because of its location between the warring states, is the first casualty. However, because of its location, during peactime the buffer is in a position to benefit economically because it may have extensive trade relations with both neighbors.

SUMMARY AND CONCLUSIONS

With the advent of highly sophisticated modern technological warfare one might argue that the reason for the existence of buffers has disappeared. It is accurate to say that jet bombers and intercontinental ballistic missiles have made the deserts, swamps, and mountains that for so long served as physical barriers to military movements immaterial to warfare if the concept of conventional warfare has been discarded by the countries of the world. None of us desire war, conventional or otherwise, but we must hope that if wars occur that they will remain of the conventional type, otherwise there is little future for the human race. Assuming that the potential for military conflicts will remain with us far into the future we must attempt to use all the resources available to prevent that potential from becoming reality: buffer states still are one important resource in keeping world peace.

Numerous instances could be cited of places and situations where a buffer state, in the traditional sense, would be beneficial. For example, evidently the demilitarized zone between North and South Korea, created in 1953, is effective, although somewhat tenuously. The countries of central and eastern Europe are still useful in preventing border skirmishes that could lead to a broader scale military conflict between Soviet and American-West European forces. Could not Aryan Iran and Arabic Iraq benefit from a buffer in their current conflict? And what about the Christians of Lebanon as a buffer between Israel and the Arab states? The idea of buffer states is old, but it apparently continues to have merit in many places and the concept should not be totally discarded simply because of the potential of high technology warfare in this latter part of the twentieth century.

In summary, a country with buffer state status is the result of two powerful states desiring a stable or neutral zone located between them. The buffer serves to keep the peace by functioning as a physical barrier between the potential combatants. Although buffer states have served as physical barriers, the geographer must examine more than such a single variable in his study of states. It is imperative that the geographer consider how all parts of the environment work together to create an end result. It has been established that buffer states are located between two unfriendly countries and are sometimes cursed, or, perhaps because of its role in their creation, blessed with a hostile physical environment. Parts of this same inhospitable environment may serve, however, as the major connection between the countries that desire spatial separation.

Thus it is evident that the location between two powers is of paramount importance in determining if a country is to function as a buffer state. The survival of buffers depends upon their ability to maintain peace between their neighbors and the willingness of their strong neighbors to resist any attempt at conquest of the buffer by another state. The buffer state, then, depends upon the ability of its neighbors for its defense because it usually is not strong enough to protect itself. The survival of the buffer state is, furthermore, enhanced by the opinion of the neighboring countries that it is in their best interests to have a small, weak neighbor rather than a large strong one that is antagonistic towards them. Thus relation with neighboring states is critical in the development and durability of states serving as buffers. The physical geography of the buffer is, however, a most important factor in that it may have served as a physical barrier separating the powerful states or served as a funnel of invasion that made the buffer states' vicinal location important to competing states within the region.

Contrary to what some believe, the usefulness of buffers is not an historical relic. Until mankind ceases to fight conventional wars and until political differences can be abolished or moderated, a need for buffer states or buffer zones will remain. With present technology, though, rugged or otherwise hostile terrain may not be a significant factor in determining the location of the buffer state: it may be more a political decision acceptable to all concerned without regard to the physical geography of the region.

In conclusion, the methods employed by geographers in the study of international relations results in several theses. According to Fitzgerald:[24]

(1) Geography establishes a close relationship between types of human organization and their environments,....

(2) The political pattern of the world is subject to ceaseless modification. . . .

(3) The interrelation of States becomes ever closer - though not necessarily more sympathetic - as man surmounts the geographical difficulties of distance, climate, and terrain. Political isolation is impossible today, as all states have been brought to realize.

NOTES

1. Preston E. James and Clarence F. Jones, eds., *American Geography: Inventory and Prospect* (Syracuse: Syracuse University Press, 1954), p. 216.

2. Y.M. Goblet, *Political Geography and the World Map* (New York: Frederick A. Praeger, 1955), p. 37.

3. Jean Gottmann, *The Significance of Territory* (Charlottesville: The University Press of Virginia, 1973), p. ix.

4. W.A. Douglas Jackson, ed., *Politics and Geographic Relationships: Readings on the Nature of Political Geography* (Englewood Cliffs: Prentice-Hall, Inc., 1964). p. 87.

5. Derwent Whittlesey, *The Earth and the State: A Study of Political Geography* (New York: Henry Holt and Company, 1944), p. 8.

6. Richard Hartshorne, "Morphology of the State Area: Significance of the State," in *Essays on Political Geography,* edited by Charles A. Fisher (London: Metheun and Company, 1968) p. 29.

7. James and Jones, p. 192.

8. Preston E. James, "Some Fundamental Elements in the Analysis of the Viability of States," in *Essays on Political Geography,* edited by Charles A. Fisher (London: Metheun and Company, 1968), p. 33.

9. Samuel Van Valkenburg and Carl L. Stotz, *Elements of Political Geography* 2nd. edition. (Englewood Cliffs: Prentice-Hall, Inc. 1954), p. 41.

10. J.R.V. Prescott, *Political Geography* (London: Metheun and Company, 1972), p. 59; and Nicholas John Spykman, "Frontiers, Security, and International Organization," *Geographical Review,* 32 (1942):440.

11. Nicholas John Spykman and Abbie A. Rollins, "Geographic Objectives in Foreign Policy," *The American Political Science Review,* 33 (1939):410.

12. *Ibid.,* p. 405.

13. Hans W. Weigert and others, *Principles of Political Geography* (New York: Appleton-Century-Crofts, Inc., 1952), p. 176.

14. "Buffer States: Their Historic Service to Peace," *Round Table,* 45 (1955):341.

15. Samuel Van Valkenburg and Carl L. Stotz, p. 51.

16. J. Murray and others, eds., *The Oxford English Dictionary* (Oxford: The Clarendon Press, 1933), volume 1, p. 127 and p. 1158.

17. Spykman and Rollins, p. 406.

18. *Ibid.,* p. 396.

19. *Ibid.,* pp. 396-97.

20. *Ibid.,* p. 403.

21. Van Valkenburg and Stotz, p. 51.

22. *Ibid.*, p. 52.

23. Lucile Carson, *Geography and World Politics* (Englewood Cliffs: Prentice-Hall, Inc., 1958), p. 32.

24. W. Fitzgerald, "Geography and International Settlement," *Nature,* 152 (1943): 589-590.

CHAPTER 2
BUFFER STATES:
THE ISSUE OF SOVEREIGNTY

JOSEPH MAILA

No attempts have been made to develop a general theory of the buffer state. The subject has always been studied within the framework of case studies relating to foreign policies of small and/or various buffer states.[1] This approach appears to leave unanswered many questions regarding the general nature and patterns of behavior of buffer states.

A general theory would initially have to address such issues in a very precise way. The intent of this paper is not to look to the requisite issues of a general theory of buffer states, but to look at buffer states from the specific view point of sovereignty status. Our argument is that buffer states are states in which the issue of sovereignty is at stake. By viewing it from this perspective we are not *only* trying to put the problem into a new framework, but we are also aiming at providing a typology of the buffer state's behavior.

GEOGRAPHY AND SOVEREIGNTY OF BUFFERS: THE COMPLEXITY OF THE DEFINITIONAL PROBLEM

Previous definitions of buffer states have emphasized their spatial location between two or more powerful states. P.B. Potter for example wrote that the term buffer state is "often used to describe a weak state, small in size, probably without foreign policy."[2] Mathisen, on the other hand, considers a buffer state as "a small independent state lying between two larger, usually rival, states (or block of states)."[3] In both definitions, the geographical criterium is combined with the political one.

The buffer state is indeed a small state sandwiched between two or more powerful neighbors. It is clear, however, that neither geography nor politics alone can qualify a state as a buffer state.

Neither Switzerland nor Lebanon is similar to Poland in terms of geographical size, yet they are, or were, as in the case of Switzerland, buffer states. On the other hand, Belgium and Holland are small states, but they cannot presently be considered buffers because of the lack of rivalry among their neighbor states. Thus, it is not only the power of geography that establishes a state as a buffer, it is also the geography of power which determines whether a state can be classified as a buffer.

The distribution of power within the regional context, i.e., balance of power among the rival states, creates the conditions for emergence of buffer entities.[4] Alternatively, the modification which may occur within the regional context of power may bring about a drastic change within the nature of the buffer state and make it lose its buffer zone status. Belgium, for example, has been for a long time a buffer state between Germany and France. However, the emergence of a new European order after World War Two created a situation in which Belgium was no longer a buffer.

Variations in the relationships between the neighbors of buffer states help to explain the changing nature of buffers. When rivalry increases between two or more powerful states surrounding a third smaller one, the latter is caught in a difficult situation where its weakness becomes evident. As a small state, a buffer is not able to change the policy of other states, and is frequently not strong enough to oppose such policies. As D. Vital explains: "the measure of state's power is the capacity of government to induce other states - or governments - to follow lines of conduct or foreign policy which they might otherwise not pursue; alternatively it is the capacity to withstand the pressure of other states or governments - which are intent on deflecting it from a course which the national interest - or the interests of its leader - would appear to require."[5] Therefore, unless the buffer state succeeds in remaining neutral, its sovereignty is threatened and at times its very existence is placed in jeopardy.

The buffer state may be compelled in certain situations to form an alliance with one of its neighboring powers. It may accept military presence on its territory and align itself with that of the strongest neighbor. However, the buffer state might be exposed to a far more dramatic situation where its unity may be endangered, and the country may be divided, as for example, Germany and Korea. Furthermore, a buffer state may no longer exist as an independent state and may be annexed by one of its mighty neighbors, as was the case with Tibet. In all of these cases, the sovereignty of the buffer state appears to be the most important issue. Thus buffer states are not only countries that differ from others because of particular spatial situations, they are also countries in which the geo-political environment affects, in a specific way, the exercise of sovereignty as a fundamental attribute of the state.[6]

SOVEREIGNTY AND THE BUFFER STATE

It has been said that "sovereignty is the criterium of the state."[7] Sovereignty is generally understood as the independent right of the state over its own territory and its autonomy *vis-a-vis* other states in the international system. Sovereignty means the right of the state alone to wield power over its territory and population. It also means the power of the state to act without being subordinated to the authority of another country. Therefore territory and autonomy are the two crucial elements in the conceptualization of sovereignty.

First, territory, as an important element of sovereignty, indicates the power and extent of a state's authority within recognized boundaries. On its territory, the state has the sole and absolute right to exercise any authority. Second, the autonomy of the state refers to the self-determination of a state in its foreign policy and independent alliances.

These two characteristics have never been pure elements and have been challenged since the Treaty of Westphalia (1648) because of changes which have occurred at social, economic, and technological levels in world society. In buffer states, the question of sovereignty is very fragile, especially when exposed to the influence of powerful neighbors. Buffer states have so many constraints working against them that the issue of sovereignty will continue to be the acid test of independence.

On the territorial level a buffer state often comes under contradictory border claims from its neighbors. Historically, portions of Poland have been claimed by Russia, Prussia, and Austria. Brazil and Argentina have considered Uruguay as a territory of their own. Uruguay, called the Banda Oriental by Argentina and Cisplatine by Brazil, has been a disputed area for a long time. Occupied at the beginning of the nineteenth century by Brazil and Argentina, Uruguay was established as an independent buffer state, thanks to British mediation, in 1828. Another example is Lebanon, which is one of the original members of the United Nations and the Arab League but has never been recognized by Syria as an independent state. From the Syrian point of view Lebanon was artificially created by the French in 1920 when the

Lebanese territory of Mount Lebanon was enlarged and extended to areas which, according to Syrian claims, belonged to former Syrian Villayets (districts) of the former Ottoman Empire.[8] Therefore Syria's intervention in the Lebanese strife was often justified by Syria's contention that Syria and Lebanon was a unique country which was divided as a result of French colonialism. Furthermore, the Syrian foreign minister did not rule out, in January 1976, the possibility that, in case Lebanon was partitioned, Syria "would not hesitate to annex parts of Lebanon which are, in reality, parts of Syria."[9]

The territories of buffer states can also be divided by powers who decide to extend their own territory or spheres of influence. Thus Poland was divided in 1772 and in the aftermath of World War Two partition occurred in Germany, Korea, and Vietnam.

On the interregional level, the buffer state's behavior may be subjected to pressure from its neighbor in order to establish alignments. The buffer remains neutral, and thus commits itself to very specific behaviors, or it forms military alliances. In the first instance, the buffer state gives up one of its most important rights, namely, the *Jus Belli* (except in self defense). In the second instance it relies on other states in order to exist as an independent country. In both cases the nature of its sovereignty is affected in a specific way.

Territorial integrity and military alliances can be used as two meaningful variables to help us understand the situation and behavior of a buffer. Whether or not a buffer state has a united territory or has concluded military alliances, is useful as an indicator of the foreign policy and overall behavior patterns of that state. A matrix combining these two elements and generating their possible outcomes is illustrated in Figure 2.1.

Territorial Integrity			+	+	−	−
Military Alliance			−	+	+	−
		Case	1	2	2	3

Fig. 2.1 Territorial Integrity and Military Alliance

When a buffer state enjoys territorial integrity and has no military alliances, as in Case 1, the state is in a posture of *neutralized sovereignty*. When a buffer has concluded a military alliance and enjoys territorial integrity or has concluded military alliance without territorial integrity (Case 2), the state is in a posture of *controlled sovereignty*. And when a buffer state has no military alliance and no territorial integrity (Case 3) the state is in the posture of what might be termed *challenged sovereignty.*

The above differentiated set of sovereignty dilemmas are of utmost importance for buffer states. These dilemmas become the source of policy and not merely an outcome of it. They determine what the buffer state will transmit or receive from the world environment and its neighbors. Because these dilemmas are so significant, they tend to weaken the policy making mechanisms and the foreign policy problems solving capability of the state. In general, because these elements are so absorbing, the leadership of a buffer state tends to be unable to search for creative, successful answers and, therefore, appears to stagnate and fail. Thus, a student of buffer states must deal with the dilemmas of sovereignty in order to be able to contribute to the politics and theory of buffers in the contemporary international system.

FOREIGN POLICIES OF THE BUFFER STATE

In order to avoid involvement in hostilities and to preserve their traditional integrity buffer states seek to remain neutral. To be neutral is voluntarily to commit oneself to non-interference in disputes of other states and the refusal of using one's territory or area for the military activities of others.

Neutrality in its legal sense results from an international treaty or from a binding unilateral declaration of the state. However, in order to be effective, the neutrality of the state must be recognized by other countries. Neutrality, like all other international relations, differs from one political context to another and one time period to another. Switzerland, for example, has made an option in favor of an absolute neutrality[10] whereas Austria has always tended to practice an active neutrality.[11] Austria has been involved in international political mediation promoting, for example, Arab-Israeli talks, and had one of its countrymen selected as Secretary General of the United Nations. Switzerland, on the other hand, is technically not a member of the United Nations. Finland is an interesting example of another kind of neutrality.[12] Finland's neutrality stems from the Finnish-Soviet treaty (The Treaty of Friendship, Cooperation and Mutual Assistance) of April 6, 1948. The treaty takes into consideration the desire of Finland "to remain outside the complicating interests of the Great Powers." More explicitly, Article 4 states that "The High Contracting Parties confirm their pledge, given under Article 3 of the Peace Treaty signed in Paris in February 10, 1947, not to include any alliance or join any coalition directed against the Soviet Union."[13]

Yet neutrality as a legal status has to be distinguished from two others, namely neutralization and pragmatic neutrality. Also, neutrality has to be distinguished from neutralism or non-alignment. The former is legally recognized as a binding status while non-alignment is an ideological or political posture which is not always followed by the countries that claim it. The Third World countries, for example, despite their non-alignment policy, may lean in fact towards one of the two super powers. Many non-aligned countries seek involvement in world affairs and do not want to stand as witnesses in the game of nations.

Neutralization is the status of neutrality of a state imposed by other countries. As C. Black explains:[14]

> In the main ... neutralization should be understood as a flexible instrumentality of statecraft. Its role is limited to the search for ways to remove minor states from arenas of destructive regional and global competition. In an area of stalemate and standoff, there is room in diplomacy for techniques designed to transform military stalemates into political stalemates. Neutralization offers the possibility for such a transformation in some circumstances, especially those wherein minor state is the scene of domestic strife and competitive intervention.

To define the relation between neutrality and neutralization "one might characterize neutralization as an alliance not to align with a specific state, and neutrality as a declaration by a state not to align with others. In this fashion, neutrality and neutralization represent dual versions of a similar posture."[15]

Neutralization occurs when surrounding neighbors or foreign powers who have claimed rights over the region agree to put an end to their conflict over a buffer state. In 1831, for example, Switzerland was neutralized by eight states; Belgium was neutralized by five states in 1831; Luxembourg was neutralized in 1867; and in the twentieth century Afghanistan was neutralized by the 1907 Anglo-Russian agreement. In this latter agreement Russia recognized that Afghanistan "was outside the sphere of influence" and Britain declared that it wanted to exercise its influence "in a pacific way."[16] On July 23, 1962, in Geneva, a "Declaration on the Neutrality of Laos" was signed by thirteen countries from Asia and Europe. It is important to note that neutralization by other states is often combined with a declaration of neutrality by the state itself.

The politics of pragmatic neutrality implies that the state without being neutral *de jure* may remain practically *de facto* so. This was the case of Belgium for a short period of its history. Although a neutral state, Belgium was nevertheless invaded by Germany in 1914. After World War One, Belgium dropped its neutrality and signed a military agreement with France on September 7, 1920. At the Locarno Conference (1925) five European countries guaranteed Belgium's frontiers. But with the threat of war becoming more real, Belgium reached an agreement with France in 1936 and terminated the 1920 accord. Thus a new trend for neutralism was proclaimed. Foreign Minister Spack stated that the new policy of Belgium was "to give assurance to all its neighbors that, in any circumstance, Belgium would not permit its territory to serve either as a passage or base of occupation for foreign armies which would profit from it in order to attack more easily another of her neighbors."[17] King Leopold's address on October 14, 1936 stated that Belgium policy "must aim resolutely at keeping us outside of the quarrels of our neighbors.[18] Therefore, during 1936-1939 Belgium practiced a policy of pragmatic neutrality, although this did not prevent the country from being invaded in 1940.

Lebanon is another case of pragmatic policy of neutrality. Although a member of the Arab League and the Arab Supreme Defense Council, Lebanon has always managed to avoid being involved in regional military conflicts. It did not participate in the Arab-Israeli wars after 1948. The unwritten National Pact of 1943 was a compromise among Christians and Muslims which, at the external level, was expected to shape an equilibrium in foreign policy. Yet, in 1958 and 1975, Lebanon was caught in situations which made it an arena of the many regional wars of the Middle East. During the 1975 war, contradictory tendencies pushed Lebanon towards Syria and other external parties, thus causing the foreign policy of pragmatic neutrality to break down.

Neutrality, whether legal or pragmatic, is not an insurance policy for success. Laos was crushed in 1971 when the United States and South Vietnam fought against North Vietnam on Laotian territory. Cambodia fell under controlled sovereignty after Vietnam gained an overwhelming position in the region. Lebanon today is a classical case of what appears to be the unfortunate future of pragmatic neutralities. It is important to assert that neutrality is not an easy commodity for small and relatively weak states. So often, buffer states find it necessary to tilt to one of their more powerful neighbors, thus encouraging domination.

Controlled sovereignty means that the buffer state, unable to disentangle itself from the pressure of the two surrounding powers, has to enter into a political-military alliance, thus relying upon one of its powerful neighbors or one of the external powers who claim interests in the region for its defense and foreign relations.

This situation may occur in two ways. The buffer may still enjoy territorial integrity, but it has to enter into a military alliance or accept troops on its soil, thus falling into the sphere of an external state. This was the case of Belgium when in 1870, during the Franco-German War, Great Britain made it clear to both Germany and France that it would not tolerate the invasion of Belgium, and in 1920, when it renounced its neutrality and signed a military alliance with France.

Unequal alliances may also occur within the framework of broader multilateral alliances. Czechoslovakia came into a buffer situation between East and West after World War Two. However, subsequently, as a part of the communist world led by the Soviet Union, it joined the Warsaw Pact and its sovereignty became linked to the larger conception of the communist theory of sovereignty.[19] On August 23, 1968, Czechoslovakia was invaded by troops of the Warsaw Pact under the rationale that the internal changes which occurred in the country constituted a threat to the whole communist world. This was known as the Breshnev theory of limited sovereignty, making it clear that the sovereignty of Czechoslovakia was a controlled one.

Controlled sovereignty may also be described as a situation in which a state is partitioned and each of its two entities concludes contradictory alliances. This occurred in Germany, Korea, and Vietnam. Unless one segment of the divided country, backed by its surrounding powers or power interested in the area, managed to invade and annex the other part of the country (such as North Korea's invasion of South Korea in 1950 and North Vietnam's conquest of South Vietnam) the two countries will remain divided, suffering foreign military presence and behaving within the sphere of influence of the greater powers. Korea, due to its location is caught between powerful neighbors and has been described by some as "a springboard for Japanese infiltration into the Asiatic mainland" and by others as a "forward base for the invasion of Japan." In view of Korea's geographical configuration, Japan thought of it as a "dagger aimed at the heart of Japan." On the other hand, Korea could equally be viewed as "a hammer ready to strike at the head of China."[20] After the Sino-Japanese War of 1894-1895, the traditional influence of China over Korea ceased, and with the Treaty of Shimonoseki (April 1895), Japan became the main force in Korea. Fighting was renewed between Japan and Russia over Korea and ended with the Russo-Japanese War. At the peace of Portsmouth (1905), Russia recognized Japan hegemony over Korea. After World War Two, the Soviet Union recovered its place in Korea, but it had to share it this time, not with China or Japan, but with the United States.

The division of Korea into two military occupational zones, North and South of the 38th parallel, was at the origin of the creation of two Korean states. South Korea is in the sphere of influence of the West, while communist North Korea is under the influence of the East. North Korea, however, has to act as a buffer between China and the Soviet Union.

In Case 3 situations neither the territorial integrity of the state exists nor a military alliance takes place. It is the case of military occupation combined with a political disintegration of the state. The challenged sovereignty is the evident manifestation of the politics of disintegration and, therefore, could be considered a complete failure of a buffer state's foreign policy. The politics of neutralization tend to create an equilibrium based on a multi-polarized symmetry towards the neighboring states.[21] Control is based on uni-polarized asymmetry facing directly another, but contradictory, uni-polarization. Challenged sovereignty is the position of dis-equilibrium and is the position of a very weak buffer state, either on the brink of internal disintegration or already disintegrated, which is unable to deal either with territorial partition or with foreign military occupation. Such cases may occur when foreign military occupation coincides with internal civil strife. Rather than a stabilized posture, the state of challenged sovereignty represents processes of breakup and frequent oscillation in behavior. Lebanon today is an illustration of this situation.

THE CASE OF LEBANON

From its independence until 1985, Lebanon has gone through four different phases and has experienced four different policies.

Because of its internal religious composition, Lebanon has succeeded in following a pragmatic policy of neutrality, avoiding regional military involvement. This policy was carefully implemented until 1975, with only one exception in 1958 when Lebanon clearly shifted to the West and followed an anti-Nasserist-Arab policy.

The policy of pragmatic neutrality was endangered by the activities initiated by the Palestine Liberation Organization (PLO) against Israel from Lebanese territory. The war between the

Lebanese factions, who either sympathized with or fought against the PLO, broke out in 1975. In 1976 Syrian troops entered Lebanon and Lebanese territory was occupied by Syrians, with the exception of small parcels in southern Lebanon which was under Israel's control. At that time Lebanon shifted towards Syria under controlled sovereignty.[22]

Following the "Peace for Galilee" operation in 1982, Israel invaded Lebanon, which was already under Syrian occupation. In order to escape this dilemma Lebanon followed a rather complex path. It combined both a shift to power external to the region, namely the United States, and at the same time tried to seek military neutrality *vis-a-vis* Israel and Syria.[23] Therefore, provisions made under Articles 4 and 6 of the May 17th Agreement banned the utilization of the territory of the contracting parties for the purpose of waging hostile actions against one another.

The opposition from Syria to the May 17th Agreement was very strong. Lebanon was compelled in March 1984 to scrap its agreement with Israel when the internal disputes were renewed and the U.S. Marines withdrew. In 1984 Lebanon shifted again in favor of Syria.

The switching patterns of behavior in Lebanon cannot fully be understood outside the internal ethnic and religious composition of Lebanon and the Middle East. Yet it is clear that its sovereignty is still challenged from Syria, which wants Lebanon to side with it against Israel. On the other hand, Israel, which wants to ensure that Lebanon will never be used to stage attacks against it, will remain in control of South Lebanon. Syria and Israel, therefore, occupy Lebanon without the framework of a military alliance. Partition of the territory between foreign forces is now a reality. The outcome of such a chaotic situation might be controlled sovereignty or permanent instability, or permanent partition of the country. Neutrality, however, can be a solution for Lebanon, if foreign troops withdraw and agree to the reestablishment of a neutralized Lebanon.

CONCLUSION

In focusing on sovereignty, independence and autonomy have been stressed. There is however, one important point found in the literature on buffer states which should be considered: the issue of asymmetric perceptions of the buffer states and their surrounding neighbors.

A buffer will always see itself as neutral, and will assert, in all circumstances, its neutrality by words and deeds. It will focus on independence, sovereignty, autonomy, freedom, and the right to exist. Whenever controlled or challenged, it will tend to disentangle itself from its threatening environment and will attempt to stick to its neutral posture, which it considers as its natural state of affairs.

Yet the perception of the buffer held by external powers does not in most cases coincide with the buffer's perception of itself. External powers paint buffers as a permanent source of problems. External neighbors of most buffers may even consider neutrality as hostile behavior. They fear the use of the buffer's territory as a launching pad against them. Thus they try to make buffers choose sides. Yet, there are some cases in which agreements on neutralizing a buffer have been reached among rival powers. Unfortunately though, the past decade has only witnessed disasters and complete breakdowns of such buffers. Laos and Cambodia, once neutralized, have collapsed. Lebanon, which followed a path of pragmatic neutrality, is going through a traumatic period of its political existence. Sovereignty of buffers, despite all claims and idealistic statements, has been sacrificed on the altars of powers' interests. The diplomacy of the buffer must, therefore, be creative enough to stress the advantage great powers can have in maintaining the neutrality of a buffer state in today's world. In a period of hard confrontation and conflicts, the buffer might play the role of a moderator, thus bringing the powers to change their attitudes and to adopt a positive view of what the world must look like. Buffer behavior must tend to develop a peaceful approach to conflict resolution and favor diplomacy over military strategies. Buffers must shape their policies more on integrated regional development than on confrontation or isolation. For a buffer, to be neutral is not to be isolationist, rather it is to neutralize war and to stress non-military approaches.

NOTES

1. T. Mathisen, *The Function of Small States in the Strategies of the Great Powers,* (Oslo: Scandinavian University Press, 1971); and M.G. Partem, "The Buffer System in International Relations," *Journal of Conflict Resolution,* (1981).

2. P.B. Potter, "Buffer State,"*Encyclopedia of the Social Sciences,* 3-4 (1930), p. 45.

3. Mathis*en.*

4. Partem.

5. D. Vital, *The Inequality of States: A Study of the Small Power in International Relations* (Oxford: Clarendon Press, 1967).

6. Cyprus, an island, might be considered a buffer in which the Greek-Turkish rivalry is taking place.

7. L. DEBEZ, *Les Principles Generaux du Droit International Public* (Paris: LGDJ, 1964).

8. E. Rabbath, *La Formation Historique du Liban Politique et Constituionnel: Essai de Synthese* Publications de l'Universite Libanaise, 1973.

9. R. Chamussy, *Chronique d'une querre. Liban 1975-1977* (Paris: Desclee de Brouwer, 1978).

10. F. Bonjour, *Swiss Neutrality: Its History and Meaning* (London: George Allen and Unwin Ltd., 1946).

11. F. Bock, "Austrian Neutrality," in R. A. Bauer, (ed.) *The Austrian Solution, International Conflict and Cooperation* (Charlottesville: University Press of Virginia, 1983).

12. G. Maude, *The Finnish Dilmemma: Neutrality in the Shadow of Power* (Toronto: Toronto University Press, 1976).

13. M. Jakobson, *Finnish Neutrality, A Study of Finnish Foreign Policy Since the Second World War* (New York: Praeger, 1969).

14. C.E. Black, et. al., *Neutralization and World Politics* (Princeton: Princeton University Press, 1968).

15. N. Choucri, "International Nonalignment," in M. Haas, *A Behavioral Approach* (New York: Chandler, 1977).

16. Partem.

17. R.C. Rothstein, *Alliances and Small Powers* (New York: Columbia University Press, 1969), p. 111.

18. Rothstein, p. 112.

19. G.I. Tunkin, *Theory of International Law* (Cambridge: Harvard University Press, 1974).

20. Y. Koo, "The Conduct of Foreign Affairs," in R. Wright (ed), *Korean Politics in Transition* (Seattle: University of Washington Press, 1975) p. 208.

21. In the case of Finland, bias in favor of the USSR is evident. The president of Finland turned down in 1948 an offer to benefit from the Marshall Plan in order not to offend the Soviet Union, which considered the Marshall Plan an American counter-offensive in Europe.

22. E. Azar, et. al., *Lebanon and the World in the 1980's* ((College Park, Md.: University of Maryland Press, 1983); and A. I. Dawisha, *Syria and the Lebanese Crisis* (New York: St. Martin's Press, 1980).

23. Leaning to a third party can be an effective strategy for a buffer. Many examples illustrate such a strategy. In 1827 Uruguay escaped from the Argentine/Brazil dilemma and leaned towards Great Britain. Belgium, in 1870, escaped the German/French rivalry by gaining the support of Great Britain. In order not to shift towards Nasserist Syria, Lebanon sought and obtained, in 1958, the aid of the United States, who sent troops there.

CHAPTER 3
SOUTHERN AFRICA: BUFFER STATES WITHOUT A CONVENTIONAL BUFFER SYSTEM

SHERIDAN JOHNS

Unlike in the Middle East, Latin America, Asia, or Europe, there have not been significant buffer states in post-colonial Africa south of the Sahara. The particular environment which led to their emergence (and sometimes prominence) on other continents has not been present in post-colonial Africa. Although there are real differences in the strength of African states and their foreign policy orientations, they have, for the most part, been preoccupied with securing their independence and altering the colonial structures inherited from the erstwhile European colonial powers. When frictions between the new states of Africa have heated they have generally been between neighboring states and have been handled often by *ad hoc* mediating arrangements through the Organization of African Unity. Although in recent years a more obvious hierarchy of states ranged according to their different economic and military strengths has become apparent, the emerging regional powers (e.g. Nigeria, Zaire) have generally been preoccupied with preserving national cohesion and have not focused externally upon potential rivalries with each other of the sort which elsewhere has been conducive to the emergence of buffer states. In this setting of international relations neither would-be regional powers, nor the much larger number of small African states, have concerned themselves with creating, or becoming, buffer states.

The partial, but significant, exception to the continent-wide pattern is, not surprisingly, found at the southern end of the continent where the relationships between regionally powerful South Africa and its neighboring states have increasingly engaged the attention of scholars. In a pathbreaking analysis in the late

1960s, rejecting earlier analyses of the region which focused either upon racial dimensions of politics of particular states in isolation or only superficially and geographically upon linkages between the states of the region, Larry Bowman argued that southern Africa should be conceptualized as a subordinate state system, largely autonomous within the global international system, in which South Africa maintained its regional preeminence primarily through unequal economic linkages which tied both its white-ruled and black-ruled neighbors to it.[1] Kenneth Grundy's subsequent book-length study provided systematic documentation to substantiate Bowman's assertion of the existence of a subordinate state system in southern Africa.[2]

Other scholars continued to analyze the region within this framework even as Portuguese rule in its colonies of Angola and Mozambique was collapsing and African nationalist goverments came to power.[3] In the wake of the changed situation in the region - and reflecting the ascendancy of an alternate paradigm for the study of international relations - the nature of linkages within the region have more recently been conceptualized within a world system approach, in which South Africa is viewed as a subimperial or semiperipheral power, subordinate to the capitalist core of North America, Western Europe, and Japan, but, by virtue of its industrializing economy, sufficiently powerful to maintain dominance over its non-industrialized and peripheral neighbors.[4] Both conceptualizations of southern Africa, whether regarding it as a regional subsystem or as integral part of the world capitalist system in which semiperipheral South Africa dominates its neighboring states, can incorporate within their analyses an examination of southern Africa as a buffer system in which the prime focus is upon the behavior of South Africa as it has sought to maintain its preeminence within the region.

With its entrenched sociolpolitical order of white minority rule challenged by blacks inside and outside the country (as well as by more distant opponents beyond the African continent), South Africa has labored diligently in the last two decades to assure that the potential threat posed by new black-ruled states on its borders and elsewhere in southern Africa could be minimized. It was only in early 1984 that the Nationalist government of South Africa seemed to have achieved a breakthrough in its previously thwarted efforts to formalize a stance of neutrality on the part of its black-ruled neighbors. The signing of the Nkomati accords between South Africa and Mozambique on March 16 marked the first time that South Africa had reached explicit and formal open agreement with one of the new black-ruled states on its borders to regulate the terms under which forces regarded as hostile by the South African state are to be controlled by the neighboring states.[5] Under the terms of the Nkomati accords Mozambique has agreed to convert itself from a hostile state providing support and transit for south Africa's exiled black opposition into a neighbor committed to denying facilities to the same opposition. The dramatic shift in Mozambique's stance marks further evolution in the buffer system which white-ruled South Africa has painstakingly sought as part of its broader determination to protect itself on a continent in which power in the last quarter century has steadily passed from white-ruled colonial states or locally-based white governments to governments representing the black majority of the population.

South Africa's quest for an adequate buffer system has been animated by its growing fears of the potential vulnerability of its system of white-minority rule. Since its accession to power in 1948 the Afrikaner Nationalist government has utilized a variety of techniques to contain threats to its hegemony within the region. A distinctive feature of its strategy has been the creation of black-ruled 'independent' mini-states out of territories within its own accepted international borders. More conventionally, outside of its borders, the South African government has utilized conventional diplomatic channels, regional economic and communications dominance, and the threat of military action (more recently and frequently actually invoked) to bend its newly sovereign neighboring states to acquiescence to its definition of an appropriate regional order.[6]

Although there are certain features of the present South African buffer system which resemble buffering arrangements devised on other continents, the South African system is more distinguished by its variance from the conventional buffer systems.[7] The various strategies which the Nationalist government has employed to advance its goal of securing its environment at the southern tip of the continent will be examined and then the buffer system which has evolved will be assessed from the dual perspective of the conformity of its features to buffer systems elsewhere and the prospects for its maintenance.

In all of its endeavors the Nationalist leadership has sought to blunt the challenge of an 'enemy' or rival which it views as seeking the demise of white-minority rule and Afrikaner preeminence. In the perception of the South African government this 'enemy' is a triple-headed hydra - militant black nationalism within South Africa, black nationalism outside of South Africa which identifies with the goal of majority-rule within South Africa, and more distant 'international

communism, led by the Soviet Union, which is seen to sustain, if
not to create, all militant opposition to the present South African
regime.[8] Confronting such an extensive and often amorphous rival,
manifesting itself both internally and externally, the South African
state has sought to construct a multi-fronted buffer system
appropriate both to its increasingly exposed position as well as to
its unusual international situation.

BUFFER STATES WITHIN

It is South Africa's 'internal' buffer states, the Bantustans, or
'homelands,' which represent the most innovative feature of the
South African buffer system at the same time that they reflect the
perhaps *sui generis* nature of the South African case. The
Bantustans were created as part of the grand design of *apartheid* to
provide separate political structures for government-approved
African political activity. In 1951, the government passed the Bantu
Authorites Act which provided for the establishment of tribal,
regional, and territorial authorities in the thirteen percent of South
Africa's land designated exclusively for Africans (and hitherto
known as the 'native reserves'). Previously moribund local
institutions, headed by 'chiefs' appointed and paid by the South
African government, were given new authority beyond the limited
responsibilities which they had previously exercised in settling
local disputes and regulating land usage. Under Prime Minister
Hendrik Verwoerd the Bantustan concept was further articulated in
the Promotion of Bantu Self-Government Act of 1959. In terms of
the legislation it was stated that Africans were not a homogeneous
group but instead consisted of a number of separate ethnic groups
distinguished by language and culture and associated with
particular land areas or 'homelands.' It was to territorial authorities
in these 'homelands' that the South African government proposed
to devolve power progressively until they were to become "self-
governing Bantu national units." Throughout the 1960s and 1970s
the South African government steadily moved to implement its
vision for the Bantustans by granting more and more power to
territorial authorities as they were created in each of the ten
ethnically-based 'homelands' recognized by the government, most
of which consisted of a number of small 'spots' of land interspersed
among the 'white' eighty-seven percent of South African territory.
The Transkei, a relatively large and basically contiguous area in
eastern Cape Province (consisting of only three separate blocks of
land), served as a showpiece model for separate development
under the Transkei Constitution Act of 1963; analogous provisions

for the remaining territories were authorized by the Bantu Homelands Consolidation Act of 1971. Although already in 1962 Prime Minister Verwoerd had recognized the possibility that the Bantustans could ultimately advance to the point where they could seek and be granted 'independence' by South Africa, it was not until 1976 that the Transkei took this option after successful negotiations with the South African government. Subsequently Bophuthatswana in 1977, Venda in 1979, and Ciskei in 1982 also became 'independent'. The other six Bantustans, Gazunkulu, KaNgwane, KwaZulu, Lebowa, Ndebele, and QwaQwa, have to date remained a part of South Africa, with KwaZulu's leader, Chief Gatsha Buthelezi, outspokenly proclaiming his intention never to seek 'independence'.

By granting 'independence' to four Bantustans South Africa has divested itself of millions of its black population since, under South African legislation, all citizens of 'independent' Bantustans automatically lose rights to South African citizenship. Yet 'sovereignity' has not brought international recognition except by South Africa and the other 'independent' Bantustans. While the 'independent' Bantustans no longer have to rely upon South African government for final passage of legislation their changed status has hardly altered the fundamental structures of dependence which tie both the 'independent' and the non-independent Bantustans firmly within the South Africa which created them. All Bantustans continue to receive substantial financial aid from South Africa enabling them to balance their budgets. All Bantustans continue to rely upon South Africa for support for their police and defense forces. All Bantustans remain unable to provide work for the overwhelming majority of their able-bodied males and must continue to send them to South Africa within the established channels of the migrant labor system in order to earn money to support their dependents still forced to remain in residence in the Bantustans. The inhabitants of both 'independent' and non-independent Bantustans remain as enmeshed within the South African political economy as they were before the establishment of the Bantustan system.[9]

As continuing dependent appendages of white South Africa the Bantustans serve effectively as buffers for the dominant white-minority government. Indeed, it appears that their existence has provided the white government of South Africa with a cushion that has enhanced its security. Their creation and steady expansion must be seen against a backdrop of an equally steady limitation of African political expression in the government-designated 'white' areas in tandem with a ruthless and relentless strengthening of government security forces applied against all opponents of the regime who have refused to accept its definition of permissable politics.[10] Black nationalist organizations, such as the African Nationalist Congress (ANC) and the Pan Africanist Congress (PAC), which seek participation in common South African political institutions, have been outlawed. Their leaders and other blacks have been denied government-accepted platforms for political expression. Many militant black nationalist leaders have been banned, imprisoned, or driven into exile. In the eyes of the South African government the only legitimate arena for African politics is the Bantustans.

Within the separate Bantustans new structures of employment and patronage have been created to provide limited opportunities in areas where other economic and political opportunities are even more limited. Emerging structures of vested interest within the Bantustans advance their own ends as well as those of the South African government in maintaining the *apartheid* system which gave them birth. Not surprisingly, almost all of the Bantustan leaders have kept South African security legislation in force - and even Chief Gatsha Buthelezi of KwaZulu seems to have terminated his intermittent overtures for some sort of *modus vivendi* with the exiled ANC.[11] In a sometimes sophisticated, and sometimes crude, fashion the South African government through the Bantustans has constructed an edifice of pseudo-sovereignity which serves to buttress its hegemony within the country.

BLACK BUFFER STATES WITHOUT

Its present considerable success with the newly-created internal Bantustan buffer states has been parallelled by success in maintaining external buffer states along its immediate borders and elsewhere in the southern African region - despite the shift to black rule which began in the region in 1964. For the most part South Africa has been able to achieve this situation of compatible external buffer states through the exercise of its superior economic power and diplomacy without formal recognition. Yet South Africa has also increasingly found it necessary to project military force outside of its (and Namibia's) borders to achieve its goals of blunting challenges from militant black nationalism in the region, particularly in the late 1970s and the early 1980s.

The first significant changes requiring adjustments in South Africa's regional buffer arrangements came in the mid-1960s with Britain's voluntary and involuntary withdrawal from southern Africa. Having rejected South Africa's invitation to become a part of the evolving Bantustan system, the moderate nationalist leaderships of the three high commission territories of Basutoland, Bechuanaland, and Swaziland (each of which was contiguous to South Africa but not to each other) negotiated independence from Britain respectively as Lesotho (1966), Botswana (1966) and Swaziland (1968), joining Malawi and Zambia to the north which had achieved their independence also under black majority-rule in 1964 in the wake of the breakup of the white-dominated Central African Federation. Rhodesia, the third component of the defunct Federation, achieved its own brand of independence from Britain when its white-minority government unilaterally declared independence (UDI) in late 1965 in defiance of both Britain and the United Nations. For South Africa the changed situation required no radical new departures, but a modification in style and strategy to accommodate the newly sovereign entities which succeeded Britain in the region. It utilized divergent approaches in dealing with its five black-ruled neighbors and its lone white-ruled neighbor.

In the cases of Lesotho (which is surrounded completely by South Africa), Botswana, and Swaziland, South Africa could build upon economic and social ties which had effectively integrated the three territories with South Africa since the nineteenth century. From the creation of the Union of South Africa in 1910 the three territories were formally linked with South Africa in a common monetary and customs union. With the advent of independence Britain's place as partner of the South African state was taken by the three African successor states who elected to maintain the Southern African Customs Union, albeit successfully persuading South Africa to renegotiate terms more to their advantage in 1969. Similarly the *de facto* monetary union was formalized as the Rand Monetary Area in 1974, although Botswana chose to withdraw and establish its own currency in 1976. As new economic activities were undertaken in each of the countries the volume of trade with South Africa increased. Transportation links through South Africa became even more essential to each of the landlocked states. Despite the closeness of economic links each of the three states refused to enter into formal diplomatic relations with the South African government. The latter, for its part, showed its flexibility by accepting its neighbors' symbolic assertions of diplomatic independence (which included, to varying degrees, verbal condemnation of *apartheid* in international fora and recognition of both African and communist states) and agreeing to new monetary and customs arrangements which enlarged the benefits accruing to South Africa's three partners without in any fashion diminishing South Africa's overwhelming economic dominance. Yet in the policy area central to South Africa's security it was able to gain private assurances that the territories of the neighboring states would not be available to exiled South African black nationalists for training or transit of armed guerrillas. No blunt public threats were needed and South Africa could accurately argue to its external critics that it was successfully coexisting with black-ruled states on its borders at the same time that it could contend to domestic critics that its immediate buffer states were being maintained as security barriers as reliable as those which had existed before their achievement of independence from Britain.[12]

It was in approaches to the more distant new black-ruled states of the region that South Africa could claim its most dramatic symbolic success in the 1960s, despite the absence of intertwining formal economic linkages which tied South Africa's immediate neighbors to her. Although Zambia's political leaders gave sanctuary to South African (and Zimbabwean) exile groups at the same time that they maintained a thriving trade with South Africa, they refused to negotiate direct agreements with the South African government - even during the mid-1970s when both governments became actively involved with each other and a range of outside powers in efforts to settle the Rhodesia/Zimbabwe conflict.[13] In contrast, tiny Malawi in 1967 startled the continent when it agreed to establish formal direct diplomatic relations with South Africa, becoming the first (and to date, the only) independent black African state to exchange envoys with South Africa. Diplomatic relations were accompanied by South African financial aid permitting the construction of a new capital in central Malawi and by expanded bilateral trade. Malawi, which had remained aloof from most of the nationalist struggles of the region, did not seem significantly to alter its foreign policy orientation, which also continued to include verbal condemnations of *apartheid.* In this fashion South Africa made Malawi a model for its declared willingness to cooperate with any African state despite its expressed opposition to *apartheid.*[14]

WHITE-RULED BUFFER STATES

It was in Rhodesia that South Africa made its most direct material commitments to sustain a neighboring state as a buffer. Along with Portugal, South Africa defied United Nations sanctions to keep the Rhodesian economy operating. From the late 1960s it gave the UDI government of Ian Smith military assistance in its struggle against the guerrilla campaigns of Zimbabwean nationalists (joined, ultimately unsuccessfully, for several years in the late 1960s by guerrillas from the ANC). Despite the growing closeness between the two regimes in the economic and military spheres South Africa refused, however, to give formal diplomatic recognition to the UDI government. Nevertheless, through the mid-1970s South Africa seemed to treat Rhodesia much as an ally, the support of which was crucial in maintaining a ring of states on South Africa's borders which would deny their territory to the slowly growing guerrilla forces of South Africa's exiled black nationalist organizations. Rhodesia under Ian Smith was, thus, an unrecognized ally which served a crucial function in buffering South Africa from more hostile black nationalism to the north.

An analogous stance was adopted by South Africa towards the Portuguese colonial government of neighboring Mozambique (as well as that of more distant Angola which adjoined not South Africa, but Namibia). Long established agreements were continued with the metropolitan Portuguese government by which black labor was recruited in Mozambique for South African mines and farms and South Africa routed a substantial portion of its trade through the Mozambican port of Lourenco Marques. When black nationalists in both territories, denied any platform for political expression by the very nature of the Salazarian system, turned to guerrilla activities in the early 1960s South Africa reaffirmed its commitment to the existing *status quo.* As the military struggle in both territories escalated and the involvement of the communist bloc with the black nationalist guerrillas deepened, the South Africans stepped up their contact with the Portuguese and almost certainly provided military, as well as moral, support to ensure the continuation of Portuguese rule. For South Africa the loss of either Portuguese territory, but particularly Mozambique, to black nationalists would raise the spectre of proximate hostile force, closely allied with 'international communism', immediately on South Africa's borders. Such a development would pose a potential threat to the South African system which could not so immediately be contained in the way that the moderate black nationalisms of Lesotho, Botswana, and Swaziland had been.[15]

With the unexpectedly speedy exist of Portugal from its colonies in 1975 in the wake of the army coup of 1974 South Africa's buffer system received a rude jolt. For the first time South Africa confronted governments in contiguous territories headed by militant black nationalists who had fought their way to power dedicated to a program of non-racial majority rule and socialist transformation. South Africa reacted differently to the challenges it saw in Mozambique and Angola. In Mozambique, where FRELIMO had achieved power unchallenged by other nationalist groups and was initially preoccupied with assistance to Zimbabwean guerrillas rather than to South African guerrillas, the South Africans indicated their willingness to accept the transfer of power and the maintenance of existing economic relationshps subject to renegotiation with the FRELIMO government. In Angola South Africa's stance was colored by its deepening embroilment in a struggle with the guerrillas of SWAPO, the Namibian nationalist movement, which stood to gain bases adjacent to Namibia with Angolan independence. The Portuguese departure came in the midst of an escalating civil war between the MPLA, backed by the Soviet Union and Cuba, and the FNLA/UNITA alliance, backed by the United States and other Western powers. Fearful that an MPLA victory would mean both bases for SWAPO as well as the advance of 'international communism' and mistakenly confident that the United States would support them, South Africa intervened on behalf of FNLA/UNITA only to withdraw several months later when it became clear that the United States would not back South Africa's military expedition. In subsequent years South Africa refused to deal with the MPLA government in Luanda; in addition, it continued military incursions into southern Angola to harass SWAPO guerrillas while giving support to UNITA guerrillas who continued to battle the MPLA government in Luanda, creating the pattern for its 'destabilization' policy extended elsewhere in the region in the early 1980s. In contrast, in its dealing with Mozambique South Africa through the late 1970s continued in its efforts to fashion a relationship of coexistence with a militant black nationalist government similar to the type of coexistence which existed with its other immediate neighbors where more moderate leaderships remained in power.[16]

'INTERNAL SETTLEMENT' AND 'DESTABLIZATION'

The 'loss' of the previously 'secure' Portuguese-controlled colonial buffer states of Mozambique and Angola heightened South Africa's need to adapt its buffer system to the changed circumstances represented by the imminent possibility of further transfers of power from white-minority governments to black-majority governments in the remaining white-controlled contiguous territories of Rhodesia and Namibia. In both territories black nationalist guerrillas were expanding their activities and international pressure from the Western powers, as well as from the United Nations, was mounting for moves to black-majority rule. To thwart the likelihood of success by the militant black nationalists in both territories (SWAPO in Namibia and ZANU and ZAPU in Zimbabwe), the South African authorities moved to deracialize their buffer arrangements through encouragement of multiracial 'internal settlements' in Namibia and Zimbabwe to bypass internationally sponsored efforts in which SWAPO, ZANU, and ZAPU were strongly represented. Simultaneously pressuring entrenched white territorial leaders to work together with moderate black politicians and encouraging black leaders opposed to SWAPO, ZANU, and ZAPU to negotiate with the South African authorities in Namibia and Ian Smith's government in Rhodesia, the South African government sought to gain acceptance for new constitutional arrangements permitting the transfer of power to multiracial governments in which blacks were prominently represented. In Namibia the South Africans used their control of the territorial administration for limited deracialization of the local constitutional structure and enhancement of prospects for the Democratic Turnhalle Alliance, a multiracial grouping headed by a local white politician, Dirk Mudge, willing to work with ethnically-based black leaders who had qualifiedly accepted South African sponsored change in the territory. In Rhodesia South Africa used its economic and military leverage to nudge Ian Smith to the negotiating table and subsequently encouraged the new government which emerged under Bishop Abel Muzorewa in alliance with Ian Smith in 1978.

When Bishop Muzorewa's government proved unable to stop the advances of the ZANU/ZAPU guerrillas allied in the Patriotic Front, and in 1979 reluctantly accepted the terms of the Lancaster House conference for Zimbabwean independence under British and international auspices, (as did the Patriotic Front), the South African government seemed to have remained convinced that Bishop Muzorewa would draw sufficient black electoral support to maintain the viability of his multiracial government in alliance with Ian Smith. It was thus a particular shock for the South African government when the ZANU wing of the Patriotic Front captured a clear majority of parliamentary seats in the new Zimbabwean parliament elected in early 1980 enabling it, in alliance with the smaller number of representatives of the ZAPU wing of the Patriotic Front, to form the first black-majority government of a fully-independent Zimbabwe. 'Internal settlement' in Zimbabwe was shown to be a chimera at the same time that prospects for the Democratic Turnhalle Alliance and 'internal settlement' in Namibia were undermined by the dramatic electoral success of the black Zimbabwean nationalists and by the staying power of SWAPO, which, like its Zimbabwean counterparts, continued its armed struggle in oppostion to the regime-supported internal institutions for black political participation.[17]

The failure of the 'internal settlement' strategy to maintain, albeit in deracialized form, the previously secure white-controlled buffers on South Africa's borders was complemented in the late 1970s by a dramatic upsurge in internal black challenge within the country and a resurgence of support for, and sabotage campaigns by, the exile-based ANC.[18] The South African government was able to contain the widespread demonstrations which erupted in Soweto in mid-1976 and the subsequent manifestations of discontent and labor unrest which have continued to simmer into the 1980s. Its determination to continue to utilize the full range of its security arsenal against internal opponents of all races has been repeatedly shown - symbolized most dramatically by the deaths in detention of Steve Biko, the Black Consciousness leader, in 1977, and Neil Aggett, a white labor organizer, 1982. Yet it has not been able to prevent the expansion of ANC activity within the country. Strengthened in exile by thousands of angry post-Soweto refugee recruits and given new potential for access to South Africa by FRELIMO's willingness to permit transit and office facilities (and the willing or unwilling toleration by Lesotho and Swaziland of an organized ANC presence), the ANC demonstrated new capabilities to challenge the South African government in many regions of the country by increasingly sophisticated attacks on military/police facilities and strategic economic installations, culminating in the sabotage of the nearly-completed Koeberg nuclear reactor in late 1982, and the car bomb explosion before air force offices in downtown Pretoria in early 1983. The success of the ANC has been reflected in public expressions of support for the ANC and renewed political activity by a range of anti-government organizations coalescing in the United Democratic Front and the National Forum which were formed in mid-1983.

The new advances by militant black nationalism and its supporters within South Africa, in tandem with the persistence of SWAPO activity in Namibia and the continuing support for exiled South African black nationalists by black-ruled states in the region, clearly accelerated South Africa's readiness to use its military and economic superiority to maintain its hegemony in the sub-continent. The strategy of 'destabilization' came to the forefront, and Mozambique joined Angola as a prime target.[19] As the unviable 'internal settlement' option played itself out in Zimbabwe, anti-FRELIMO dissidents, grouped in the *Resistencia Nacional*

Mocambicana (MNR) lost their base of logistical and military support with the demise of the Rhodesian government. South Africa stepped in to give new sanctuary to the MNR which apparently had not received significant direct support from it in the mid-1970s. With renewed resources and promising prospects for expansion in a Mozambique weakened by both brutal Rhodesian attacks in the late 1970s and economic dislocation and drought in the 1980s, the MNR successfully expanded its capabilities to challenge FRELIMO authority and further disrupt the fragile economy of the country. South Africa itself took direct action against ANC targets in Mozambique, conducting commando forays and bombing attacks in the wake of major ANC sabotage successes within South Africa; it also undoubtedly gave logistical support for sabotage against the petroleum storage and transportation facilities which Mozambique wanted to reopen for Zimbabwe.

South Africa's aggressive stance against Mozambique was replicated against Lesotho when its embattled regime permitted ANC activists to assemble in its capital. South African commandoes raided ANC headquarters in late 1982, killing both ANC members as well as women and children, and support seems to have been given, as well, to domestic opponents of Chief Leabua Johnathan engaged in guerrilla activities against his government. In Angola the South African military successively extended its penetration within the country in an effort to eliminate SWAPO bases while simultaneously maintaining support for UNITA in its campaign against the MPLA government. Elsewhere in the region South Africa has hinted at its willingness to give military training to opponents of other neighboring regimes (most notably to dissidents from Zimbabwe after the disburbances in Matabeleland of 1982-83).[20] It has also not hesitated to flex its economic muscles, particularly before Zimbabwe, by restricting the transit of petroleum and the supply of railway cars, crucial to the Zimbabwean economy until alternate links through Mozambique are restored. With its 'destabilization' tactics (which had roots in earlier commando raids into Zambia against SWAPO bases and occasional delays in supplying goods in transit through South Africa to states in the region) South Africa has displayed the external face of its 'politics of survival', its ultimate readiness to use force to persuade its weaker opponents to accommodate its security interests.[21]

From South Africa's perspective the 'destabilization' strategy has begun to reap a harvest which suggests the inauguration of a new stage in its evolving regional buffer system. Mozambique has acquiesced in shifting its stance towards South Africa. The present joint Angolan-South African monitoring machinery to ensure the implementation of the terms of the 'truce' agreement of February 16, 1984, between the two countries could be translated into a longer term arrangement, possibly linked with either regional or internationally-recognized machinery to permit elections in Namibia and the transfer of power from the present South African authorities to a black-majority Namibian government. Zimbabwe might now be more willing to negotiate with South Africa at the ministerial level, a procedure which it has rejected since the achievement of independence. In such a fashion South Africa's most recently independent black-ruled neighbors are being drawn back towards the buffer state status which they occupied under white-minority rule. As such they would join South Africa's older black-ruled internationally-recognized neighbors - although without necessarily giving the formal diplomatic recognition which Malawi alone has done.

CONSTELLATION VS. SADCC

In 1979, shortly after replacing Prime Minister B. J. Vorster, Prime Minister P.W. Botha and his colleagues began the articulation of a proposal for the creation of "a peaceful constellation of southern African states with respect for each other's cultures, traditions, and ideals." The proposals as they were elaborated in subsequent pronouncements systematically outlined South Africa's ideals of a regional order in which all states would join together to strengthen and extend institutions for cooperation in the economic and technological spheres and would consult upon possible common approaches to other problems, including the 'Marxist threat', through formalized councils of states and international secretariats which would serve executive functions.[22] Membership in the constellation was to include South Africa, 'independent' Bantustans, and recognized sovereign black-ruled states in the region. The constellation concept was rejected by all except the 'independent' Bantustans and, indeed, South Africa's sovereign black-ruled neighbors responded with new efforts to disengage from South Africa's economic embrace through the creation of the Southern African Development Coordination Conference (SADCC) which drew together Zimbabwe and the five frontline states most closely involved in its struggle in the 1970s (Angola, Botswana, Mozambique, Tanzania, and Zambia) as well as the remaining black-ruled states in the region (Lesotho, Malawi, and Swaziland).[23]

Despite the initial failure of South Africa to attract its neighbors into a formally established constellation South Africa did not stop its efforts to draw its neighbors closer. Its surprise offer of June, 1982, to transfer two pieces of Bantustan territory to Swaziland can be seen as an imaginative 'soft' diplomatic gambit within the premises of the constellation concept to counterpoint the 'hard' destabilization strategy being pursued against Mozambique, Lesotho, and more distant Angola. With the offer to cede to Swaziland the South African Swazi Bantustan of KaNgwane and the Ingwavuma district of northern KwaZula stretching from Swaziland to the Indian Ocean, the South African government dangled an attractive prospect before the conservative Swazi government then headed by its entrenched traditionalist leader, King Sobhuza - lands controlled by Swazi authorities in the precolonial nineteenth century would be returned to them and simultaneously landlocked Swaziland would gain access to the sea. The boundary shift promised multiple benefits to South Africa - the elimination of a particularly unviable Bantustan whose inhabitants would become citizens not of an 'independent' Bantustan but of an internationally recognized sovereign state; the deepening of Swaziland's already great economic dependence upon South Africa inasmuch as a majority of its citizens would then be working in South Africa; the territorial aggrandizement of a buffer state facing antagonistic Mozambique; and the hope that Swaziland might be more willing to join the constellation formally at some future date. Fierce opposition by the leaders of KaNgwane and KwaZulu, supported by successful challenges within the South African courts, led the South African government, in mid 1982, to establish a commission under Chief Justice Rumpf to further investigate the proposal and then to shelve the plan in early 1984.[24]

Although the Swazis have not recovered their patrimony and South Africa did not reap the full benefits of its scheme, nevertheless Swaziland's utility as a buffer state was improved through the maneuver. The 1984 revelation of the 1982 signing of a non-aggression accord between Swaziland and South Africa suggests that Swaziland traded the prospect of future territorial aggrandizement for an immediately operative agreement to limit the use of its territory as an organizational and transit point for ANC guerrillas.[25] The recent expulsions of ANC members from Swaziland offer confirmation that South Africa continues to reap the benefits of its aborted plan for the divestment of Bantustan lands.[26]

The episode points up the ongoing utilization of diplomatic tools (including, for the first time, offers of boundary adjustment) to raise the viability of South Africa's buffer system.

Simultaneously harassed by 'destabilization', blandished by constellation-inspired diplomacy, battered by harsh drought in the early 1980s, and unable collectively through SADCC (or individually) to mobilize substantial outside foreign assistance, both recalcitrant militants and more sympathetic conservatives have yielded to South African pressure in the early 1980s. South Africa has not been able to achieve a return to the pre-1974 regional *status quo* nor has it yet been able to extend the constellation designed to replace it outside its borders, but it does seem to have reconstituted a regional buffer system which enhances its security for the short term. For the longer term its goal of a regional constellation remains.[27]

SOUTH AFRICA'S BUFFER SYSTEM IN PERSPECTIVE

The South African buffer state system of the 1980s is at variance from more conventional buffer systems - as it was in its earlier form in the 1960s. A buffer system usually assumes two large rival states, roughly equally powerful, between which there are smaller and much weaker states contiguous to both large rivals. The smaller and weaker states, whether one or more, incapable themselves of determining the outcome of the rivalry between their powerful neighbors, act to preserve their own security by refusing to enter into alliance with either of the two larger rival powers which may or may not also be members of more encompassing rival alliances.[28] In the regional state system of southern Africa there are not two large rival powers with smaller and much weaker states between them; instead there is one dominant powerful state, South Africa, (directly controlling Namibia), and eight neighboring states, five of which (Botswana, Lesotho, Mozambique, Swaziland, and Zimbabwe) are contiguous to South Africa and three of which (Angola, Malawi, and Zambia) have no direct border with South Africa but are either contiguous to Namibia or historically tied to South Africa through links forged in the period of British colonial rule. In the eyes of the Nationalist government of South Africa there does exist a single potentially powerful regional rival - black nationalism, rooted in South Africa, but also supported externally in the region (and beyond), and dedicated to the destruction of the existing white-dominated sociopolitical order. In its efforts to mitigate the threat of this non-state regional rival South Africa has acted in many ways similar to a state faced with a powerful rival state by moving to prevent any neighboring state from close alliance with its declared opponent. Although South Africa's neighboring black-ruled states have limited maneuverability by virtue of their weakness and the lack of a strong proximate black-ruled state to rival South Africa, they have attempted to keep their distance from South Africa. In so doing they have shown behavior similar to that of some buffer states elsewhere geographically caught between two proximate larger state rivals.

South Africa, as the powerful architect of the regional system, has been successful in recrafting a buffer state network in the 1980s, which, together with internal policies suppressing dissent, provides a partial shield against black nationalism in South Africa and its supporters northward on the continent. The South African buffer system is unique in its two-tiered nature and in the geographical location of its components. One tier of buffer states, the 'independent' Bantustans, are spots scattered in the midst of South Africa's own territory, given 'sovereignity' as a device to enhance their credibility as part of the overall program of separate development which is central to apartheid. Through their 'sovereignity' they have been made eligible to play a role in a South African-defined constellation system of international relations in which states with different sociopolitical orders will be joined together in common structures to maintain the regional *status quo* under South African hegemony. The second tier of buffer states, consisting initially of white-ruled allies (unrecognized Rhodesia and Portuguese-controlled Angola and Mozambique) and newly-independent black-ruled states, now consists entirely of Black-ruled states (with the continuing exception of South African-controlled Namibia). Either explicitly through accords (in the cases of Mozambique and Swaziland) or tacitly through diplomatic understandings (in the cases of the other states which have not signed agreements but have agreed to limit the activities of South African exiles), the neighboring states have yielded to South Africa's will.

SOUTH AFRICA'S DIPLOMATIC WEAPONS

South Africa's policies of the last few years, not only towards Angola, Mozambique, and Zimbabwe, but also towards Swaziland and Lesotho particularly, have given it the opportunity to display the full range of its arsenal for regional strategic diplomacy. Its blunt weapons have consisted of air and commando strikes on the bases of South African exiled nationalists complemented by the financing and training of guerrilla opponents of neighboring regimes, in Angola and Mozambique (and also in Lesotho and probably in Zimbabwe),[29] as well as logistical support for economic sabotage against key transport and fuel facilities (utilized in Mozambique). South Africa has also effectively used its economic strength and geographical advantage to deny rail transport facilities temporarily (in the case of Zimbabwe particularly) and to limit border movement (in the case of Lesotho). Its actions highlight vulnerability and encourage acquiescence. The instrumentalities of economic pressure and denial of communications have been continually supported as well by the 'soft' tools of direct diplomacy, through secret meetings (in the case of Swaziland), less visible interchanges of communications and middle-ranking officials, and also through upper level meetings and formal agreements, capped by the signing of the Nkomati accords by President Samora Machel for Mozambique and Prime Minister P.W. Botha for South Africa.

Since South Africa's nearest potential rival state (or states) on the continent (e.g. Zaire, Nigeria, Algeria, Ethiopia) are weak individually relative to South Africa and distant (and preoccupied with internal affairs) South Africa's even weaker neighboring buffer states do not have the option which buffer states elsewhere have had of choosing to lean towards one of two proximate rivals. Nor have the southern African buffer states had particular success in pursuing a "third power strategy." The Western powers have refused to give more than very limited military support (e.g. to Botswana and Zambia during Rhodesian UDI), and their economic aid has never met the targets which states of the region have established (whether it was support for Zambia, Botswana, and Malawi in the wake of sanctions against Rhodesia, or funds for Zimbabwean reconstruction after independence, or assistance for SADCC projects). Furthermore, and crucially, the Western powers have never been willing to cut their important trade and investment ties with South Africa - (although they have to varying degrees, particularly since 1977, complied with the United Nations arms embargo upon South Africa). The communist powers have also proved limited in their capacity and willingness to aid states in the region with the notable exception of Angola where Cuban troops and Soviet weapons have buttressed the MPLA regime - (although their aid has not been able either to prevent South African incursions into southern Angola nor to achieve suppression of the South African-supported UNITA guerrillas).

Constrained by their isolation and powerlessness in the shadow of the South African colossus, the neighboring states have only had one option - to sustain, in effect, a policy of uneasy neutrality in which stances of individual states towards the South African government and its black nationalist opponents have been nuanced in keeping with specific vulnerabilities and differing sympathies for particular South African exiled nationalist organizations. The recent experience of Mozambique has demonstrated how even a most militant opponent of the South African government can be forced to accept South African terms for terminating active support for nationalist exiles. South Africa's neighboring states have all again been molded into its second tier of buffer states. From South Africa's perspective they are neutral in the sense that they do not directly support the organizational and military activities of South Africa's nationalist opponents nor are they yet willing to enter into the constellation offered by South Africa and thus lend legitimacy to the South African regime and its 'independent' Bantustans, the first tier of South Africa's buffer states. From their own perspective the neighboring states have been neutralized from acting fully upon their continuing commitment to bring an end to white minoritty rule in South Africa. In the regional context of southern African inequality full and activist neutrality, balancing between proximate rival states or blocs, on the Austrian or Swiss model, has never been a viable option for South Africa's neighbors.

LIMITATIONS OF THE BUFFER SYSTEM APPROACH FOR SOUTHERN AFRICA

The South African buffer system does not display a balanced, almost binary, distribution of power between two rival states, with smaller weaker state(s) maneuvering, or being maneuvered, through strategies of neutralization, leaning to one rival state or the other, or seeking third-power support, to maintain themselves inviolate and free from invasion by the larger neighbors.[30] The preeminence of South African state power and the absence of a rival state in the region with capabilities approaching those of South Africa highlight the limitations of conceptualizing the interrelationships between South Africa and its neighbors as a buffer system of the conventional type. Similarly, the lack of options for buffering diplomacy open to South Africa's neighboring states underlines their dissimilarity to buffer states positioned between two large and powerful states. Nevertheless, South

Africa's behavior towards its neighbors as it has sought to enhance its security in a more threatening international environment does have the earmarks of the actions of one of the large powers in a conventional buffer systems. From the perspective of the Nationalist government South Africa does face a potentially powerful and threatening rival which must be blocked by creating buffers against its advance. From the perspective of the other states in southern Africa, however, the power of the South African state and the policies of the Nationalist government which controls it are more fruitfully considered as the actions of a Gulliver threatening its Lilliputian neighbors. Unable to find Gulliver asleep or ropes strong enough to tie him, and with no rival Gulliver in sight to appeal for help, South Africa's neighbors must resign themselves in the immediate future to existence as dependent states subordinate to the dominant regional power.

South Africa, however, manifests not only the behavior of a dominant regional power but also that of one of the two major powers in a buffer system. In this sense it is of interest to consider the southern African system as a partial buffer system, a conceptualization complementary to that of a subordinate state system in which South Africa is the "subsystem dominant" regional power. Seeing the system as a buffer system also complements analyses considering South Africa as a subimperial power seeking to improve its semiperipheral status in the world system.

HOW VIABLE IS SOUTH AFRICA'S BUFFER SYSTEM?

South Africa's reconstructed buffer system of the 1980s seems to hold promise in the short run as a means for South Africa to continue to protect its sociopolitical order and its position as the preeminent regional power surrounded by a *cordon sanitaire*. In the 1970s the viability of the system was threatened by the collapse of the Portuguese empire and by the success of the Zimbabwean nationalist guerrillas. South Africa has clearly stemmed the disintegration through its activist 'destabilization' and diplomacy of the early 1980s which has forced its most militant regional state antagonists to reintegrate themselves within the buffer system. Should it permit Namibia to become independent (even under a SWAPO government) it would also seem possible for South Africa to continue to utilize its overweening military, economic, and diplomatic strengths to keep Namibia within any marginally modified version of the regional buffer system. In the immediate future it is neither likely that the Soviet bloc or the Western powers will project themselves into southern Africa in a massive fashion nor will potentially strong African states elsewhere on the continent realize their latent power. South Africa's black ruled neighbors thus will neither be able to lean to the side of a strong black continental rival to South Africa nor will they be able to invoke effectively a third power strategy to change their present status. Limited maneuverability within an uneasy neutrality will remain their only alternative.

The most immediate threat, if any, to South Africa's buffer system is most likely to arise within South Africa itself through the contradictions of its own dynamic sociopolitical order. An increasingly mobilized and crucial black labor force, interacting with the growing number of better educated blacks which the modified structures of *apartheid* are unable fully to accommodate, will pose new challenges to both the South African government and to the governments of the 'independent' Bantustans. In response to such challenges black nationalism will have opportunities internally to deepen and widen its organization and capacity to undermine white-minority rule, even if in the short run its capacity for sabotage by guerrillas is limited. Heightened tensions within the poorest and worst governed of the 'independent' Bantustans (e.g. the Ciskei)[31] could become the Achilles heel of the buffer system. The costs of staunching their vulnerability (and coping with widening dissent within South Africa) will stretch South Africa's capability to deploy resources to deal with the second tier of buffer states outside of its borders. For the immediate future the threat to South Africa's buffer system (and to its *apartheid* sociopolitical order) will come primarily from within the country and not from outside - despite a continuing hostile international environment in which *apartheid* will remain almost universally condemned and South Africa will remain a pariah state.

NOTES

1. Larry W. Bowman, "The Subordinate State System of Southern Africa," *International Studies Quarterly, 12* (September 1968): 231-261.

2. Kenneth W. Grundy, *Confrontation and Accommodation in Southern Africa: The Limits of Independence* (Berkeley: University of California Press, 1973).

3. Sympathetic reevaluations of Bowman's analysis can be found in Timothy M. Shaw, "Southern Africa: Cooperation and Conflict in an International Sub-System," *Journal of Modern African Studies, 12* (December, 1974):633-655 and Susan Aurelia Gitelson, "The Transformation of the Southern African State System," *Journal of*

African Studies, 4 (Winter, 1977):367-391. A collection of essays by eighteen authors analyzing southern Africa from the springboard of Bowman's analysis is found in Timothy M. Shaw and Kenneth A. Heard (eds.), *Cooperation and Conflict in Southern Africa: Papers on a Regional Subsystem* (Washington: University Press of America, 1976).

4. Timothy M. Shaw, "South Africa, Southern Africa and the World System," in Thomas M. Callaghy, *South Africa in Southern Africa: The Intensifying Vortex of Violence* (New York: Praeger, 1983), 45-68. Shaw's analysis marks a further evolution of the views expressed in his 1974 article (see n. 3) as well as in subsequent articles, Timothy M. Shaw, "International Stratification in Africa: Sub-imperialism in Eastern and Southern Africa," *Journal of Southern African Affairs,* 2 (April 1977):145-165 and Timothy M. Shaw, "Kenya and South Africa: 'Sub-imperialist States,'" *Orbis,* 21 (Summer 1977):375-394.

5. For the text of the Nkomati accords and the speeches of President Samora Machel and Prime Minister P.W. Botha see "Supplement to AIM Informatation Bulletin No. 93" (Maputo: Mozambique Information Agency, 1984), 1-17. The full text of the accords and extracts of the speeches are also found in *South African Digest* (Pretoria: Department of Foreign Affairs), March 23, 1984, 3-7.

6. A recent extensive assessment of the evolution of South Africa's regional policy in Southern Africa (but not one cast explicitly in regional subsystem terms) is to be found in Deon Geldenhuys, "South Africa's Regional Policy," in Michael Clough (ed.), *Changing Realities in Southern Africa: Implications for American Policy* (Berkeley, Institute of International Studies, University of California, 1982), 123-160. The subject is also treated from the perspective of South African foreign policy strategy (rather than from a regional subsystems approach) in Sam C. Nolotshungu, *South Africa in Africa: A Study of Ideology and Foreign Policy* (Manchester: Manchester University Press, 1975), 114-258.

7. Amplification of this point is made subsequently in analysis starting on p. 24.

8. The flavor of the conceptualization of the South African government of the nature of the 'enemy' threat can be found in Republic of South Africa, Department of Defence, *White Paper on Defence 1977* (Laid upon the Table in the Senate and the House of Assembly by the Minister of Defence, 7.

9. A careful assessment of the significance of 'independence' for the Bantustans if provided by Newell M. Stultz, "Some Implications of African 'homelands' in South Africa" in Robert M. Price and Carl G. Rosberg, *The Apartheid Regime: Political Power and Racial Domination* (Berkeley: Institute of International Studies, University of California, 1980), 194-216. The analysis is amplified with respect to the Transkei in Newell M. Stultz, *Transkei's Half Loaf: Race Separatism in South Africa* (New Haven Yale University Press, 1979). A divergent assessment, explicitly disagreeing with Stultz, is to be found in Roger Southall, *South Africa's Transkei: The Political Economy of an 'Independent' Bantustan* (New York: Monthly Review Press, 1983), 281-304, but particularly 297-300.

10. The process and machinery by which African rights have been limited and civil rights circumscribed for all South Africans is concisely delineated in Study Commission on U.S. Policy Toward Southern Africa, *South Africa: Time Running Out* (Berkeley: University of California Press, 1981) 48-79.

11. For an examination of the tense relationship between the ANC and Chief Gatsha

Buthelezi see Thomas Karis, "The Resurgent African National Congress: Competing for Hearts and Minds in South Africa" in Thomas M. Callaghy, *South Africa in Southern Africa,* 217-223.

12. The evolution of relations between South Africa and Botswana, Lesotho, and Swaziland into the early 1970s is traced in Nolotshungu, *South Africa in Africa,* 130-155. A more recent update describing the deterioration in relations, particularly with Lesotho, is found in Bernard Magubane, "Botswana, Lesotho, and Swaziland: South Africa's Hostage's in Revolt", in Thomas M. Callaghy, *South African in Southern Africa,* 355-370.

13. On Zambia's shifting relationships with South Africa see Douglas Angling and Timothy M. Shaw, *Zambia's Foreign Policy: Studies in Diplomacy and Dependence* (Boulder: Westvies Press, 1979), 272-309. Another perspective is provided from an enthusiastic supporter of South Africa's policy in F.R. Metrowich, *South Africa's New Frontiers* (Sandton, South Africa: Valiant Publishers, 1977), 53-64.

14. For discussion of the reasons for Malawi's willingness to expand South Africa's offers of economic assistance into diplomatic recognition see Nolotshungu, *South Africa in Africa,* 192-218 and Carolyn McMaster, *Malawi - Foreign Policy and Development* (London: Julian Friedman, 1974), 88-112.

15. Analysis of the evolution of South Africa's links with Rhodesia and Portugal through the early 1970s is also provided in Nolotshungu, *South Africa in Africa,* 162-190.

16. Delineation of South Africa's policy towards Angola and Mozambique (Including the post-1980 shift to antagonistic 'destabilization' in Mozambique) may be found in Thomas M. Callaghy, "Apartheid and Socialism: South Africa's Relations with Angola and Mozambique in Callaghy (ed.), *South Africa in Southern Africa,* 267-322. For more specific information on Mozambican-South African relations see Mario Azevado, " A Sober Commitment to Liberation?: Mozambique and South Africa 1974-1979", *African Affairs, 79 (October 1980): 567-584.*

17. For a summary of the evolution of South African policy in Namibia through the early 1980s see John Seiler, "South Africa in Namibia: Persistence, Misperception and Ultimate Failure" in Thomas M. Callaghy, *Southern Africa in Southern Africa,* 165-190.

18. The rise of the ANC is assessed against the backdrop of broadening black political and trade union activity in Karis, "The Resurgent African National Congress". See also Joseph Lelyveld, "Black Challenge to Pretoria", *New York Times,* October 12, 1983.

19. For assessments of the 'destabilization' policy see Deon Geldenhuys, "The Destabilization Controversy: An Analysis of a High-Risk Foreign Policy Option for South Africa", *Politikon 9* (December 1982): 16-31 and Richard Leonard, *South Africa at War: White Power and the Crisis in Southern Africa* (Westport, Connecticut: Lawrence Hill & Co., 1983), 86-95.

20. See, for example, statements by Prime Minister P.W. Botha indicating the willingness of his government to consider requests for aid from "anti-communist guerrilla forces in southern Africa"; Botha indicated that, "if it is in the interests of South Africa and stability on our borders, we shall certainly consider it." *New York Times,* February 17, 1983.

21. The internal dimensions of the 'politics of survival' as they were devised in the early 1960s have been delineated in Newell M. Stultz, "The Politics of Security: South Africa under Verwoerd, 1969 -," *Journal of Modern African Studies,* 7 (April 1969):3-20.

22. For articulation of the "constellation" concept by South African officials see *Address by the Honorable P.W. Botha, Prime Minister, Carlton Centre, Johannesburg, 22 November 1979* (Pretoria: Department of Foreign Affairs, 1979) and *Address by the Hon. R.F. Botha, South African Minister of Foreign Affairs, to Members of the Swiss-South African Association in Zurich, on 7th March 1979* (Berne: South African Embassy, Press Section, 1979). Assessments of the constellation concept by South African scholars include: W.J. Breytenbach, *The Constellation of States: A Consideration* (Johannesburg: South Africa Foundation, 1980); Deon Geldenhuys, "Regional Cooperation in Southern Africa: A Constellation of States," *International Affairs Bulletin* 2 (1979):36-72; Wolfgang H. Thomas, "A Southern African 'Constellation of States': Challenge or Myth?," *South Africa International,* 10 (January 1980): 113-128; and Wolfgang F. Thomas, "South Africa and Black Africa: The Future of Economic Integration," *Politkon 6* (December 1979): 103-135.

23. Among the many analyses of SACDD are Michael Clough and John Ravenhill, "Regional Cooperation in Southern Africa: The Southern African Development Coordination Conference," in Michael Clough (ed.), *Changing Realities in Southern Africa,* 161-186, and Richard F. Weisfelder, "The Southern African Development Coordination Conference: A New Factor in the Liberation Process," in Thomas M. Callaghy, *South Africa in Southern Africa,* 237-266. See also Christopher R. Hill, "Regional Cooperation in Southern Africa," *African Affairs,* 82 (April, 1983):215-239. For the papers of the first SADCC meeting, including the Lusaka Declaration of April 1980, see Amon Nsekela (ed.) *Southern Africa: Toward Economic Liberation* (London: Rex Collings, 1981).

24. For a report of initial opposition in KaNgwane and KwaZulu see *New York Times,* June 18, 1982. The decision to withdraw the plan, along with an account of the South African government's handling of the matter, is discussed in *Washington Post,* June 20, 1984.

25. See *Africa Research Bulletin: Political Social and Cultural Series,* 21 (May 15, 1984):7201BC-7202AB.

26. *New York Times,* July 15, 1984.

27. As Prime Minister P.W. Botha put it on the occasion of signing the Nkomati accords with Mozambique, "I have a vision of the nations of Southern Africa cooperating with each other in every field of human endeavour; a veritable constellation of states working together for the benefit of all on the basis of mutual respect." Supplement to AIM Information Bulletin No. 93 (Maputo: Mozambique Information Agency, 1984) 16.

28. This definition is a distillation of a more formal and mathematically precise definition offered in Michael Greenfield Partem, "The Buffer System in International Relations," *Journal of Conflict Resolution,* 27 (March 1983):16.

29. For Zimbabwe's case against South Africa see *Washington Post,* June 23, 1984.

30. For elaboration of how these three strategies can be exercised by buffer states in conventional buffer systems see Partem, "The Buffer System," 19-25.

31. For a description and assessment of the vulnerabilities of the 'independent' Ciskei see Joseph Lelyfeld, "Misery in a South African 'Homeland'," *New York Times Magazine,* September 25, 1983, 37-39, 54-55, 58-63.

CHAPTER 4
BUFFER SYSTEMS OF MIDDLE AMERICA

PHILIP KELLY

Middle America is a fragmented geographic region, weak in relation to larger states, yet possessing a central and strategic location which attracts outside interference and authority. Originally inhabited by a variety of Amerid peoples, whose complicated immigration patterns still are seen throughout the area in isolated islands, jungles, valleys, and plateaus, the region later became exposed to an additional array of races and nationalities in the centuries after discovery by Europe. The Spanish introduced unassimilated African slaves to the Caribbean; the Dutch, English, French, and North Americans brought their own cultures and attracted immigrants from Africa, Asia, and elsewhere. A melting pot for unifying the fragmented parts was not feasible because formidable geographic barriers and rival colonial jurisdictions prevented amalgamation. Turmoil of subsequent centuries extended and solidified these cleavages, and today we continue to see Middle America disunited, exposed to outsiders' interventions, and consequently without an independent or neutral voice in international affairs.

Within the scope of this chapter, Middle America includes Central America, Panama, Mexico, northern South America, and the islands of the Caribbean Sea. Hardly a compact or united geographic territory within itself, it merits a regional label, in my opinion, because of its buffer position between North and South America and between the Atlantic and Pacific Oceans. For convenience, the terms "Middle America," "Caribbean," "Caribbean Basin," and "Basin" will be used interchangeably.

Among types of areal configurations, I argue that four are appropriate as contemporary models for interpreting the Caribbean as a world region:[1]

buffer system: regions which isolate and separate other areas from each other.

spheres of influence: regions which are dominated by one foreign state or alliance.

shatterbelts: regions in which two or more outside Great Powers compete for control.

neutral or independent political zones: regions which are not strongly penetrated by any foreign powers.

It is contended in this chapter that Middle America is a natural buffer system, permanently existing because of the Basin's rugged terrain and its central location. In fact, two unique buffer dimensions, occur a series of internal buffers within Middle America and a Caribbean-wide buffer which affects political happenings in adjacent territories.

In addition, transpiring simultaneously with these buffers, and influenced by them, spheres of influence and shatterbelts likewise occur in Middle America, rotating their appearances based upon regional and international events. I maintain below that at present a shatterbelt exists in the region. In contrast, it would be quite unlikely to expect the Caribbean to be a sphere of influence or a neutral or independent entity, in large part because of disruptions created by the buffers existing there.

REVIEW

For five hundred years, Middle America has alternated between being labeled by scholars and statesmen either a sphere of influence of Spain, Britain, or the United States, or being labeled a shatterbelt, caught between power struggles of large nations. Spain established paramountcy over the region after discovery until mid-seventeenth century. Dutch, French, and English territorial and economic inroads into the Basin gradually eroded this dominance, the Dutch in Curacao (1630) and Surinam (1652), the French in Guadalupe and Martinique (1635), and the English in Barbados (1624) and Jamaica (1655). Following the demise of Spanish control, Middle America became entangled in European warfare, particularly between France and England after 1739, and the region changed to a shatterbelt configuration. The English by the early nineteenth century successfully asserted their hegemony over the Caribbean, whereupon this sphere of influence transferred to the United States after 1895. I have argued elsewhere[2] that Middle America in the 1960s returned to a shatterbelt because of the Soviet-Cuban alliance, revealing another historic shift in the Basin's sphere of influence/shatterbelt rotation. These eras are listed in Table 4.1 below:

TABLE 4.1
Caribbean Spheres of Influence/Shatterbelt Eras

1520s - 1650s	Spanish Sphere of Influence
1659 - 1820s	Shatterbelt
1820s - 1890s	British Sphere of Influence
1890s - 1960s	United States Sphere of Influence
1960s - present	Shatterbelt

Not ever during this period of alternating eras has the Caribbean Basin taken an exclusively neutral or independent character, never breaking the above tendency for Great Power intervention in the region. Middle America's strategic location, its mineral and agricultural wealth, and its political weakness derived from fragmented geographic and demographic features, have continually made it an arena for intervention and control by large outside nations.

Although less recognized in the extant literature, a buffer status likewise is characteristic of Middle America. Unlike spheres of influence, shatterbelts, and neutral or independent political zones, all of which are mutually exclusive, Caribbean buffers have appeared permanently throughout the entire period simultaneously with the first two phenomena. A variety of interesting and important buffers within and beyond Middle America may be described, based upon the area's uniqueness as a world region and its history of Great Power rivalry or control.

To me, buffers are territories which separate and isolate other geographic areas from each other, caused by the qualities of rugged topography, racial or demographic variances among peoples, smaller centrally located countries, territories suffering political breakdown, strategic land or maritime choke points, agreements for non-involvement by large powers, or large and sparsely inhabited spaces. These buffer separations normally possess some type of geopolitical consequences in the foreign policies of adjacent and interested foreign states. Buffers may reside within regions or countries, functioning to block communications and to lessen areal unity. Some of these sub-system buffers located within the Caribbean Basin are described below. In addition to sub-system or internal buffers, a region-wide Middle American buffer exists which separates or isolates much larger territorial and maritime spaces and whose impact projects well-beyond the bounds of the Caribbean. Today, Brazil and the Soviet Union, in my opinion, benefit from these buffer features; comparable United States objectives are made more difficult to attain. Lastly, I believe that dynamic and significant linkages among buffers, shatterbelts, spheres of influence, and neutral or independent political zones occur with respect to Middle America.

INTERNAL BUFFERS

Middle American topography once was described to a Spanish king by crumpling a segment of paper, then allowing it partially to unfold. This resemblance shows the Caribbean to be primarily an unpatterned collection of highlands, valleys, inland seas, and islands, features encouraging political and economic diffusion rather than unity. Such terrain creates a multitude of buffer cases, some dynamic in reflection of shifting national alignments, others determined naturally by their permanent geopolitical position. Had North America approximated Middle America's terrain, a similar varigated patchwork of small states and fragmentation might have arisen there as well.

Central America provides several examples of buffer phenomena. The republics of El Salvador and Honduras, traditional antagonists, separate Guatemala and Nicaragua, the two primary powers of the area. This buffer corridor prevented attempts during the nineteenth century to forge regional political union at the instigation of both Guatemala and Nicaragua, and it later represented a major reason why the recent Central American Common Market was unable to succeed in joint economic development. Ironically, the El Salvador-Honduras war of 1969 strengthened this buffer corridor. If Guatemala today were directly to border Sandinista Nicaragua instead of weaker Honduras, frontier strife probably would be much more serious and escalation to regional warfare more likely. Neutralist and unarmed Costa Rica likewise could be labeled a buffer, separating her northern neighbors from Panama. In sum, there is no rational reason for the existence of six weak and antagonistic Central American states, other than the chaotic geographic source which has spawned these buffers and thus the separations and turmoil.

Mountain plateaus and intervening jungles kept Panama and its canal potential disconnected from northern and southern Hispanic neighbors. It is interesting that the isthmus, so vital to commerce and so central to Middle America, itself exhibited a strategic buffer which drew as a magnet the hegemonic ambitions of the United States. The isolation of Panama and North American continental objectives combined to eventually bring United States control over the canal zone.

The United States in the twentieth century has shown a keen interest in Central American political stability, a factor tied to her protection of the vital isthmian transit. Favoring a divide-and-conquer approach, she continuously sought a balance between Nicaragua and Guatemala in hope of maintaining the El Salvador-Honduras buffer corridor. Further, the United States has utilized strong ties with Guatemala for preventing Mexican penetration into Central American affairs. In this latter regard, the United States fears a possible Mexican sphere of influence over these territories and traditionally has aimed to divert the Republic's interests from pointing southwardly. The Guatemalan buffer serves this deflecting purpose and is reflected in the close United States-Guatemala relationship during much of the twentieth century. Mexican peace plans for resolving contemporary turmoil in Nicaragua and El Salvador are disregarded by the United States in part to limit Mexican influence in Central America.

Mexican Americans or Chicanos, a largely unnoticed but nevertheless important nationalist groups which could be considered a part of Latin America as well as the United States, increasingly are seen as cultural and potentially as political "bridges" between Anglo and Latin America.[3] Currently numbering more than seven million citizens, fifth among ethnic backgrounds within the total United States population, Chicanos are unique in that a majority reside near the southwestern border with Mexico, their original homeland. Villarreal and Kelly assert that:[4]

> No major nationality group except Mexican Americans may claim a domestic territorial perspective with political overtones, seen in the 'Aztlan' concept, a very weak yet potentially significant secessionist suggestion for Chicano leadership of a 'Southwestern Quebec.' These two unique features, cultural and geographic, as well as

other traits, extend Mexican Americans naturally
and inevitably into the international realm.

This Aztlan nationhood of Chicano mythology, spanning territory
from Texas to California, likewise represents a buffer between the
two Americas. Here could rest a future facility for cultural
understanding, a neutral area for resisting contacts between the
two cultures, or a zone for perpetuating racial antagonism.

The Guiana highlands, the Andean mountains, and the Amazon
jungle effectively divide the northern rimlands of South America
from the continent's central and southern regions. Considered
more Caribbean in orientation than South American, the foreign
policies of Colombia, Venezuela, Guyana, and Surinam[5] are more
concerned with problems in Central America, Cuba and the United
States than with events of the Southern Cone. These geographic
obstacles, which isolate territories, buffer the politics of the two
South Americas, fragmenting the continent and retarding
development and integration of the Amazonian and Andean
hinterlands.

Position of islands and straits in the Caribbean creates several
important buffer situations. The eastward Atlantic island strings,
the Bahamas, Hispanola, Puerto Rico, and the Lesser Antilles,
separate the Atlantic from the Caribbean Sea and obstruct access
to interior spaces. This factor has influenced naval strategies from
the early buccaneers to contemporary submarine warfare. Cuba
itself figures as a buffer by its isolating the northern from the
southern Caribbean and in this way blocking the United States from
Jamaica, Panama, and northern South America.[6] Long considered
the heartland of Middle America, Cuba as a Soviet ally has meant
the decline of United States regional hegemony, allowing other
republics of Middle America to assert independence from northern
domination as well. The lessening of United States influence has
tended to make buffer systems within Middle America more
noticeable and to augment their political impact.

Maritime straits in Middle American waters reveal buffer
characteristics. An overwhelming proportion of strategic minerals
imports enter the United States via the Gulf of Mexico and
Caribbean Sea, enroute through the Mississippi waterway where
they are destined for processing plants and factories in the Middle
Western industrial heartland. United States Atlantic and Pacific
ports in contrast absorb relatively small amounts of such materials,
for local industries do not handle large sums of these minerals and
rail systems from coastal harbors to midwestern plants cannot

compete with the efficiency and convenience of central river barge transport. Hence, because the primary funnel for strategic minerals is the Caribbean, no matter whether the African, Australian, or Latin American source,[7] the region of most immediate United States sensitivity for guarantee of maritime passage of these materials clearly is Middle America, particularly in four clusters of choke points which could easily disrupt traffic if attacked during war. These particular choke points include the Panama Canal, the Straits of Florida, the Yucatan Channel, and the several Lesser Antilles passages.

Strategic materials destined for gulf ports originating from southern African sources must pass through the Mozambique Channel, the Cape of Good Hope, the Atlantic Narrows, and the Florida Straits, each of which pose promising opportunities for enemy interdiction. South American trade paths first cross the Atlantic Narrows, then may traverse the Dominica Channel, the Trinidad Passage, the Carios Passage, the Saint Vincent Passage, and/or the Guadalupe Passage of the Lesser Caribbean Antilles, and later northward through the Yucatan Strait. Caribbean strategic minerals travel a similar direction, sans the Atlantic Narrows. Minerals shipments from Australia to the United States extend through choke points situated along southern Australia before facing the open Pacific, the Panama Canal, and the several Caribbean passages. In each of these four Middle American choke areas, geographic restrictions to passage buffer one area from another.

In sum, buffers within Middle America are numerous, created by topographical and other disrupting features which have contributed to often chaotic geopolitical relationships among the nations of the region and with states beyond the Caribbean. For the most part, these buffers thwart regional unity and independence, isolating particularly the weaker states. I believe that internal buffers have prevented Middle America as a whole from itself asserting independence or neutraility, and therefore, local states have become pawns to larger states' interventions as a result. Buffer-created fractionalization apparently has assisted strong foreign powers for five hundred years toward establishing spheres of influence or shatterbelt bases over the Caribbean, revealing a strong linkage among buffer, sphere of influence, and shatterbelt configurations. These linkages, as well as their extraterritorial projections of influence shown in the Middle America-wide buffer, will now be examined.

EXTERNAL FUNCTION

From its central position astride Atlantic and Pacific Oceans and between North and South America, a Caribbean-scope buffer exerts a strong impact upon the international relations of large outside states who hold interests in the region. For example, I maintain that Brazilian and Soviet Union objectives currently are enhanced by this larger Middle American buffer perspective. In contrast, attainment of United States defense requirements are made more difficult because of the Basin's peculiar spacial dimensions. Most of this section will explore these features of the Caribbean buffer's external impact.

The fact that the Central American land buffer between North and South America effectively impedes Europe and Africa from direct access to Asia has contributed to a variety of geopolitical consequences. Absence of natural Atlantic to Pacific passageways through Middle America diminished Western penetration of China, Japan, and elsewhere in the East. Europeans and Africans instead settled predominately in America, and not Asia, making the New World an arena not only for racial blending and antagonism but also for exploiting a rich environment with new ideas and a wide-variety of immigrant classes. Middle America probably blocked extensive Asian contact with Europe and Africa as well.

By limiting exchange between oceans despite the relatively short distances involved, the isthmian buffer increased the strategic importance of certain territorial and maritime zones throughout the Americas which were to be considered potential or actual inter-oceanic transit routes. The several Caribbean and Gulf of Mexico isthmian areas, in Panama, Nicaragua, and Tehuantepec, drew particular foreign notice. Certain continental routes as well have become similar magnets of international transit rivalry, some of these including the Northwest passage of Canada, the southern straits of Magellan, Beagle, and Drake, the southwestern region of the United States, and the several Andean passes of Bolivia and Ecuador in South America's interior.

Controlling these oceanic passages have posed serious diplomatic problems for the United States and for Brazil, each being continental powers desiring access to both oceans. In the case of the northern republic, the attainment of California made control of a Middle American canal a vital national interest. Panama remains a key to North American continental unity as well as to United States projection of influence onto the rimlands of Eurasia.[8] For Brazil, the "March to the West" meant domination of the strategic Charcas Triangle of Bolivia, the alleged "heartland" of South America and gateway to the Pacific.[9] Recently, her interest likewise extends to the southern passages and to Antarctica as intra-oceanic avenues of commerce and power.[10]

In addition to blocking western pentration to the East, Middle America reduces contact between North and South America. One consequence of this separation is that the southern continent never has come under United States dominance. Nor has South America experienced a shatterbelt in which the United States competed in the area against another Great Power rival. (Nevertheless, Spain, England, and Portugal dominated South America under a sphere of influence or rivaled each other within a shatterbelt during much of the region's European-directed history.) Today, South America, from the Amazon and Andean watersheds to the Southern Cone, continues to be free of European and United States control, showing it to be one of the few world areas at present which is independent of Great Power penetration.

Because of South American isolation from the United States for reason of the Caribbean buffer and internal buffer-induced Central American strife, and the waning of European impact during the nineteenth century, several geopolitical patterns have emerged in the region's international relations which would not have surfaced had these foreign powers been able to interfere. Two historians of South American diplomacy[11] discovered a balance of power configuration among Southern Cone nations operating during the nineteenth and early twentieth centuries. Child suggests this pattern can be applied to contemporary politics and extended to Caribbean South American states as well, thus forming a continental linkage of alliances and antagonisms.[12] (See Fig. 4.1. Bold horizontal and vertical lines signify international rivalries; dashed diagonal lines indicate harmonic relationships.)

FIG. 4.1
South American Balance of Power

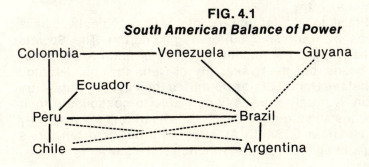

Child argues that this balance pattern has returned to South America because United States and European influence has disappeared, resulting in the resumption of traditional antagonisms. In part, the Caribbean buffer's location enabled these balances to re-appear.

I have written elsewhere that Brazil appears on the verge of being the hegemonic power of South America, fitting a role of continental rule maker and enforcer, stabilizier and integrator. My reasoning is contained in this passage.[13]

> Why should Brazil be in a position to enforce regional order? First, among South American nations, Brazil, as a geopolitically satisfied country, has the most to lose from uncontrolled regional strife, in lessened international prestige, economic prosperity, internal development, and even possible loss of Amazon territories. With these strong interests at stake, Brazil possesses ample incentive for performing pacifier and integrationist roles. Second, Brazil has necessary power for projecting influence across the continent, and her central location, bolstered by an improving transportation network, further enhances this qualification. Third, Spanish American neighbors lack sufficient unity or power to form an effective bloc against Brazilian hegemony, and in most cases incentives for cooperating with Brazil outweigh any advantages for opposing her hemispheric objectives. Last, South America no longer is under outside Great Power political control, making it feasible for Brazil to occupy the strategic vacuum which has ensued.

In the latter case, Brazil's ability as a hegemonic power to fill the region's political vacuum is a direct consequence, in my opinion, of the Middle American buffer, within which the United States has become entangled and from which Brazil enjoys its present isolation from the north.

Similar to Brazil, the Soviet Union's international objectives have been advanced by Caribbean buffer fragmentation. The Soviets traditionally have lacked sufficient influence in Latin America for establishing bases, but the availability of Cuba for socialist-bloc alliance against the United States permitted their first military entry into the region. Not only were they now able to consolidate their hold on territories and straits in the Basin's heartland but also they could widen isolation of South America from northern territories and encourage rebellion in Central America and elsewhere.

From a United States foreign and security policy perspective, the buffer system of Middle American poses a variety of very serious difficulties. The United States has sought stability along its frontiers, a policy first emerging in reaction to weaknesses in Spanish Florida and Louisiana,[14] later extending to political vacuums in Texas and the Pacific, and more recently reaching to turmoil throughout the Caribbean Basin and in some Eurasian rimland areas. A security threat arises against the United States not immediately from frontier power vacuums themselves but from possible enemy military intrusions into these vacuums which could threaten the United States core. Contemporary revolution and depression in Middle America do not endanger United States defenses, but serious consequences accrue from enemy armed alliances with radical anti-United States countries of the Caribbean. These vacuum spaces in fact are buffers; they separate the United States from allied or neutral states and signify anchors onto which foreign powers may attach themselves.

With this frontier policy, the worst-case scenario for United States security is a Middle American shatterbelt because this condition, by its inherent nature, means the existence of rival military bases in the Caribbean, North America's best alternatives figure to be either a United States sphere of influence or a completely neutral or independent Middle America, both of which preclude enemy encroachments. Buffer qualities within Middle America. I argue, contribute to the weakening of United States hegemony, prevent the emergence of Caribbean independence, but prompt instead a shatterbelt configuration in the region. Therefore, buffers have contributed to a loosening of North American control and have provided opportunities for Soviet Caribbean inroads.

Because Washington's post World War Two vision of the most dangerous threat to her vital interests is Soviet expansion, defense strategists naturally stress Eurasia, not Latin America, in their immediate military calculations. The essence of United States security policy since 1947 has been to project military force effectively onto certain Eurasian territories so as to prevent inclusion of these into the Soviet empire.[15] Three terminals of contemporary American power projection are Western Europe, the Persian Gulf, and East Asia; additional zones of Eurasia involvement have emerged from time to time as well. Consequently, the United States security perimeter lies in Eurasia, not in America, and a "fortress America" conception, a quarter-sector sphere, and similar defense plans where Latin America becomes an equal partner of the United States have never been widely contemplated by Pentagon analysts.[16]

Within this Eurasian thrust, Latin America's contribution to North American defense, from the United States geopolitical viewpoint, lies in these areas: a) prevent hostile bases from arising in the hemisphere; b) enhance United States military efforts with bases, material, and troops; and c) assist in protecting transit routes utilized for importing resources to America and for projecting United States power overseas.[17] This Latin American defense contribution is secondarily important to United States strategists, who count primarily on hemispheric acquiescence toward United States security efforts beyond the New World.

Focusing upon this aspect in his classic work, *America's Strategy in World Politics: The United States and the Balance of Power,* Spykman maintained:[18]

> There is no possibility of achieving an adequate integration of the states of the New World in the face of German opposition, and even if there were, the balance potential of the Americas would still be inadequate to balance the Old World. Because of the distribution of land masses and military potentials, a balance of power in the transAtlantic and transPacific zones is an absolute prerequisite for the independence of the New World and the preservation of the power position of the United States. There is no safe defensive position of this side of the oceans. Hemisphere defense is no defense at all. The Second World War will be lost or won in Europe and Asia. The strategic picture demands that we conduct our military operations in the form of a great offensive across the oceans. If our allies in the Old World are defeated, we cannot hold South America; if we defeat the German-Japanese alliance abroad, our good neighbors will need no protection.

Spykman predicted United States encirclement and eventual defeat if "the three land masses of the Old World can be brought under the control of a few states and so organized that large unbalanced forces are available for pressure across the ocean fronts." In the possibility of invasion, a loyal Latin America would be no compensation for the loss of the Eurasian balance of power, and the United States could be strangled into submission by the vast resources of the encircling nations. This geopolitical scenario was significantly to influence post war containment policies of George

Kennan and others,[19] a security approach which has continued to the present day.

The buffer of Middle America tends to limit this United States extension of power to Eurasia and to disrupt her hemispheric defenses as well. Projecting military force would be quite difficult so long as vital choke point buffers in the Caribbean were susceptible to enemy interdiction, such as Soviet ally Cuba intends those adjacent her shores to be. In addition, the United States simply cannot afford to ignore Middle American turmoil on her southern frontier, and consequently she must partially retrench from Eurasia involvement to protect her New World flank as a result. Finally, Middle America separates North America from potential South American allies, restricting United States leadership in South Atlantic and Pacific defense and her ability to coordinate a northern and southern quarantine of the Caribbean buffer.

The central location of the Middle American buffer isolates and separates other areas from each other, similarly to the functioning of sub-system buffers within the Caribbean Basin. For each level of geopolitical impact, these buffers closely interact with other regional configurations, primarily spheres of influence and shatterbelts, and these connections have characterized the historic political perspective of the entire Basin and its ties to other territories as well. Some of the shapes of this nexus are drawn in the section which follows.

ANALYSIS

In comparison to shatterbelts, spheres of influence, and neutral or independent political zones, buffers are unique geopolitical entities in a variety of special ways. For example, they may operate within sub-regions of fairly limited scope, as was noted in Central America and elsewhere in the Caribbean, and simultaneously occupy a complete region. Each of the other configurations normally do not exist in both isolated sections and in the whole region concurrently. Spheres of influence indicate absolute authority over a certain tier of states by one outside power or alliance. Anything less than preponderance is not an influence sphere. Neutral and independent zones must be free of all outside domination; foreign bases within the area cannot transpire. Shatterbelts are regions where rival Great Power bases exist, an arena of potential conflict escalation which cannot be reduced to smaller dimensions.

Buffers differ by projecting an impact to adjacent regions. Because the Caribbean shields South America from the United States, Brazil may be able to assert hegemonic leadership over the Southern Cone, a feat Mexico cannot attempt relative to Central America, being under the political shadow of its northern neighbor. Where the other geopolitical constellations seem to exert an external influence, it usually means those regions are buffers also, and it is from this latter source that an impact beyond the immediate region is created.[20]

A further variation among the four configurations derives from the permanency of buffers; they continue to occur despite other political transformations within a region. This constancy is because buffers originate from unique geographic qualities, terrain, demography, vacant spaces, choke points, and the like, and from strategic position, both of which usually do not change. Unlike other regional models, buffers are conditioned more directly by an areas's immediate geographic attributes and position. In contrast, neutral or independent zones only arise when outside major powers do not intrude into their areas, spheres of influence emerge only after one Great Power is in areal command, and shatterbelts are born of two or more foreign competitors vying for territorial control.

Because buffers function to separate and to isolate adjacent territories, they sharply differ from prominent characteristics of the other configurations. Shatterbelts are noted for Great Power rivalry, spheres of influence for their exclusive control by one major outside power, and neutral or independent regions for an absence of foreign political involvement. Buffers are compatible with the presence of any level of outside states' entry. Finally, as shatterbelts, spheres of influence, and neutral or independent zones are mutually exclusive, they cannot function simultaneously with each other. An independent area cannot also be a sphere of influence, and neither can be a shatterbelt. Nevertheless, a buffer comfortably performs its functions simultaneously with all three, both in its internal and external aspects.

Could a Caribbean neutral or independent political zone someday replace or become an addition to the sphere of influence-shatterbelt rotation which has regularly transpired in Middle America for the past five centuries? Does there exist a potential for a federated Middle American state, or at least a widely recognized zone of neutrality, to arise? I believe this possibility to be very remote, based upon the buffer characteristics inherent to the Caribbean Basin. First, the United States likely will remain deeply involved in Middle America for the foreseeable future. She must be so, for the region will continue to be her most vital frontier defense area. Second, the prominence of the Basin's fragmenting internal and external buffer qualities, and the Soviet's consequent alliance with Cuba, will assure the continuance of a Caribbean shatterbelt. Third, at present no United States rival, not the Soviet Union or Brazil, possesses sufficient power in Middle America to induce a withdrawal of outside bases from the Caribbean. Hence, an international sponsoring of neutrality or independence for the region is not likely. Four, any shift away from a shatterbelt would be a rotation again toward a United States sphere of influence, which could occur if the Soviet Union were to reduce its interventions in Middle America.

I am also of the opinion that a resumption of a United States sphere of influence over the Caribbean is not possible under present circumstances. Conditions in the Basin are ripe for a shatterbelt instead. Middle America literally is torn apart now, particularly in a political sense, buffered internally from one section to another and attracting the establishment of rival Soviet and United States military alliances. And the Cuban-Soviet alliance seems healthly, despite occasional strains of partisanship. Consequently, neither a sphere of influence nor a neutral or independent status is evident because currently Middle America cannot be freed of the escalation of Great Power confrontation. It appears most probable, therefore, that a Caribbean shatterbelt will characterize the region for the remainder of the twentieth century.

In many respects, aspects of the Caribbean buffer and shatterbelt appear to resemble each other quite closely. Each enhances the other's visibility and importance within regional and international geopolitics. For instance, buffers normally reflect and stimulate a fragmented environment, a condition favoring the rise of shatterbelts. This is because buffers provide more opportunities for foreign states to establish armed footholds in Middle America, a situation which would not be permitted during spheres of influence or neutral-independence predominance. Likewide, shatterbelts increase the significance of buffers, both internally to the area and in their external projection. The Cuban buffer paved the way for Russian penetration of the Caribbean, hence a shatterbelt emerged. From this event, the rise of Central American and other subsystem buffers to greater prominence was facilitated as well as was the advance of Brazilian hegemony in the Southern Cone and the increasing difficulty of United States power extensions toward Eurasia. The buffer of Middle America likely has contributed to a rise of additional Eurasian shatterbelts as well. In these ways, the

Middle American buffers and shatterbelts reinforce each other, making the emergence of both spheres of influence and neutral or independent zones much less realistic.

In another sense, shatterbelts reflect buffer characteristics themselves. They reduce direct confrontation among Great Power homelands by deflecting this rivalry to more isolated regions.[21] Competition between the United States and the Soviet Union is played out in the Caribbean, where escalation is less threatening than in Middle Europe or East Asia and where control over surrogates or allies can be more flexible. In another case, a potential for conflict between Brazil and the United States is hidden by both the shatterbelt and the buffer system of the Basin.

SUMMARY

In conclusion, Middle America is a natural buffer zone, held permanently in this mode because of its rugged terrain and its strategic location. Two particular buffer features stand out: a series of subsystem internal buffers throughout the Basin which have tended to fragment political relationships and a region-wide buffer which has separated adjacent areas from each other, posing problems or opportunities for large foreign states involved in Caribbean affairs.

But, these buffers of Middle America never operate in vacuum; they instead hold close linkages to other types of regional configuration. Consequently, these relationships, such as we have seen in Middle America, must be studied in unison and not separately. In the Caribbean, buffers exert a disrupting impact on international affairs during shatterbelt eras and tend to be quiescent if spheres of influence and neutral or independent constellations predominate. Likewise, strong buffers facilitate the emergence of shatterbelts but tend to restrict spheres of influence and neutral or independent zones from developing.

How will these geopolitical relationships influence future politics in the Caribbean Basin? I would suggest several outcomes for immediate decades ahead, based upon the tandem association in Middle America of buffer and shatterbelt. First, if the Soviet presence in the Caribbean continues undisturbed despite United States opposition, a shatterbelt will remain in place along side prominent internal buffers and external buffer projections. Middle America consequently will continue to be a security problem for the United States and a foreign policy opportunity for Brazil and for the Soviet Union, factors which may press these states toward more involvement in the Basin. Second, turmoil and depression in Middle America may increase because of stronger buffer capacities as well as more significant Great Power intrusions. Finally, greater Caribbean tensions could either erupt someday into a serious United States-Soviet Union escalation toward war similar to the 1963 missile crisis over Cuba, or force the Soviets to withdraw their power from Middle America, a retrenchment caused by Russian failures elsewhere in addition to America. In the latter case, the Basin itself. Perhaps for other world buffer areas, potential again.

In these respects, the buffers of Middle America contribute more to a rise of shatterbelts than to a rise of spheres of influence and of independent or neutral political zones. Combined with a strategic Caribbean location, these buffers invite additional outside military intervention and frequent rivalry among Great Powers because they create regional hemispheric disunity and thus bring a built-in susceptibility for escalation of tensions within and beyond the Basin itself. Perhaps for other world buffers areas, potential antagonists are separated and isolated, bringing some possibility for peace. But in Middle America, buffers seem to encourage foreign intervention, either toward spheres of influence or toward shatterbelts. This attractiveness to outsiders, more than other aspects, appears to be the distinguishing quality of the Middle American buffer system.

NOTES

1. For more analysis of shatterbelts, see P. Kelly *(Political Geography Quarterly)* and S. Cohen, "A New Map of Global Geopolitical Equilibrium: A Developmental Approach," *Political Geography Quarterly,* 1 (1982):223-241 and S. Cohen, *Geography and Politics in a World Divided* (New York: Oxford University Press, 1973). For spheres of influence, see C.S. Gochman and J.L. Ray "Structural Disparities in Latin America and Eastern Europe, 1950-1970," *Journal of Peace Research,* 16 (1979):231-254 and for buffer systems, M.G. Partem, "Buffer Systems in International Relations," *Journal of Conflict Resolution,* 27 (1983):3-27.

2. P. Kelly, "Escalation of Regional Conflict: Testing the Shatterbelt Concept," *Political Geography Quarterly,* accepted for publication.

3. A.B. Rendon, *The Chicago Manifesto* (New York: Macmillan, 1971).

4. R. Villarreal and P. Kelly, "Mexican Americans as Participants in U.S.-Mexico Relations," *International Studies Notes,* 9(1982):1-6.

5. J. Ewell, "Development of Venezuelan Geopolitical Analysis Since World War II," *Journal of Interamerican Studies and World Affairs,* 24 (1982):295-320.

6. A.T. Mahan, *The Interest of America in Sea Power: Present and Future* (Boston: Little, Brown, and Company, 1918).

7. Congressional Budget Office report on foreign sources for strategic minerals, November 1983, as reviewed in the *Christian Science Monitor,* December 12, 1983, pp. 24-25.

   While many of these minerals could be replaced by substitutes or synthetics, the cost and time elements for conversion would be significant, and thus beyond the capability for a short duration conflict. U.S. Department of Commerce, *Mid-American Ports Study,* 1 (1979), and U.S. Department of Commerce, *Essential World Trade Routes,* (1975).

8. J. Child, "Military Aspects of the Panama Canal Issue," *U.S. Naval Institute Proceedings,* 106 (1980):46-51.

9. M. Travassos, *Projecao Continental do Brasil,* (Sao Paulo: Editorial Nacional, 1947).

10. H.T. Pittman, "Geopolitics in the ABC Countries: A Comparison," Paper presented before the Western Political Science Association, (1983), Seattle, Washington.

11. R.L. Seckinger, "South American Power Realities During the 1820s," *Hispanic American Historical Review,* 56 (1976):241-267.

12. J. Child, *Geopolitics and Conflict in South Amereica: Quarrels Among Neighbors,* (New York: Praeger, 1985).

13. P. Kelly, "Geopolitical Tension Areas in South America: The Question of Brazilian Territorial Expansion," *Texas Journal of Political Studies, accepted for publication.*

14. S.M. Bemis, *A Diplomatic History of the United States,* (New York: H. Holt and Company, 1936).

15. N.J. Spykman, *America's Strategy in World Politics: The United States and Balance of Power* (New York: Harcourt, Brace, and Company, 1942); E.B. Atkeson, "Hemispheric Denial: Geopolitical Imperatives and Soviet Strategy," *Strategy Review,* 4 (1976):26-36; and C. Gray, *The Geopolitics of the Nuclear Era: Heartlands, Rimlands, and the Technological Revolution* (New York: Crane, Russak, 1977).

16. J. Child, "Latin America: Strategic Concepts," *Air University Review,* 27 (1976):27-42.

17. D.F. Ronfeldt, *United States Security Policy in the Caribbean* (Santa Monica: Rand Corporation/paper No. 316, 1983).

18. Spykman, p. 457.

19. Gray, *The Geopolitics of the Nuclear Era.*

20. Shatterbelts obviously would make an important external effect if political rivalries within such areas were to spark serious escalation to international war, a characteristic of shatterbelts. Beyond this exception, nevertheless, shatterbelts, similar to spheres of influence and to neutral or independent political zones, show an internally-directed focus.

21. S. Cohen, *Geography and Polities in a World Divided,* (New York: Oxford University Press, 1973).

PART 2

REGION AND COUNTRY CASE STUDIES

CHAPTER 5

EASTERN EUROPE: THE BUFFER EFFECT OF A CORDON SANITAIRE*

OLAV FAGELUND KNUDSEN

*The cordon sanitaire worked also the other way round, though this was less perceived for some years. It excluded Russia from Europe, but it also excluded Europe from Russia. Ina perverse way, the barrier designed against Russia became Russia's protection.

(A.J.P. Taylor. *The Origins of the Second World War.* New York: Atheneum, 1961, p. 37)

INTRODUCTION

The purpose of this chapter is to assess and explain the buffer effect of a belt of smaller states located on the periphery of a great power, *in casu* the Soviet Union. Here "buffer effect" means the degree of "resistance" of such smaller states to encroachments from the great powers, whether nearby or farther away. The concept will be elaborated further later in the chapter. First, the general subject will be introduced in stepwise fashion, beginning with identification of the problem, moving to conceptual underpinnings, and finally and most importantly, application of the concepts to the case of Eastern Europe.

THE PROBLEM IN PRINCIPLE

All great powers and empires have sooner or later had to face the question of where their ultimate perimeter is to be. Even if in their expansive phases they have been able to keep their boundaries undefined and steadily moving outward, a time always came when they had to delimit their boundaries. If this has been a difficult issue to the great power, it has been a matter of existence itself to the smaller neighbors on its border. The size of the territory effectively controlled will reflect the power of the ruling group. Where several groups control adjacent areas, the drawing of boundaries will indicate their relative power position. However, there will always be uncertainties that keep boundaries from being exact power representations. Some are geographical, or topographical. Others are socio-cultural, particularly ethno-linguistic, or economic. Moreover, power in itself is often a vague phenomenon, seldom unequivocally clear to the parties involved except when wills are being tested to the limit. In the interim, the reputation for prevailing serves as a usable substitute. A reputation for power can make the effect of a demonstrated power edge linger on for an extended time without any true confrontations taking place.

The distinction between what is part of the state and what is outside it is therefore always in a political sense unclear, even if it may be clearly defined on a map and in the actual physical terrain. The political neighbor-relation revolves around this ambiguity.

Boundaries, then, are rough power divisions; they show where the exclusive control in each side declines sharply, although in our case sharper on one side than the other. In Karl W. Deutsch's perspective the universal variety of patterns of social communication - each pattern being at the base of a community - may in itself be a precondition for the exercise of power.[1] The domain of power tends, perhaps, to become coextensive with a given pattern of social communication. Deutsch's perspective provides a reasonable interpretation of the limits to lateral extensions of power.

Boundaries are not absolute. The ambiguity of the great power's boundary is at the very heart of the small neighbor's existence. Not only is the small state at the mercy of the great power; at the other end of the relation, the great power also feels threatened by its small neighbor. That threat, while often imaginary, may at times turn out to be real. Even a small state may be able to conspire with others against the great power's security, perhaps even letting its territory be used for such purposes. In a sense, therefore, the great power's acceptance of the continued existence of a small neighbor represents its decision to run a calculated risk: that of leaving what is outside its boundary, or part of it, to the discretion of others, even as it still aspires to the maximum possible influence over what happens there.

Eastern Europe, historically an area of multiple, crisscrossing empire boundaries, will be analyzed as a region in which the larger portions have for substantial periods been firmly in the grip of one or another of the great powers. Over time, however, there have also been substantial changes in overlordship, with power shifting back and forth. The nations of the region have, moreover, long been part of the greater economic system of Europe. In the following, the relationship of Eastern Europe to the neighboring great powers and to the European system as a larger entity, with emphasis on the two most recent generations, will be discussed.

TYPES OF RELATIONSHIPS
BETWEEN GREAT AND SMALL POWERS

Several factors are involved in making up the relationship of power disparity on the fringe of a great power. One is the *degree of control* exercised at any given time over the smaller state by the larger - contemporary Finland, Poland, and Czechoslovakia illustrate different points along the continuum. Another factor is the question of whether an opposing great power is also involved - the *symmetry* factor.[2] Conceivably the degree of power disparity may be reduced or cancelled out by the appearance of a rival great power. The two factors are related: The greater the interest and involvement of a rival great power, the smaller the degree of control exercised by one side only. Conversely, as the degree of great-power symmetry declines, the possibility of unilateral great-power intervention increases. For the relationship to be operative there would conceivably be a threshold, a certain minimum level of great-power involvement that had to be exceeded before the degree of symmetry could be expected to influence the degree of control. As we shall presently see, the relationship between symmetry and control is central to what is called "the buffer effect."

A third factor is the *attractiveness of the small state to the great power(s)*. This factor concerns the possession by the small state of something desired by the great neighbor or its opponent, whether a mineral resource, a potential military base site, or some other attractive item. The implications of this kind of factor for small state survival are not clear-cut. Conceivably, to the small state such "great-power lures" could be liabilities equally as well as being assets. If they attract both great-power sides equally they would reinforce the symmetry factor. However, if great-power interest became extreme, that might bring the great powers together for a joint exploitation of the small.

A fourth and final factor concerns the intrinsic *strength of the small state* itself. Military power is one aspect. Domestic, or internal, cohesiveness is another: The greater the degree of internal conflict, the smaller the external strength of the unit. Commitment to independence among the elites and population of the small state is a third aspect. The other side of the coin is the extent to which there are elements of dependency reducing the strength of the small state, and what degree of dependency is involved.

The foregoing factors affect the situation of all small states situated on the fringe of a great power. In the following the focus will be somewhat narrowed to examine what may be called "buffer relationships" in particular.

BUFFER SYSTEMS

An area may be referred to as a potential *buffer area* if it is controlled by one or more small states and located between two opposing - and much greater - powers. There are three key defining characteristics: Contiguity, a substantial power disparity between the great and small powers involved, and rough power parity between the great. The complete collection of great and small powers may, as suggested by Michael G. Partem, be termed a potential *buffer system*.[3] The term *buffer state* traditionally refers to a relatively small state that separates areas controlled by two opposing great powers.[4]

The buffer phenomenon can be conceived as an effect, the resultant of a variety of causal factors. The buffer effect may be defined as the degree of "resistance" of a buffer area to outside encroachments, superficially observable as the persistence over time of the small states of the buffer system as independent political units. The strength or weakness of the buffer effect in empirical cases is a question on which some time will be spent in the following.

According to Partem, "The logic of the buffer system dictates that neither (great power) can dominate the system."[5] Indeed, a central point of a strong buffer effect is that neither great power attacks or encroaches on the state in between, because they deter each other.[6]

On the other hand, a side effect is presumably that tension and conflict between them is subdued. As in other deterrence relationships, however, the system may become unstable for a variety of reasons. If the strategic importance of the buffer area is not equally great to both great-powers, that would be one element of instability. If the commitment of the small buffer state's leadership to continued independence decreases, that could be another.

In reality, of course, the overall buffer effect may vary both between individual cases and over time. The specific variables which seem to influence the strength of the buffer effect may be summarized as follows:

A. variables related to the symmetry factor:

1. the degree of power parity (ratio of capabilities) between the great powers;

2. the degree of equality of salience of the buffer area to the great powers (also linked to the attractiveness factor);

3. (a function of the preceding two:) the probability that each great power would resist an attempt by the other to attack or intervene in the system's small state;

4. the apparent cost to each great power (as perceived by themselves) of subduing the small state (also linked to the factor of small state strength);[7]

B. variables related to the control factor and to that of small state strength:

5. the degree of power disparity (ratio of capabilities) between great power/small state;

6. the commitment to continued independence on the part of the buffer state's leadership, especially desire for freedom from great power influence or intervention, as evidenced in recurring public statements and visible acts.

The intensity of conflict between the opposing great powers is an exogenous variable. Here it can simply be treated as a constant, assuming that it is fairly high (though not extreme - that might introduce a new dynamic element).

The variables are hypothesized to be positively related to the buffer effect. In other words, the way they interact (especially items 5 and 6) serves to maintain the buffer system, keeping the small-state part of the system from becoming on the one hand too weak (leading the system to collapse), and on the other hand too strong, so that it becomes a prospective alliance partner to either great power. In this analysis cases will mainly be examined in which one or more of these conditions are only weakly present or fail to occur.

THE *CORDON SANITAIRE*

The term *cordon sanitaire* was used by the French to denote their containment policy towards the new Bolshevik state and its small western neighbors after World War One.[8] More generally, and disregarding the pejorative connotations, it may be used to refer to a relationship in which a string of small powers on the perimeter of a great power are made by a rival great power to serve as a barrier - or themselves seek to form one - in order to isolate, and insulate, the great power from the rest of the world. Hence it may be a strategy by which a great power seeks to shut out the world, perhaps in order to consolidate its internal power position; or it may be a strategy employed by another great power "on the outside" seeking to hem in the target power and contain its influence. The Monroe Doctrine sought to establish a type of *cordon sanitaire* in the Western Hemisphere in the nineteenth century, and subsequent U.S. policies have in one way or another pursued the same goal with some success even up to the present time.

A *cordon sanitaire* may take the form of an asymmetric pattern of alliance or association. The extent to which the small states are being controlled in the process may vary from negative great-power influence at one end of the spectrum, consisting simply of denial of the area to its opponent, to absolute dominance at the other end. The difference between denial and dominance may be illustrated by the situation of Finland since 1948 vs. that of the rest of Eastern Europe in the same period; or possibly by the situation of Central America as opposed to that of Eastern Europe.

The success of a policy to establish a *cordon* may hinge on the extent to which the small neighboring states are able to cooperate with the external instigator(s) on the need for such action, and/or the extent to which the instigator is able to control what goes on inside the small states.

Clearly, as a policy the *cordon sanitaire* has strong defensive connotations, regardless of why or by whom it is pursued. It is not exclusively defensive, however. If initiated "from the inside," it may be combined with an expansionist strategy, seeking to add new territory to the area controlled. Some, perhaps, might call that a policy of seeking "security in depth." Conversely, if rooted on the outside, the policy may be used by the outside power(s) as a springboard for the ultimate conquest of the state behind the *cordon*.

In short, the *cordon sanitaire* has two main functions. The first one overlaps with that of the buffer area: separating a great power from another great power or group of powers. The second function is to enlist the support of political elites in the area for the *cordon,* or - failing that - to control the politics of the area, at least where foreign policy is concerned, in ways inimical to the interests of the opposing great-power side.

SYMMETRIC VARIATIONS:
THE BUFFER COMPLEX

Combining aspects of the two preceding sections, one might conceive of a system that is partly controlled by one side, partly by the other, and partly uncontrolled by either. At the center there would be an uncontrolled core area consisting of one or more non-aligned states. In the wider setting around the core, there would be several more or less contiguous small states, under the influence or partial control of opposing great powers. In a model or ideal type as discussed here, rather than any specific case, the influence and control exercised by the great powers would decline gradually as the distance from their own borders increased. This type of system is considered as a "buffer complex."[9] In this kind of complex some states "lean" to one side, others to the other side, while some are non-aligned. The buffer effect is conceived as before; i.e., as the degree of "resistance" of a buffer area to outside encroachments, but this time with the added proviso that within the area there may be a declining degree of resistance to outside pressure as one moves from the center towards the periphery. What distinguishes the buffer complex from other buffer areas is above all that the buffer effect at the center may "spill over" - to a greater or lesser extent - to the surrounding small states. Hence it may be hypothesized that the stronger the buffer effect at the center, the greater its geographical extension beyond the core area. The reasons for this will be elaborated in the following.

In confronting the surrounding great powers, the small states of the complex derive added protective strength from the aggregated effects of mutual relations amongst themselves. To the extent that they are actively cooperating with each other, and are strongly committed to preserving their independence, their protection from great-power control may be enhanced. The Nordic region, whose so-called "Nordic Balance" emerged after 1948, illustrates this.[10] If conditions are right, the overall effect may be a flexible kind of strength, repulsing encroachments from both (or all) adjacent great powers. Some degree of outside influence or even control over foreign policy and domestic politics in the peripheral states may be expected to occur, however, because the peripheral countries of the complex are more likely to have their own relationships to outside powers, and so each may experience less of the simultaneous kind of pressure from both great powers which often relieves the situation of the ordinary buffer state.

The stability of a buffer complex hinges on the success of each small member in resisting unilateral great power pressures. In short, the small members of the buffer complex will tend to prioritize their mutual peaceful relations over and above their individual bilateral relations with their respective great powers. This amounts to a regional solidarity - thinking of the possible ramifications of new foreign policy moves, not just to one's own state, but also to neighboring states.

In a real-world example Nordic states, to fend off great power pressures, argue that any demand for change in the status quo in one country is bound to lead to demands for similar changes by other great powers in other countries. For a long time, the prospect to either superpower gaining a new concession in the Nordic region while giving the opponent a similar advantage has not appeared desirable, and so the region has gained some protection from the existing constellation of forces.

The buffer complex may begin unraveling, however, if the argument about similar concessions to competitors does not take hold and the revisionist great power persists in its demands. The outside powers may in fact both (all) come to feel that it would be better if the two (or all) of them controlled more of the buffer complex directly.

Another and even more destabilizing element would be introduced if one of the small states were to conclude on its own that it wanted a closer relationship to "its" outside great power.[11] The danger here, of course, is that this could trigger demands for "compensation" from the other great-power side. In short, the buffer complex has flexibility and strength, but also a built-in element of instability.

If there is conflict among the small powers in the complex, the likelihood of fending off great power pressures naturally becomes much reduced. Indeed, the greater the amount of small-power conflict, the weaker their position in the over-all buffer system, and the weaker the buffer effect of the complex itself. Infighting among the small, then, is one reason why a buffer complex may collapse.

To the extent that the core area falls under the control of the surrounding great powers, the buffer effect thereby disappears. Though always a matter of degree, the buffer effect (in the context of the buffer complex) is definitionally contingent on some minimum level of resistance to great power encroachments at the core. As great power control over the core increases beyond that level, we would be dealing with an ordinary, direct great-power confrontation, which should be seen as a conceptually distinct phenomenon. In the following, the above mentioned concepts are applied in order to improve our understanding of Eastern Europe.

AN ANALYSIS OF THE EAST EUROPEAN SYSTEM

The establishment of the current (post-1948) state of affairs in Eastern Europe must be seen as a step in a gradual process of change initiated when the stable condition of previous centuries started giving way. During the nineteenth century, the Ottoman Empire experienced a long period of decline, erosion and ultimate disintegration which repeatedly jolted the European balance-of-power system. The process continued until the beginning of World War One.

By 1917-18 there were, in addition to the highly significant Ottoman decline, no less than three empires and great powers which collapsed around the Vistula and Danubian basins. Rapidly and almost simultaneously they fell, setting all of the East European nationalities free in a vast power vacuum. Russia collapsed from within, Austria-Hungary and Germany [12] from external strain - but all ultimately from the stresses induced by the war.

This triple collapse affected the northern part of Eastern Europe more directly than the southern part, many of whose nations had already gained their independence previously. However, the notorious instability of the Balkan south, compounded by the beginning decline of Austria-Hungary and by Russia's attempts to replace her, were important contributing factors to the outbreak of the great war. Ironically, then, the changing of great power positions, as they were competing to dominate the area, also helped to bring about the ultimate break-down of the Eastern dominance system itself.

In sum, while at the time of the Congress of Vienna of 1815 Eastern Europe was subject to a reasonably stable system of domination, over the next century that system dissolved almost completely.

The story of Eastern Europe in this century is the account of a progressive transition from the collapse of one system of dominance to the establishment of another, from multi-power dominance to single-power hegemony.[13]

In the analysis that follows an examination of the latter part of this transition will be sought by relating historical events to the main analytical factors initially outlined. Since 1918 the buffer effect for Eastern Europe seems to have been weak. The theme of the analysis will be that a weak buffer effect is probably related to the intensity and degree of symmetry of great-power interests in the area.

There are good reasons to consider the question in two stages - before and after World War Two. In the inter-war period, when no great power controlled Eastern Europe, one might have thought - as did many contemporary observers - that conditions were quite favorable for a buffer effect. The late 1930s proved them wrong. Then, with the war, conditions changed drastically. After 1945 there were unique opportunities for a fresh start: Previous regimes erased in Eastern Europe, two new great powers opposing each other over the shaping of the future in Europe. Yet, once, more the changes were different than many had expected - or hoped.

Not until the end of the war, in 1919, were the immediate political implications of the long imperial decline in Eastern Europe apparent. Chief among them was a widespread disintegration of power. The Versailles Conference, understandably, was not much concerned with that aspect, but focused rather on the promise of seeing so many long-oppressed nationalities liberated from foreign domination. In the Wilsonian spirit, the conference granted self-determination to all major national groups in the region.

The authority of the settlement rested with the victorious powers of the west, who had no particular designs or interests of their own in Eastern Europe. Hence, when they accepted the regional power vacuum which ensued, it was by default rather than design.

The inter-war period saw the consequences of Eastern Europe's political breakdown and of the Versailles settlement on the European system at large: In addition to an unsettling lack of any discernible power structure, there were neighborly conflicts, authoritarian excesses and silly demonstrations of small-power arrogance. Interacting with such minor disturbances and political deficiencies were other post-war developments, above all the stepwise restitution of German power - only superficially overcome in 1918 - and the slower stabilization of Bolshevik power in Russia.

By about the mid-1930s signs of serious stress were visible, in the shape of mounting tension, at different points in the European system.

Some of the stress originated in the war itself, such as the anti-Bolshevik interventions in Russia by British, French and U.S. forces; also the territorial immodesty of the Poles after they had successfully beaten back the Red Army from Warsaw in 1919-21. However, much of the internal East European stress had literally been built in at Versailles. The Baltic states and Poland (the part that was recognized as Polish by the Peace Conference) were carved out of formerly Russian and German territory. Most of Austria-Hungary was reshaped into Czechoslovakia, Hungary and an Austrian successor state, and parts of it were transferred to the new Yugoslavian state, joining together the Serbians and numerous other strong nationalities, notably the Croats and Slovenes. Romania received Bessarabia (formerly Russian) and Transylvania (formerly Austro-Hungarian), decisions never accepted whether by Russia or Hungary. In response to their new situation, Czechoslovakia, Romania and Yugoslavia soon (1920-21) got together to form the *Little Entente,* a set of alliances directed primarily against revisionist Hungary.

In the meantime Germany, though defeated, had not been crushed. The Versailles settlement was, territorially speaking, considerably less favorable to Russia than to Germany. A restoration of German power could not be ruled out. The widespread rejection of the Versailles settlement in the German population gave that potentiality clear international relevance. After 1925 Western fears were calmed by the Locarno Treaty, in which Germany explicitly accepted her new western borders. But Locarno never had an eastern counterpart. To the contrary, Germany unambiguously cited the eastern borders as targets for future revision. Hitler's accession to power became a catalytic factor, releasing these tensions in revisionist action.

Both Russia and Germany had been absent from - and subsequently also rejected - the territorial settlement of Versailles. However, for a buffer effect to be present, the great powers next to the buffer area must accept the status quo. In the inter-war period Germany and Russia, both European outcasts, had a common inclination to reject the status quo - as demonstrated by their surprise Rapallo Treaty in 1922 and ultimately confirmed by the Molotov-Ribbentrop Pact in 1939, which divided all of Eastern Europe between them.

The small neighbors between Germany and Russia did not seem to grasp the wider implication of these tendencies - or, if some of them did, they were unable to gain the necessary political support to institute defensive measures. Other preoccupations got in the way. Indeed, among the East European nations there was scarcely any feeling of solidarity, nor any realization of a need for it. There was no sense of being in the same boat, tossing about between Scylla and Charybdis. When they were not preoccupied with their own territorial claims, East European political leaders seemed almost exclusively concerned with the Russian political threat. As one of them observed, "If the Germans come, we will lose our freedom, but with the Russians we will lose our souls."[14]

As we shall see, these preoccupations had long been nurtured by Western policies in the region, particularly the French policy - succeeding the policy of direct intervention in Russia and conceived to continue the anti-Bolshevik line when intervention failed.

In the internal post-war politics of the region France and Russia were the main potential counterweights to growing German power. But France, whose primary concern since 1919 had been to keep Germany weak, also wanted to prevent the westward spread of communism. Many French feared Bolshevism almost as much as they feared the renewal of German ambitions. Applied to Eastern Europe, these two French goals may at first have seemed compatible. Encourage a strong Eastern Europe, and the result might be both a barrier to communism and a counterweight to Germany.

In fact, a *cordon sanitaire,* counterbalancing a "German-Hungarian bloc" and a "Russian bloc," was an early goal of Romanian policy after the war.[15] Other East Europeans were more concerned with other dangers, especially the threat from revisionist Hungary. To the extent that their fears converged, this motivated the succession of treaties that grew into the *Little Entente.* France, after some initial hesitation, supported these developments and from 1924 joined the treaty system herself. But the region was hard to fit into the ideal French (and Romanian) scheme. For one thing, Poland and Czechoslovakia were France's chief access points. However, these two states were unable to get along, being divided by border disputes. For another complication, Italy soon entered the East European scene in a diplomatic competition of sorts with France, eventually concluding an agreement with Hungary that stirred up strong enmities and contributed to keeping the area divided.[16]

Equally serious, perhaps, Eastern Europe was hardly a potential great power even if the states in the area had all welded together. Militarily they were weak. If containing German eastward expansion had been a serious French goal, then Russian backing ought to have been a welcome addition in supporting countries like Poland or Czechoslovakia. But that, of course, would mean cooperation with the Bolsheviks. Not until Hitler's take-over in 1933 were the French willing to consider that alternative. (The Russians, for their part, had been equally reserved towards the Western powers and were not ready, either, to cooperate with the French until that time.)

Part of the problem of France's eastern policy was that whatever strength Eastern Europe represented lay more in motivation - especially aversions - than in military muscle. East European sentiments, in addition to being divisive within the region, were clearly less anti-German than anti-Russian. Had the East European nations been politically cohesive and militarily strong, Germany - as well as Russia - would have had to take that strength into account. Such political and military strength could have been an independent and impartial power factor, propping up Eastern Europe in resistance to encroachments from either side, Russian or German. But to the extent the French were preoccupied with the *Cordon sanitaire* as a way to contain Bolshevism, their 'build-up' of Eastern Europe was robbed of any neutral flavor. Subsequently, the coming to power of rightist, quasi-fascist regimes in Poland and other countries in the area did little to improve the situation.

The East European trends reflected not just anti-communist sentiment, but also anti-Russian feeling. Many East European countries, having been created literally at Russia's territorial expense, had reason to fear Russian moves to revise the Versailles settlement. Granted, those that had been created at Germany's expense hardly slept any better for it, but the ideological factor was much weaker. In short, among the two motivations for the French policy only one - that of isolating Russia, strategically, the less important motivation - was really served by France's eastern allies.

As long as the German threat seemed remote, the French policy was all right. But the moment Hitler acceded to power, the problem became acute. Now France needed the Russian link. Still, both sides moved slowly. Only in 1934 did the Soviet Union join the League of Nations. Another two years were required before a Franco-Soviet agreement was completed. Then, very little was ever done at the military level to give substance to the relationship.

Despite obvious common interests, the political distance remained too great.

As the likelihood of war increased during the 1930s, French priorities became more uncertain. France had wanted Eastern Europe to supplement her power in confronting Germany, or diverting Germany's attention from the West; she never intended to commit herself to a war with Germany in order to save her Eastern allies. The building of the "Maginot line" illustrated this. To protect her allies from Germany, France would need to move offensively; not just sit in waiting behind a wall. The French "regarded their Eastern alliances as assets, not liabilities; bringing protection to France, not commitment."[17] French inconsistencies came to a head over Czechoslovakia in 1938.

In the Eastern belt Czechoslovakia was somewhat an exception. She was neither strongly anti-Russian *nor* militarily weak; in fact, she was militarily quite well prepared to defend herself.[18] At this point, however, the French (and the British) were concerned above all to stay out of armed conflict. France wanted to keep German attention focused eastward, but was not prepared to get involved. The Russians saw the implications and may have been ready to act alone in Czechoslovakia's defense.[19] But for the Soviet Union to honor her commitment to Czechoslovakia she needed (in addition to a request) permission to transit Romanian territory or airspace, or conceivably that of Poland; yet the actual granting of such permission was regarded as rather unlikely given the basic orientation of the regimes involved.

In the end, Czechoslovakia found herself with two nominal - and uncoordinated - supporters. To Prague, being defended by Russia but not France was out of the question, until at the very last moment, when the only alternative was surrender. Given the changing French preferences, Czechoslovakia had made the worst possible choice.

Underlying the symmetry dimension is the question of the degree of salience of the buffer area to the relevant great powers. For the buffer effect to work, the area must be seen as important by leading status-quo powers. When salience is high to revisionist powers, trouble may be brewing.

In the inter-war period the salience of Eastern Europe to status-quo powers was consistently high only to France. As a matter of fact, for a long time there was only one other power - Britain - that fit the status-quo description, and British indifference to Eastern Europe was hardly a novelty at Munich in 1938.

Soviet policy in this area may superficially seem ambiguous, but is perhaps better characterized as unstable: "Do whatever it takes to ensure survival." From 1933 on, the Soviet Union became increasingly status-quo oriented. There was a five-year period during which three great powers - France, the Soviet Union, and Germany - were strongly and actively concerned with the fate of Eastern Europe. It turned out to be an unfortunate combination. To official Weimar Germany, the eastern part of the Versailles settlement was unacceptable. No less to Hitler's Germany: Eastern Europe was the living space of the future and *ipso* facto a vital interest.

The Bolshevik regime broke off from the traditional Tsarist obsession with Eastern Europe, Constantinople and the Straits. Indeed, until Hitler came to power, Stalin seems not to have regarded Eastern Europe as a vitally important area, nor had Lenin before him. Germany, however, was important - to Lenin as the eventual scene of revolution; to Stalin as a powerful capitalist country - but Eastern Europe held little interest, except for its possible role in a capitalist encirclement scheme. With Hitler coming to power there was a new kind of challenge. Now there was a recognizable threat - physical as well as ideological - to the socialist state. The Soviet reaction was predicated above all on the need to safeguard the Russian socialist experiment against this new German threat: support the status-quo for Eastern Europe as long as that could keep the Germans at bay - and even seek the cooperation of the Western powers in the process; but turn revisionist if the status quo policy were to fail.

The Soviet status-quo phase petered out as its lack of success became increasingly clear. The Soviet demands for Finnish territory in 1938 are hard to see as anything but revisionist, even if they were presented by the Russians as a defensive move.

Other Soviet moves in 1939-41 make it no easier to see Russia in retrospect as a stable status-quo power where Eastern Europe is concerned, even if the motives may have been basically defensive and the annexations were undertaken in a state of near-desperation.

The pressures on the Versailles system peaked with the Czechoslovakian crisis in 1938. From this point on, an acelerated erosion of the established European order took place. During 1939-41 the eastern belt was rapidly digested by Germany and Russia. As we know, the meal failed to satisfy either Germany's appetite or Russia's fear of starvation.

The lack of internal regional stability in the inter-war period stands out. Clearly, Eastern Europe did not take on the appearance of a buffer complex during this period. The Versailles Treaty brought about a settlement in Eastern Europe that was satisfactory primarily to the weak, not to the strong - at least not to those of the strong that cared most intensely about the area. Change - even drastic change - was wanted by most of those who might be able to bring it about.

French policy, potentially a stabilizing factor, was diverted to anti-communist purposes. Thinking they could make a *cordon sanitaire* constrain Russia and at the same time absorb some of Germany's external pressure, France ended up with a policy that worked only against the Russians. Even as a one-way instrument it did not function very well. It probably antagonized the Soviets more than it constrained them, and also brought home the fact that Russia's string of western neighbors could be used against them. The coincidence of French and German purposes may have looked less coincidental at the receiving end.

On a different level, the two most powerful malcontents were still highly unequal. Versailles - and a civil war - had left Russia a good bit weaker than Germany. Even if Russian power increased tremendously during the 1930s, she still was not the counterweight to Germany that she had been - or seemed to be - in 1914. Russian power was also undermined by the reluctance of the West to join in a serious alliance with the Soviet Union. Hitler's confidence in that factor seemed well placed and was part of the undermining process.

With almost all interested powers, discontented with the status quo, and most status quo powers being mildly indifferent, the system had poor prospects of long-term survival.

The German attack on Russia, along with the Japanese attack on the United States were contests which came to determine the shape of the post-war power balance. The Second World War, unlike the First, did more than just trigger collapse. It led to the emergence of a new set of leading powers.

There was more, however, than just the shifting balance of power - even if fundamental at this point - which determined the fate of Eastern Europe. Indeed, the bisection of Europe was gradually produced by the confluence of a number of more specific factors, among which were the following:

(1) Russia's practical monopoly in pushing the Germans back from The east;

(2) the agreement at Yalta that Russia was to have "friendly regimes" on her western borders;

(3) the totality of Germany's defeat;

(4) the weakness of Britain and France after the fighting ended; and

(5) the gradual substitution of U.S. power for the collective collapse at the Center and West of Europe.

When the Russians finally turned the tide and chased the Germans home, the absence of other participants on the Eastern front was a straightforward consequence of the grand pattern the Allies had chosen for the final push. Churchill's idea of Western armies moving up east of the Alps from the Mediterranean had failed to win Roosevelt's support and was predictably opposed by Stalin. The wider consequences, in terms of post-war great-power relations, were probably seen more clearly by the British than by the Americans.

Stalin's demand for "friendly regimes" was hard to oppose effectively the way it was phrased. The Yalta agreement sanctioned it for lack of an alternative acceptable to all. In the aftermath of the war, with Russian troops all over Eastern Europe, the enforcement of this vague phrase came, as it were, automatically, Its ultimate Russian interpretation did not come out, however, until early 1948, when the central party line was clamped down over East European attempts to define distinct national "roads to socialism," and a coup was instigated in Czechoslovakia.

As an aside, Poland's situation is worth mentioning in this connection. Churchill and Roosevelt sought to counter Stalin's demand for "friendly regimes" by inserting in the Yalta agreement a call for free elections. They had Poland particularly in mind. But the strategic reality of postwar Poland proved more weighty than free elections could ever be. Poland was moved westward at Germany's expense - just as she was allowed to move eastward after World War One at Russia's expense. This time it was Russian troops that gave Poland the power she needed - not Polish ones. Since that time Poland has been utterly dependent on the Soviet Union to guarantee her western border.

The totality of Germany's defeat in 1945 was largely a planned event, brought on - in a longer time perspective - by experiences after World War One; in the shorter perspective by the allied goal of unconditional surrender. But in a more immediate sense it also resulted from the improvised Russian strategy of immediately dismantling much of the economic infrastructure in their occupation zone. Germany was destroyed not only as a military power, but also as an economic power. The postwar division of the country, which had not been planned by the allies, but grew out of their subsequent disagreements, insured the long-term stabilization of a Germany weaker than her potential.

The weakness of France and Great Britain was probably a matter of long term change, accelerated by the consequences of the war. However, their decline added to the effects of the disappearance of Germany from the structure of European power. Here was another instance of power collapsing in the central part of Europe's political system - but this time affecting areas further west.

Although Russia quickly took over the eastern half of the system, there was no rapid countermove in the west. The British appeal to the United States in early 1947 - focused initially on the Eastern Mediterranean - along with concurrent events in East-West relations, made the United States reconsider its plans to withdraw from Europe. The Truman Doctrine (March 1947) offered financial and military assistance to free peoples threatened by communist aggression. In June of that year the Marshall Plan added depth to the financial side by enabling European countries to purchase American goods using American grants. It also got European economic cooperation started in the framework of the OEEC. Further developments in 1948 solidified those decisions and set in motion the negotiations leading to NATO's founding in the spring of 1949.

Thus, in contrast, to the collapse of 1917-18 and its aftermath, after 1945 no uncontrolled center was allowed to remain in the European system. Europe was divided neatly in two.

The new system established by 1948 has proven rather durable. Judging by the propensity of either side to resist intervention attempts by the other, it is a strongly asymmetric system. (Only the Russians intervened there, and the United States never resists other than verbally.) In periods this low degree of symmetry has even been declining. Throughout, the inclination of the USSR to intervene has been rather high.[20] The Western powers have mostly, and perhaps wisely, foregone their opportunities to get involved. The Hungarian uprising in 1956 was met with tremendous sympathy in the West but was, politically speaking, ignored. In the case of Czechoslovakia - whether in 1948 or in 1968 - there was, again, outrage, but little or no counterpressure. In 1948 strong reactions all over Western Europe eventually flowed into the creation of NATO, but there was no reactive push to restore the subverted democracy of Czechoslovakia. In 1968 the Johnson administration even gave explicit notice that it would not interfere with the Soviet measures.[21]

The West has also refrained from getting into more subtle forms of involvement. Yugoslavia went her own way after 1948. Despite her subsequent membership in several West European international organizations, she has never been a channel of Western influence into Eastern Europe. That also goes for Romania's maverick line in foreign policy since the late 1950s, which may have garnered influence for Romania in some contexts and quarters, but has hardly been the wedge for the West that some expected it to become. More recently, the Reagan Administration's way of reacting to events in Poland since 1981 may be a deviation from the pattern of leaving Eastern Europe to the Russians.

Through the entire period, Germany - and Berlin in particular - have been in the focus of pressures and counterpressures between east and west; predictably, since this is where their spheres of influence intersect and to some extent overlap. The division of Germany reflects the degree of parity between the great powers in Europe as a whole. Superficially there has been a rough parity here for a long time. But a real concern is the degree of parity in the most restricted geographic area of Eastern Europe.

Taking the geographical dimension into consideration, the power balance in Eastern Europe is heavily lopsided in Russia's favor. Even in Western Europe, from a geo-strategic point of view, the potential Soviet advantage is hard to overlook.[22] Mutual strategic deterrence may have righted the balance, but it has not kept the superpowers out of Europe. On the contrary, they have - each in their own characteristic way - taken half of it under their protective wings and influence.

The closest neighbor tends to be the most concerned. Since the 1930s conditions in Eastern Europe have never been as important to a western power as they have been to Russia. The major powers of the West pulled out of their engagements in Eastern Europe during the 1940s. Regardless of current American political rhetoric, those ties are not likely to be reestablished in any important way in the foreseeable future. The stability of the U.S. relationship with Russia is important to the West - probably sufficiently so to make it unlikely that it will be jeopardized by meddling in matters vital only to Russia. Part of the current long-term asymmetry, then, is due to the continued low salience of Eastern Europe to the West.

During the 1920s and 1930s there may have been only one factor inhibiting great-power intervention in smaller East European states: The likelihood that other great powers would follow the act. That inhibition, part of the notion of the buffer complex, has not been present since 1945. However, it may still be worth considering what has happened to the cost of intervention during this period. It has been suggested above that the higher the apparent cost of subduing a small state, the lower *(ceteris paribus)* the propensity to intervene.

There is a companion to that hypothesis: The more extensive the demands put on the small power by the great, the higher the likelihood of non-compliance, and the greater the need for eventual intervention. As Stalin found, keeping troops on the spot is one way to solve that problem. But as his successors found, the troops-and-tanks solution, in addition to being expensive, tends to bring on a vicious circle: It generates hatred in the local population, which in turn increases the need for troops.

Relaxing the demands on the small neighbor is another possibility. Since the end of the Stalin era that has clearly also been attempted by the Russians, but the trouble that followed in the wake of Khrushchev's anti-Stalin speech in 1956 illustrates that even this approach has limited utility: As long as some control is felt to be mandatory the basic difficulty remains.

A better alternative from the Soviet viewpoint would be to try to improve the combined legitimacy of the local regimes and their compliance with Russian wishes, a strategy which has in fact been pursued. However, plain political logic - as well as post-war events in the region - indicate these objectives are not necessarily compatible. The Soviet leaders do not seem to have found any hard-and-fast solution. On a couple of occasions interventions have not been forthcoming when one might otherwise have expected them; perhaps significantly, they have mostly concerned Poland (in June 1956, 1970, and 1980-81). However, Soviet actions in the 1956 and 1980-81 cases lend themselves to conflicting interpretation; one version might argue that these were interventions as good as any, even if troops were not put into more than symbolic action.

Since 1948 the domestic politics of the East European countries has basically been played out in the tensions between what is thought to benefit the legitimacy of the regime and the kinds of policies the Russians prefer. The recent example of *Solidarnosc* is a difficult challenge for the other East European regimes. The leaders of Poland, Hungary and Bularia - even the East Germans and Czechoslovakians - are looking for concessions in areas other than union freedom. Still it remains an open question just when the free trade-union idea is going to come back to haunt them all.

On balance, then, the cost of Soviet intervention in Eastern Europe seems to have been increasing steadily since the 1950s, but especially during the 1970s and 1980s. On the other hand, the legitimacy of some kind of socialism or "state capitalism" in Eastern Europe may still be fairly strong in most of the countries concerned. Such trends may be working slowly together towards a more stabilized, and a slightly more independent, region.

What, then, might be an appropriate characterization of the East European borderlands during this period? Much like in the 1920s, Eastern Europe serves as a *cordon sanitaire,* only this time with the primary function of protecting the USSR from Europe - and the world. But contrary to Taylor's suggestion concerning the '20s and '30s, the protection no longer seems to work both ways. Western Europe does not appear to have any reason to feel safer after the new territorial status quo of the early 1970s, even if Russia does. Topping it off, ironically, neither side seems to actually have that feeling of security.

No doubt the over-all level of armaments in Europe is too high to nourish feelings of mutual trust. However, as long as the Soviet Union needs troops in Eastern Europe to assure its own hegemony there, the side effect of inspiring West European fear and distrust is going to stay on and encourage new armaments efforts on the Western side. The Soviet need for internal control in Eastern Europe - only remotely a matter of defense - is indeed to blame, therefore, for the general East-West impasse in that part of the world.

CONCLUDING REMARKS

Could the East European *cordon sanitaire* develop into a buffer complex over time? As long as Germany remains divided, that would seem unlikely. A divided Germany, moreover, is Russia's most fundamental premise for the established European order. No matter how neutralist - to the point of submissiveness - a reunited Germany were to be, the U.S.S.R. would be unlikely to tolerate the creeping rivalry over Eastern Europe that would ensue.

Europe as a whole has evolved into something akin to a buffer complex after the bisection of the late 1940s, but it has always had a soft center: The uncontrolled portions - the neutrals Austria, Finland, Sweden and Switzerland - have been rather small and weak, and not unambiguously "controlled" either, compared to the more controlled portions. As a result the two superpowers confront each other directly in Central Europe, increasing and perpetuating the tension in the European system as a whole. The buffer effect in this kind of system is so weak as to be almost nonexistent.

It is conceivable that the West European nations could use the post-45 Nordic example of a buffer complex more actively in an effort to promote Russian restraint in Eastern Europe. That, however, would require a new policy in Bonn. If the West Germans were to initiate, quite cautiously, a somewhat more distant relationship to the United States, they might be able to use that as a leverage for coaxing and nudging the Russians - with judicious backing from other European nations, east or west - into a less assertive stand in the East. Bonn could utilize this as an approach to achieving a closer relationship with East Germany. But a significant buffer complex would only evolve from that if Germany were somehow reunited and permitted a nonaligned status between East and West.

In concluding the discussion it bears repeating that the point of the buffer concept is the implication of a buffer effect - a restraint, on the part of the great powers, from intervention and meddling in countries located in the middle, and an attendant limitation or even reduction of great power tension and conflict. We have seen, however, that the buffer effect does not follow in any straightforward manner from the intermediary position of a small state or goup of small states. Indeed, perhaps the key lesson of the foregoing examination of Eastern Europe is how far the buffer effect is from being an automatic function of location.

NOTES

1. Karl W. Deutsch, *Nationalism and Social Communication, An Inquiry into the Foundations of Nationality.* 2nd ed. (Cambridge, Mass.: The M.I.T. Press, 1966) pp. 75-82, 104-106.

2. By our definition, the degree of symmetry is greater the more equal the power of the outside parties interested in the small state. The degree of control may more suitably be regarded as a dual factor, in that it applies both to foreign policy and to domestic policy. Control over foreign policy is probably more common than control over domestic policy. Domestic control on the part of a big neighbor is not likely to occur without foreign policy control also being effected. On the other hand, foreign policy may often be controlled without any meddling in domestic affairs taking place.

3. See Michael G. Partem, "The Buffer System in International Relations," *Journal of Conflict Resolution,* 27 (1983):16 for a more elaborate definition. On the term buffer state see, in addition to Mathisen and Partem, *Encyclopedia of Social Science,* 1930 ed., s.v., "Buffer State," by P. B. Potter.

4. There is a built-in ambiguity here which the existing literature does not resolve. Several positions may be discerned, of which three will be cited. In one view the buffer effect derives from the intrinsic strength of the small state; in another view it derives from the stalemate of the two opposing great powers over their interest in the area between them. Partem apparently inclines to the latter view, although his use of comtemporary Cambodia as an example makes his position less than crystal

clear. Potter seems to take a third position, treating strength or viability as irrelevant or uninteresting, inasmuch as he regards all Eastern European nations in the 1920s as buffer states. In our view it is difficult to regard the intrinsic strength of the small state as a phenomenon unrelated in the state's "extrinsic strength," or to overlook the connection of these factors to the rivalry of the small state's neighboring great powers and to other power.

5. Partem, p. 10.

6. However, the buffer idea also often implies that the buffer is expandable. Thus, West German defense minister Manfred Worner recently expressed satisfaction that "France no longer regards Germany merely as a buffer," *Aftenposten,* January 25, 1986 .

7. Valerie Bunce, "The Empire Strikes Back: The Transformation of the Eastern Bloc from a Soviet Asset to a Soviet Liability," *International Organization,* 39 (1985): 1-46.

8. See, e.g., Taylor, pp. 35ff; and Robert L. Rothstein, *Alliances and Small Powers* (New York: Columbia University Press, 1968), pp. 128-178, esp. pp. 140ff.

9. I reserve the term "buffer system" for the aggregate of all the great and small powers involved in a buffer relationship. In short, the most general term used here is "buffer area", which may take the form either of a "buffer state" if one state only (or if the small states in the intermediary area are considered individually) or "buffer complex" if we are concerned with a more complex relationship as described in the text.

10. Arne O. Brundtland, "The Nordic Countries as an Area of Peace," in *Small States in International Relations,* eds. August Schou and Arne O. Brundtland (Stockholm: Almqvist & Wiksell, 1971). Cf. Rothstein, p. 31 and pp. 193-4.

11. There is an important exception to this, namely if the objective is to improve relations with the *great power* on the *opposing* side, Kekkonen used this point to defend his close relationship with the Russians: The better the ties with Moscow, the easier it would be for Finland to improve her relations with the west. Subsequently Norway's Foreign Minister Knut Frydenlund used the same arguments: The better Norway's relations with the United States, the better the prospects for improving relations with Russia. See Knut Frydenlund, *Lille land - hva na? Refleksjoner on Norques utenrikspolitiske situasjon,* (Oslo: Universitetsforlaget, 1982).

12. Germany did not strictly speaking collapse, but in terms of her loss of territorial control and foreign influence the effects were the same.

13. The stability of that hegemony is open to debate. For the view that it is slowly moving away from hegemony see (e.g.) Daniel N. Nelson, "Burden Sharing in the Warsaw Pact," in *Alliance Behavior in the Warsaw Pact* (Boulder: Westview Press, forthcoming 1986).

14. Polish marshall Smigly-Rydz, as quoted by Max Jakobson, *The Diplomacy of the Winter War* (Cambridge: Harvard University Press, 1961), p. 92.

15. Rothstein, p. 140.

16. Taylor, pp. 37-38. Rothstein, pp. 145ff.

17. Taylor, p. 38. See also Rothstein, p. 228.

18. David Vital, *The Survival of Small States. Studies in Small Power/Great Power Conflict* (London: Oxford University Press 1971), pp. 14-17.

19. Vital, p. 50. Also: Jonathan Haslam, *The Soviet Union and the Strugglew for Collective Security in Europe,* 1933-39 (London/New York: Macmillan Press/St. Martin's Press 1984), pp. 191-192.

20. See Stephen S. Kaplan et al., *Diplomacy of Power: Soviet Armed Forces as a Political Instrument* (Washington, D.C.: The Brookings Institution, 1981) for a comprehensive and systematic overview of Soviet uses of armed intervention in Eastern Europe and elsewhere.

21. Jiri Valenta, *Soviet Intervention in Czechoslovakia, 1986. Anatomy of a Decision* (Baltimore: The Johns Hopkins University Press, 1979); Richard Falk, "Zone II As A World Order Construct," in *The Analysis of International Politics,* Essays in Honor of Harold and Margaret Sprout, eds, J. Rosenau, V. Davis & M. East (New York: Free Press, 1972). See also Jiri Valenta, "The Explosive Soviet Periphery, "*Foreign Policy,* (1983) 84-100.

22. This is not the military capability argument, which is somewhat harder to evaluate, and where it may be easier to underestimate Western potential. However, the most important task of the Western position is to counter the geo-strategic disadvantage.

I gratefully acknowledge the support of The Norwegian Research Council for Science and Humanities as well as the Department of Political Science of The University of Kentucky. My thanks to colleagues Jens A. Christopherson, Vincent Davis and Arild Underdal for useful comments on a previous draft.

CHAPTER 6

THE ALBANIAN LANDS: CONTINUITY AND CHANGE IN A BUFFER REGION

ALBERT M. TOSCHES

The inherent contradiction of a buffer region is that despite the intention of reducing the threat of direct conflict between hostile states, its existence as a sphere of competitive influence often leads to serious political and military confrontations. For centuries prior to the establishment of an independent Albania, and, subsequently, up to the present time, the lands inhabited by the Albanians in the southern Balkans retain this characterization within changing historical and political contexts.

Tradition, toponymic and other evidence suggest that the Albanian lands encompass the entire western portion of the Balkan Peninsula. However, while this extensive territory was populated by the ancient Illyrians, from whom the modern Albanians claim descent, a more strictly defined region is identified on the basis of more specific evidence of the Albanian historical and political experience. This area lies in the center of the southern Balkans bounded on the west by a line extending along the river Drina to the Gulf of Kotor and on the east by the line of the Vardar and Morava rivers, and from the river Sava in the north to the Gulf of Corinth in the south (Fig. 6.1). A considerable extent of coast is included from the Gulf of Kotor to theGulf of Corinth facing the Strait of Otranto, which links the Adriatic Sea to the central Mediterranean. The interior is mostly rugged and mountainous, and except for peripheral lowlands, such as the Adriatic coastal plain, relatively extensive zones of low relief are found only in the interior tectonic basins that form the Kosova Plain and the Dukajin Basin. Of special

111

Fig. 6.1
The Albanian Lands In History

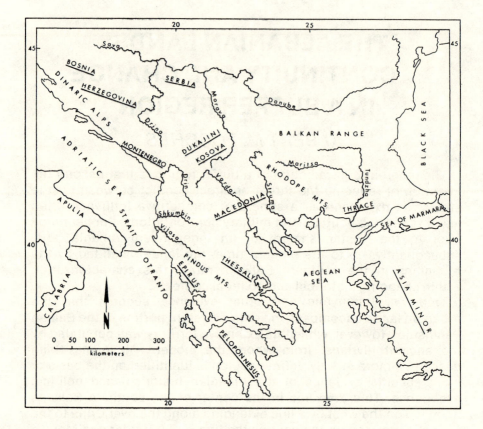

significance for agriculture and settlement both here and throughout the western Balkans are the numerous limestone depressions *(Doline, polje)* scattered throughout the region in various sizes. Otherwise, the many small river valleys have been important both for settlement and communication within the rugged terrain. They are more numerous to the south where they are oriented toward the southeast than in the north where they are directed more toward the east.

While the last among the Balkan peoples to secure their national independence, the Albanians were clearly among the first to occupy the region, in the person of the ancient Thraco-Illyrians. The Illyrians distributed themselves throughout the western Balkans, but there is dispute as to the extent of their indigenous settlement. In support of Albanian claims, it is argued that this area constituted not only the region of the Shkumbin and Devoll basins, the Adriatic coastlands and the districts of Shkodra and Korce, but extended beyond the river Drin to the Kosova Plain and beyond.[1] Together with Albania proper this region would presently include areas of western Macedonia, southeastern Montenegro and an extensive portion of southern Serbia. The counterpoint to this argument is that these extended areas were settled by Albanians subsequent to earlier Slav occupation during a period of considerable dislocation and migration.[2]

Disputes over the origins of Albanian settlement aside, a broad distribution of Albanians in the southwestern Balkans is recognized throughout the nineteenth and into the twentieth century.[3] They formed a substantial and often compact element well beyond the boundaries of present-day Albania: to the northeast as far as the Leskovac Basin and the region of Nyssa (Nis); to the east beyond Lake Ohrid to the districts of Prilep and Manastiri (Monastir); to the south to western Thessaly, throughout Epirus, and as far as the Gulf of Corinth. These were the lands of the Albanian *ethnicum* where a continuity of Albanian settlement since Illyrian times could be argued, but where other Balkan peoples would assert their own national and historic claims.

Whatever the extent of their national territory the Albanians found themselves within an ethnic frontier where different cultural and political currents converged, but the distinctiveness of the Albanian element persisted. Among the Indo-European languages Albanian occupies an independent place though with considerable influence from Latin, Greek, Slavic and Turkish sources. Unfortunately, the literary expression of the language had to await the acceptance of a common dialect and the adoption of a unified alphabet which did not occur until late in the nineteenth century. Nevertheless, language was to be the most important formative element in the development of Albanian national consciousness.[4]

The imprint of religion upon the Albanian lands was even more complex in its result. Although predominantly Christian until the middle of the fifteenth century the divisions in Christianity were mirrored in the disposition of the northern (Gheg) Albanians toward Rome and the southern (Tosk) Albanians toward Constantinople. After nearly five centuries of political and cultural domination by the Ottoman Empire, however, the great majority of Albanians would profess Islam. This condition would strikingly differentiate them from the surrounding Orthodox Slavs and Greeks, although the Islamization of many Serbs and Macedonians (together with the existence of Orthodox Albanians) would often blur the ethnic boundaries.[5] The fact is, that as Islamization spread among the Albanians, they were distributing themselves in more compact fashion within the ethnic frontier.

Until the late nineteenth century a recognized lack of political unity among the Albanians was both a distinctive feature of their situation and a weakness which the surrounding political formations sought to exploit. The primary social and political unit continued to be the tribe or fis, which consisted of one or more ancestral stocks which were further differentiated into a number of extended family units. They were generally distributed in isolated territorial units and dispersed settlements in response to the difficulties of communication in the mountainous terrain and the poverty of agricultural land and resources. Although this form of social and territorial organization militated against a broad national unity, it nevertheless provided an objective basis for the self-government of Albanian tribes on their own land.[6] While providing cohesion and continuity when the overriding imperial or state systems were exhibiting weakness or disintegration, it also supplied sufficient coherence to resist integration within hostile territorial frameworks.

The situation of the Albanian lands as a crossroads and frontier of interaction and conflict among various economic, cultural and political interests has been an enduring reality. Even before the Christian Era the region had become the center of a commercial network linking Europe with the eastern Mediterranean lands. Consistently on the frontiers of imperial control it would become an arena of competition among emergent nation states. Three distinct ethnic formations would converge here with the Albanians striving to resist the efforts of the Greeks and Slavs to encroach on their national territory. The cultural and political development of the Albanian lands as a buffer zone, within the context of regional interaction and conflict, represents a major chapter in the historical and political geography of the southwestern Balkans.

THE IMPERIAL PERIOD

The reality of the geographic situation of the southwestern Balkans, as the strategic link between central Europe and the eastern Mediterranean, was recognized by the Ottomans no less than by the Romans and Byzantines. Effective control was especially crucial when the area was transformed from a spearhead of expansion to a military frontier in the eighteenth and nineteenth centuries.

The design and function of Ottoman administration served to heighten the antagonisms among the nationalities of the Albanian lands and ensure the divisions among the Albanians themselves. In the seventeenth and eighteenth centuries the Ottoman Empire was divided into large units called *eyalets,* that were further subdivided into *sanjaks* of varying size and population. The Albanian lands were distributed among at least twelve *sanjaks.*[7]

Following an administrative reform in the middle of the nineteenth century the *eyalets* were replaced by smaller entities called *vilayets* as the first order administrative units (Fig. 6.2). While intending to provide greater recognition of national characteristics, Albanians would continue to be distributed among four *vilayets:* Shkodra, Janina, Manastiri, Kosova. These were also subdivided into *sanjaks* which, although more uniform in size and population than previously, were smaller and more numerous.[8] The intention was to ensure greater effectiveness of administration and control while minimizing tendencies toward greater unity among the Albanians as well as the other nationalities.

To secure Albanian support and cooperation, the Ottoman authorities encouraged the traditional Albanian distrust of the Slavs. From the seventeenth century a policy to resettle Albanians throughout Kosova, western Macedonia and as far as the Leskovac Basin was viewed by the Albanians as an attempt to recover ancestral lands from the Serbs as much as an Ottoman effort to create a defensive zone. Placement of Albanian villages among the Serbs and Bulgarians could be intended to prevent Slav encroachment on Albanian lands, as much as to maintain surveillance of Serb activities for the Ottoman authorities.[9]

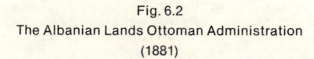

Fig. 6.2
The Albanian Lands Ottoman Administration
(1881)

SERBIA

MONTENEGRO • Peja • Novi Paza

• Pristitina

• Prizrendi

⊙ Shkodra

⊙ Shkupi

Dibra •

• Durres

• Elbasan

⊙ Manastiri

Berat • • Korca Selaniku ⊙

• Serfixhe

• Gjirokastra

Boundary
––– Vilayet
•••••• Sanjak
––– International

• Janina GREECE

• Preveza

N

Islamization among the Albanians served as both a support and instrument of Ottoman administration. Some accepted Islam, with its associated privileges, since, as Christians, the alternative under Ottoman rule was social and economic deprivation, and most recognized in their acceptance of Islam a further element of security against the Slavs. But as more than two-thirds of the Albanian population came to accept Islam, they became more sharply differentiated from the Christian Slavs and Greeks and tended to lose their ethnic identity. The subject nationalities considered the Albanians as synonymous with 'Moslems' and 'Turks' and instruments of their subjugation with whom cooperation against Ottoman domination was impossible.

BALKAN NATIONALISM

AND THE FIRST PARTITION

The development of nationalism invariably involves an identification with a more or less defined territory.[10] In a region of complex ethnic and cultural diversity, such as the southwestern Balkans, nationalisms often arise with associated conflict over 'national territory' and 'ethnic boundaries' and become steadily more destructive and difficult to control. On the frontier of the declining imperial system of the Ottomans the Albanians confronted the increasing territorial nationalism of the Slavs and Greeks. In political terms the dubious choice for the Albanians was between support for the Ottoman imperial system which had manipulated their sense of territoriality and submerged their national identity, and common cause with emergent nation states to whom the Albanians were an indistinguishable part of the oppressive system of the Ottomans.

First to exhibit intentions for territorial expansion in the region were the Montenegrins, ethnic Serbs who had escaped into the mountains of the western Balkans after the Ottoman conquest. The principality of Montenegro emerged as a semi-independent enclave at the southern end of the Dinaric Alps at the beginning of the sixteenth century. By the end of the eighteenth century her territory impinged upon the Albanian lands in the vicinity of the Shkodra Basin and in the coastal region where her territorial objectives would continue to be focused throughout the nineteenth century.

While the Montenegrins were the first to threaten the integrity of the Albanian lands, the Serbs would have the greatest impact upon the political and territorial status of the region. The focus of the modern Serb state was in the rugged and forested Sumadija district south of Belgrade - far from the core of medieval Serbia, which had largely been abandoned by the Serbs and where the Albanian population had continued to increase. Serbia managed to expand her territory within a framework of conditional autonomy, so that by 1833 it included most of the area of the Belgrade Pashalik and reached the vicinity of Nis.[11] Outlying areas of Albanian settlement were incorporated and the Albanians subjected to harassment and expulsion in a manner characteristic of the advance into the Albanian lands at later periods.[12] Future expansion within the framework of a 'Serbian Idea' was seen as an attempt to fulfill historical goals that had been interrupted by the Ottoman conquest and to incorporate all Serbs into a single state.[13] Medieval Serbia and much of northern Albania were included within the territorial scheme.

Greek pretensions toward Epirus and western Thessaly were contained within the broader framework of the "Megale Idea."[14] The future Greek state was meant to incorporate not only ethnic Greeks, but all Hellenized inhabitants of adjacent lands. The inclusion of southern Albania could be justified because of its Orthodox population while the existence of ethnic Albanians in the Greek lands could be denied. While the political circumstances did not allow for the full realization of territorial goals at the time of Greek independence (1830), this rationale would continue to be a basis for territorial claims.

The territorial ambitions of Bulgaria conflicted with those of both Serbia and Greece and involved the Albanians of western Macedonia and southern Serbia. A similar romantic concept envisaged a Bulgarian state whose territory would conform to the limits of the medieval Bulgarian empires. Within its boundaries would be included all of Macedonia and a large area extending westward beyond Lakes Prespa and Ohrid.

After the Russo-Turkish War of 1877-78 Montenegro succeeded in greatly enlarging her territory and population. The amount of arable land was substantially increased and many new towns were acquired including Podgorica, Shpuza, Tivari and Ulqini. A small coastal strip was also obtained that extended from Ulqini to the mouth of the Boyana River. Montenegro derived considerable economic and strategic value from these areas at the expense of Albanian territorial interests, while many Albanians were displaced and forced to retire beyond the newly-established boundary.

The acquisitions of the Serbs were more considerable in their extent and impact on Albanian lands and population. Serbia confirmed her possession of the entire Leskovac Basin and the districts of Kurshumlia and Vranja together with the major center of Nis. Thousands of Albanians who were established in these regions were subjected to wholesale confiscations and evictions and forced across the new international boundary.[15] Their departure was followed by a systematic colonization of these districts by the Serbs, anxious to affirm their historic claim. Large numbers of Albanian refugees settled to the north of Prishtine and increased the Albanian concentration in Kosova.[16]

Greece was able to secure territory in Thessaly, though except for Arta and Preveza failed to obtain any territorial concessions in Epirus. Bulgaria was deprived of territorial gains in western Macedonia, though she would continue to pursue her claims there in competition with Greece and Serbia.

Afer 1878 the entire region of Albanian settlement became a zone of transition in which political control was insecure and uncertain. Territories acquired by Montenegro and Serbia corresponded to the concept of "settlement frontier" in that effective control had yet to be achieved despite the establishment of *de jure* boundaries.[17] The remaining large area of Albanian settlement was a "political frontier" in that international boundaries were temporary or transitional in nature and effective administration was lacking.

The Greeks and Serbs sought to extend their influence in the contested zones through cultural penetration as much as through military confrontation with the Ottoman authority. A policy of Hellenization was pursued in southern Albania through the establishment of Greek schools and the monopoly of the Greek Orthodox Church, while the Serbs established numerous schools and churches throughout Kosova and maintained two seminaries in Prizren.[18] The Ottoman administration generally acquiesced in these policies, partly because of pressure from the European powers but mostly because it encouraged division among the Albanians and competition between the Serbs and Greeks. In essence, the region was a true frontier zone of uncertain political control on the periphery of five competing territorial political systems - the Ottoman Empire, Austria-Hungary, Serbia, Montenegro and Greece.

For more than thirty years subsequent to the Congress of Berlin, the danger to the integrity of the Albanian nation and territory steadily increased. Together with the territorial pretensions of the Slavs and Greeks and the interference of the European powers, the inconsistency of the Ottoman Administration made the Albanian response to the situation extremely complicated. Initial support for

Ottoman authority in the political frontier was often viewed as an attempt to promote the broader aims of Ottoman and Austrian policy rather than an effort to preserve Albanian territorial integrity.[19].

Recognizing the limitations of unilateral military action for the advancement of their political aims and the prevention of a further partitioning of Albanian territory, many Albanians emphasized an intellectual response to the situation.[20] Concerted efforts were applied to unify the language and develop a standardized alphabet, as well as to overcome the mutual suspicions and antagonisms among Moslem, Catholic and Orthodox Albanians. The increased literary output of prominent expatriate Albanians gave formal expression to the Albanian cause.

The diplomatic response centered initially upon a plan to create a single, autonomous Albanian vilayet by uniting the four vilayets of Shkoder, Kosova, Janina and Monastir. Apart from interfering with their territorial ambitions the Balkan states rejected this proposal since it would separate large number of Slavs and Greeks and maintain Ottoman authority in the region. Nor were the Ottomans willing to allow the precedent which an autonomous Albanian unit would establish. A completely independent Albanian state as an alternative was not seriously advocated by Albanian spokesmen until, left without options, the creation of an independent Albania gained acceptance as a means of preserving at least a portion of Albanian national territory from being acquired by the Slav states and Greece.

THE SECOND PARTITION AND ITS AFTERMATH

The events of 1912-13 resulted in the effective partitioning of the core of Albanian territory and population and radically altered the political and territorial context. The appearance as well as the reality of Ottoman authority disappeared and the region was subsequently partitioned among four territorial political systems. Altogether nearly two-thirds of Albanian national territory would be permanently separated from the new Albanian state and half of all Albanians would become a political minority distributed among the surrounding states. Henceforth the character of social, economic and political development in the Albanian lands would unfold separately within the distinct administrative frameworks of the Albanian national state and those of the regional nation states and their successors.

The existence of the Albanian state has always depended on timely support by an extraregional power, expediently viewing Albania as an instrument to promote its own territorial, political and economic interests against those of regional states or other external powers. Such was the case when the Albanian Provisional Government sought political and territorial recognition for an independent Albania. The Albanians proposed a state of considerable territorial extent that would incorporate those areas where Albanians were either preponderant or in a clear majority - the old vilayets of Shkoder and Janina in addition to substantial portions of the former vilayets of Monastir and Kosova. (Fig. 6.3). Austria-Hungary and Italy supported the concept of a 'big' Albania, recognizing that "the larger Albania became, the more quickly would she establish herself as a progressive and prosperous State, a 'buffer' against Pan-Slavism, and a 'buffer' between the two powers themselves . . . "[21] But while they opposed the efforts of the Balkan allies, supported by Russia and France, to reduce the coastal zone and the depth of territory to be allotted to Albania, they acquiesced in the annexation of substantial portions of Albanian national territory to the extent that their own economic and political interests were not affected.

Until the First World War the conflicting strategic and economic interests of Austria-Hungary and Italy converged in their support of Albanian independence and territorial integrity. Austria-Hungary sought to frustrate Slav aspirations in northern and eastern Albania to prevent the expansion of Russian influence in the southwestern Balkans, while Italy opposed Greek control of southern Albania as a direct threat to her security in the Adriatic. At the same time both Austria-Hungary and Italy strived to prevent each other from extending and consolidating each other's influence in Albania. The perception was clearly that the existence of a conditionally independent Albanian state was necessary to prevent further intrusions by the Slavs and Greeks toward the Adriatic, as well as to reduce the threat of conflict between Italy and Austria-Hungary themselves.

After World War One Italy was initially thwarted in the attempt to assume a mandate over all of Albania. She assumed greater influence in Albania after 1925 due largely to an expanded economic role which included both loans and direct investment for transportation and construction projects and a predominance in trade relations.[22] Despite efforts by the Albanian government to mitigate Italian influence by expanding trade with other states and improving relations with Yugoslavia, Italy gradually increased her

Fig. 6.3
Partition Of The Albanian Lands
(1912-1913)

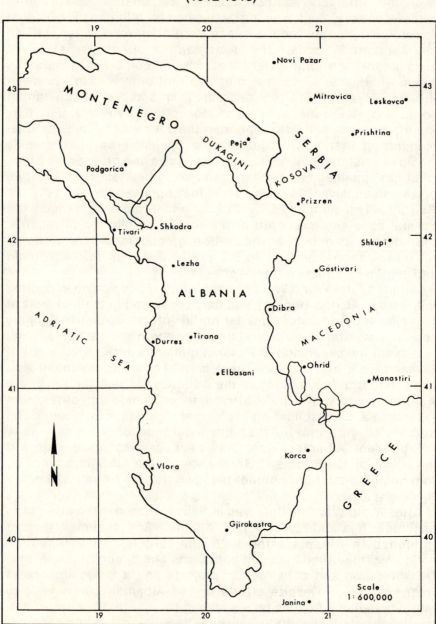

Scale
1:600,000

political and military role. As Yugoslav interest declined and Albania increasingly sought to assert her political sovereignty, Italy decided on direct action to secure her political, economic and strategic objectives. With the Italian invasion and occupation of Albania in 1939, the Albanian lands were fully partitioned and without any independent national identity.

Internal unity and stability was sufficiently difficult to achieve even without the interference of external forces. No Albanian government was able to overcome completely the local and regional antagonisms, often fomented and supported by foreign elements, until Ahmed Zogu established himself as king in 1928. Surprisingly, there were some successes as in the formation of a centralized administrative structure focused on Tirana, improvements in transportation and communication, an improved financial situation and progress toward the systematic exploration and development of mineral resources.

Probably the major achievement of Albania during the Interwar Period was the assertion of her personality as a sovereign and independent political entity. At international conferences and through the League of Nations articulate spokesmen eventually succeeded in convincing the world of Albania's national and territorial distinctiveness. Unfortunately, claims to the partitioned Albanian lands in Yugoslavia and Greece were unlikely to gain effective international recognition and support.

While maintaining a consistent political and territorial interest in the new Albanian state after 1912, the Slav states and Greece not only focused attention on the security and functional control of their new international boundaries with Albania, but were also equally concerned with establishing firm control in those portions of the Albanian lands which they had recently annexed. Administrative policy was designed to effectively integrate these areas within new social and political systems toward which the Albanian population was suspicious and often hostile. Consequently, a systematic effort to reduce separatist and irredentist tendencies among the Albanians became a distinctive feature of administrative policy during the Interwar Period.

Greece had obtained a mixed population of Orthodox and Moslem Albanians through the acquisition of the southern portion of the vilayet of Janina. Consistent with a policy of identifying nationality with religion, Greece refused to recognize the ethnic distinctiveness of the Orthodox Albanians while Moslem Albanians were considered as Turks. This attitude of non-recognition tended to justify the virtual proscription of Albanian linguistic and cultural expression as well as the repatriation or explusion of ethnic Albanians to Turkey.[23] At the same time these ethno-religious arguments continued to support Greek territorial claims to portions of southern Albania with an Orthodox population.

The Albanians within the Yugoslav state were more numerous and compact in distribution than in the Albanian lands under Greek administration. From a core in the Kosova and Dukajin (Metohija) Basins and the adjacent highlands, they extended into southeastern Montenegro and western Macedonia and remained numerous but less compact in the southern and eastern parts of Serbia proper and central Macedonia. Between 1921 and 1948 official Yugoslav statistics indicate that the Albanians maintained a consistently high rate of natural population growth (over 2 percent per year compared to a national rate of 1.5 percent) and showed an absolute increase of over 70 percent from 450,000 to 750,000-or from 3.7 to 4.8 percent of the total national population.[24]

A widespread though compact distribution of Albanians throughout 'Old Serbia' and western Macedonia is recognized on 1924 census maps which show only a few Slav enclaves, while in most communes Albanians comprise at least 75 percent of the total population.[25] Most of the Albanians were Moslem with a small minority of Catholics, easily distinguishable from the largely Orthodox Serbs, Montenegrins and Macedonians who were located in proximity to Albanian districts or in mixed settlement areas. The Albanians were much too numerous and well established to be ignored or easily displaced.

These facts notwithstanding, the statistics also indicate a decline in the Moslem proportion of the population of the Kosova and Dukajin (Metohija) plains during the first half of the Interwar Period. From 1921-1931 this proportion declined from 75.1 to 68.8 percent while the Serb Orthodox population increased from 21.2 to 27.3 percent of the total in the same period.[26] This was a direct result of the policy of internal colonization under which large numbers of Serbs and Montenegrins were settled within Albanian districts, while the local Albanian Moslem populations were often forced to abandon their traditional lands.

The official rationale for the policy of colonization was to alleviate the serious argicultural overpopulation and low agricultural productivity that characterized much of Montenegro as well as parts of Serbia proper and Bosnia-Hercegovina. Lands made available consisted of public lands, parts of large estates, and reclaimed lands, but also included unused or abandoned lands resulting from the displacement of he Albanian population. The colonization program had established nearly 10,000 families and 40,0000 - 50,000 persons in 'Old Serbia' by 1930.[27] By 1940, nearly a quarter million hectares of arable land had been distributed in the districts of Pec, Urosevac, Kosovska Mitrovica and Prizren alone.[28] Together with a standard allocation of arable land each family was provided with a residence in a new or expanded village in which a *zadruga* organization prevailed, with houses aligned on straight and broad streets in contrast to the enclosed *kula* of the Albanians. In the Dukajin Plain (Metohija) villages between Pec and Djakovica contained the greatest number of colonists while the largest of the new villages were found in the Kosova plain between Vucitern and Urosevac.[29]

The economic goals of the program of internal colonization were not achieved due to the lack of sufficient organization and supervision, insufficient investment, and a limited appeal because whole family units were required to participate.[30] Greater security and control in the settlement frontier were obtained through the establishment of several thousand Serbs and Montenegrins in areas of compact Albanian settlement. But by displacing Albanians and otherwise excluding them from any positive consequences of agrarian reform, interwar Yugoslavia missed an opportunity to stimulate integration and improve the prospect for stability and progress in the social and economic development of the Albanian minority.

Throughout the Interwar Period the efforts of the Yugoslav government to establish effective political and administrative control within its territory were impeded by a number of circumstances: regional differences in legal and administrative traditions, the varied social and cultural background of an ethnically diverse population, strong regional contrasts in economic development, and a history of conflicting nationalisms. A highly centralized political and administrative system was adopted to prevent these national and regional associations from hindering political unity and threatening the territorial integrity of the state.

Under the Ottoman administration the Kosova Vilayet had encompassed all of Old Serbia (i.e. Kosova and western Macedonia), northern Macedonia and the districts of Novi Pazar and Plevlja, and consisted largely of a compact Albanian population. This territory was now extended to include the rest of Yugoslav (Vardar) Macedonia, and its sizeable Macedconian and Serb population, within the new province of South Serbia, one of eight *provinces* established in the early post-war period. The provincial system was replaced in 1922 with a centralized prefectural system based on thirty-three *oblasts* which fragmented historic and ethnic regions while supposedly conforming to natural, social and economic conditions. Kosovo Oblast was an elongated region, extending from the Albanian border to the vicinity of Nis, which excluded areas of compact Albanian population while including some Serb districts.[31] The administrative reorganization of 1929 replaced these units with nine *banovinas,* which again largely avoided ethnic and historic associations (Fig. 6.4). The territory and population of Kosova was consequently divided among the banovinas of Morava, Vardar and Zeta.

The creation of a system of supposedly functional regions across ethnic and historic boundaries was unrealistic in considering that functional relationships within such "rationally efficient" regions could supplant traditional relationships within the historic regions. Stress within the Yugoslav administrative and territorial framework developed between two sets of functional relationships - a social/cultural set based on historic associations, and a political/economic set based on the rationale of centralized control and defined in economic terms. Kosova with the adjacent areas of Albanian settlement represented but one regional sub-system with a histrocial distinctiveness which the territorial administrative system of interwar Yugoslavia hoped to erase. Unlike other regions, however, the extreme social, cultural, and economic backwardness of Kosova prevented the articulation of a regional political response to the policy of centralization. At the same time political development, as a positive movement toward the goal of wider participation and cooperation among groups within a territorial political system, made little progress among the Albanians within the Yugoslav state.

LATER DEVELOPMENTS AND RECENT TRENDS

During World War Two most of the area of compact Albanian population in Kosova, western Macedonia and southeastern Montenegro was united with Albania, which had been under Italian occupation and control since 1939. There subsequently developed a number of resistance movements united in their opposition to the Italians and Germans, but in conflict over the post-war disposition of the Albanian lands as much as over social, economic and political ideologies. Some Albanian units in Yugoslavia attached themselves to the Partisans under the leadership of the Yugoslav

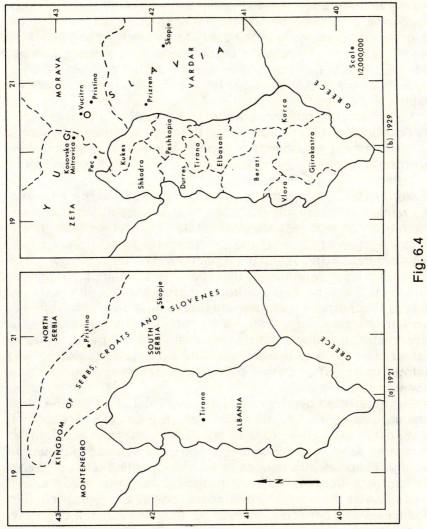

Fig. 6.4

The Albanian Lands In The Interwar Period

Communist Party and hoped to obtain support for maintaining the unity of Kosova with Albania. The YCP not only rejected this proposal but refused to support republic status for Kosova in the projected plan for a Yugoslav federation after the War. In Albania the anti-Communist National Front also supported retention of Kosova and Metohija but was opposed by the National Liberation Movement, dominated by Communists and dependent on the YCP, which agreed that these regions should be restored to Yugoslavia. The accession to power by the Communists in both Yugoslavia and Albania, therefore, seemed to render the partition of the Albanian lands as permanent and remove the issue as a matter of territorial dispute.

The collapse of political authority in the Albanian lands during the Second World War would not be followed by permanent change in the international boundary regime, but the new political and territorial systems instituted within the region would effect profound changes in social and political development and territorial status. While the territorial distribution of the Albanians has remained essentially the same, the distinctive frameworks of the highly centralized Albanian state, the democratic though unitary system of Greece, and the Yugoslav federal system have had a differential impact on the Albanian *ethnicum.*

Albania was determined that her third attempt to achieve functional political and territorial sovereignty would succeed. Toward this purpose a largely isolationist and autarchic state has evolved characterized by efforts to reduce foreign influence and dependence, a policy of rigid centralization in programs for social and economic development, and an extreme nationalism with historic roots but amplified by the experience and prospects of Albanian communism.

Having rejected overtures for improved relations from the West, Albania was obliged to maintain a close political and economic relationship with the Yugoslavs, despite historic differences. Increasing economic dependence, however, was accompanied by growing Yugoslav interference in Albanian political affairs.[32] When this activity culminated in a proposal to unite Albania with Yugoslavia at the time of the Yugoslav-Soviet ideological conflict, Albania severed her economic and political ties with the Yugoslavs in 1948.

For the next ten years Albania functioned as an ideological buffer between Yugoslavia and the Soviet block and profited both economically and politically. Substantial Soviet support allowed Albania to initiate major programs for the social and economic transformation of Albanian society on the Soviet model. At the same time Soviet military support through the Warsaw Pact represented a meaningful guarantee of territorial integrity. These arrangements were secure until the Soviet-Yugoslav rapprochement and de-Stalinization policies of the late 1950s were perceived as potential dangers to Albanian political and territorial integrity.[33] It was felt that these developments encouraged Yugoslav pretensions toward Albania and threatened to weaken internal constraints felt to be necessary to prevent instability and division.

The dramatic role of Albania in the Sino-Soviet ideological dispute has been thoroughly discussed and analyzed. Albania's collaboration with China did not merely provide mutual ideological support but offered a readily available alternative to the loss of political and economic support from the Soviet Union. While economic disruptions were severe and could not be fully addressed with Chinese aid alone, many projects were completed and new ones initiated. Sufficient progress toward economic management and self-sufficiency had been made by the late 1970s such that adjustments to the dislocations following the subsequent break with China could more easily be made. Disagreements had increased as China broadened her contacts with the West and embarked on her program of economic rationalization and modernization. Once again Albania refused to compromise in support of policies viewed as potentially disruptive of her social, economic and political system, and proceeded to withdraw completely into political and economic isolation.

A highly centralized approach to social and economic development that demands strict allegiance to the state and party is the basis upon which Albania strives to maintain national unity and defend against foreign influence. The degree of uniformity and absolutism goes well beyond the Stalinist model in concept and practice and has been formalized in the 1976 Constitution.[34] Cultural expression and social activity are tightly controlled while the practice of religion is totally proscribed. The complete abolition of private property is extolled as well as the total collectivization of agricultural land. Heavy industrialization remains the prime economic directive and Albania is alone among the East European communist states not to have at least experimented with economic reform. Apart from the morality as well as the success or failure of these measures in achieving social and economic goals, they can be viewed as a response to the disruption, partition and foreign domination of the Albanian people that has often resulted from historic divisions in social and cultural outlook.

A distinctive nationalism combines the ancient traditions with the ideological and statist principles of the Albanian communist system. It is the ultimate support for the principles of autarchy and centralization upon which the future of the Albanian state and nation are professed to depend. While never losing sight of the struggles of the Albanian people for nationhood and independence, the Socialist Peoples Republic of Albania is posed as the manifestation of traditional hopes achieved under Communist leadership. Support for Party and state becomes a serious duty toward the preservation of Albanian nationality and the existence of national principles.[35]

CONCLUSION

Persistence of instability and dynamic change have always characterized the Albanian lands in the southwestern Balkans. A most striking feature of the political history of the Albanians has been the ability to maintain their ethnic distinctiveness and attachment to national territory. The long physical and cultural isolation of the Albanian lands may be partly responsible, but this cannot explain the failure of successive territorial political systems to disrupt or suppress the Albanian nation or the political and territorial expression of Albanian nationality. The reality of the Albanian nation has finally obtained political recognition within formal territorial frameworks through which regional as well as international concerns have been expressed. While the situation of the Albanian lands may preserve the appearance and function of a buffer, the continued assertion of Albanian nationality and territorial sovereignty will have increasing impact upon regional and international affairs.

NOTES

1. Alain Ducellier, "Genesis and Failure of the Albanian State in the Fourteenth and Fifteenth Century," in *Studies on Kosova,* edited by Arshi Pipa and Sami Rapishti (Boulder: East European Monographs, 1984), pp. 4-5.

2. Henry R. Wilkinson, "Jugoslave Kosmet: The Evolution of a Frontier Province and its Landscape," *Institute of British Geographers, Transactions and Papers,* no. 27 (1955):178-190.

3. H.N. Brailsford,*Macedonia: Its Races and Their Future,* (1906), p. 35.

4. Stavro Skendi, *The Albanian National Awakening* (Princeton: Princeton University Press).

5. Henry P. Baerlein, *A Difficult Frontier* (London: Leonard Parsons, 1922); and Jovan Cvijic, "Geographical Distribution of the Balkan Peoples," *Geographical Review,* 5(1918):345-361.

6. Edith Durham, *Some Tribal Origins, Laws and Customs of the Balkans* (London: George Allen and Unwin, Ltd., 1928), p. 92.

7. Zvonimir Dugack , ed., *Istorijski Atlas* (Zabreb. 1970), p. 32; Aleks Buda, et. al., eds., *Historie e Popullit Shgiptar,* (Tirana: State University of Tirana, 1967), vol. 1 and 2, p. 35.

8. Buda, p. 228.

9. Brailsford, pp. 90-91.

10. Hans Kohn, *Nationalism: Its Meaning and History* (Princeton: D. Van Nostrand Co., Inc., 1955).

11. Dugacki, p. 53.

12. Sadulla Brestovci, *Albanian-Serbian Montenegrin Relations, 1830-1878* (Prishtine: Instututi Albanologjik i Prishtines, 1983), p. 270.

13. Paul N. Helin, "The Origins of Modern Pan-Serbism - The 1844 Nacertanije of Ilija Garasanin: An Analysis and Translation," *East European Quarterly,* 9 (Summer 1975): 153-171.

14. Charles Jelavich and Barbara Jelavich, *The Establishment of the Balkan National States, 1804-1920* (Seattle: University of Washington Press, 1977), p. 77.

15. Brailsford, p. 279; and J. Swire, *Albania: The Rise of a Kingdom* (New York: Richard R. Smith, 1929).

16. Cvijic, p. 353.

17. John R. V. Prescott, *The Geography of Frontiers and Boundaries* (Chicago: Aldine Publishing Company, 1965).

18. Swire, pp. 64-65.

19. Wayne S. Vucinich, *Serbia Between East and West: The Events of 1903-1908* (Stanford: Stanford University Press, 1954), pp. 32-33.

20. Skendi, Chapters 4-7 and 15.

21. Swire, p. 150.

22. *Ibid.,* pp. 459-466.

23. *Ibid.,* pp. 467-470.

24. Paul F. Myers and Arthur A. Campbell, *The Population of Yugoslavia* (Washington: Government Printing Office, 1954), pp. 16 and 54.

25. Henry R. Wilkinson, *Maps and Politics: A Review of the Ethnographic Cartography of Macedonia* (Liverpool: University Press 1951), p. 259.

26. Myers and Campbell, p. 126.

27. Marcel Larnaude, "Un village de Colonization en Serbie du Sud," *Annales de Geographie,* 39 (1930):321.

28. Hivzi Islami, "Les Recherches Antropogeographieques dans le Kossova," *Gjurime Albanologjike, Seria e Shkencave Historike* (1-1971), 1972, p. 162.

29. Milislav Lutovac, "Danasnje Naseljanje Metohije," *Glasnik Geografskog Drustva,* 20 (1934): 62; and Kosovska Ristic, "La Colonisation et les Villages des Colonistes dans la Plaine de Kosova," *Bulletin de la Societe Serve de Geographe,* 38 (1958):137.

30. Jozo Tomasevish, *Peasants, Politics and Economic Change in Yugoslavia* (Stanford: Stanford University Press, 1955), pp. 330-331.

31. B.Z. Miloevic, "The Kingdom of the Serbs, Croats, and Slovenes: Administrative Divisions in Relation to Natural Areas," *Geographical Review,* 15 (1925): 71 and Plate II.

32. Nicholas C. Pano, *The People's Republic of Albania* (Baltimore: the Johns Hopkins Press, 1968), pp. 58-87.

33. *Ibid,* pp. 111-134.

34. Peter R. Prifti, "Albania's New Constitution," *Balkanistica,* 5 (1979):59-69.

35. *Ibid.,* pp. 62-63.

CHAPTER 7

THE GEO-POLITICAL DEMISE OF LEBANON: CONSEQUENCES OF A POLITICAL AND MILITARY BUFFER

R.W. McCOLL

Lebanon involuntarily became a political and military buffer between Israel and its Moslem neighbors as a matter of geographic necessity. Lebanon does not sit between any of the combatants - as is the case with most classic buffer states. The geopolitical function that Lebanon came to play was as a neutral battleground. It was an easily accessible area where Israel and its numerous enemies - the PLO, PLA, Syria, Jordan, Libya, and others could fight in clandestine assassinations and terrorism or in formal battle, but without direct threat to their own populations and territory. This was the geo-political role gradually assigned to Lebanon. It is a role and function as well as geo-political model of increasing applicability to modern politics and contemporary military technologies.

BACKGROUND

While its population contains representatives of virtually every religious and political faction to be found anywhere in the Middle East, Lebanon was the only formal Christian state in the Middle East.

Lebanon is a small country, only 125 miles long and 50 miles wide at the widest part. The coastal plain is narrow and interrupted by spurs of the Lebanon mountains. It has no natural resources that would attract outsiders, and in fact the historic role of the coastal area was trade and fishing (Phonecians). Its politics and economics are such that Lebanon is not a necessary partisan in the Arab-Israelli conflict. For decades it was considered to be the "Switzerland of the Middle East" both by its own people and by most of the Arab nationals in contiguous states. Lebanon had been one of the few safe locations in the region. Sophisticated, Francophile, a banking center and playground for the rich, Lebanon also was considered to be the only successful democracy in the region.

How could a country with so many apparent advantages lose both its neutrality and now, apparently, its national sovereignty and identity as a separate state and become a buffer/battleground? Do the events that led to the virtual demise of Lebanon provide lessons in the geo-politics of neutrality and the consequences of becoming a buffer? The following study traces the geo-political history of Lebanon from its creation to what apparently is its demise. This chronology provides clear indications as to what political and geographic elements brought about Lebanon's loss of neutral status. More importantly, this case history provides important lessons for other states that seek to remain politically neutral in today's increasingly polarized political world.

Lebanon, and the Lebanese, were a creation of extra-regional powers and politics. The country is a classic example of the interplay of politics and geography in what remains essentially a tribal/clan highland/mountaineer sociology. Lebanon sits in and affects events in the twentieth century, but its internal politics and behavior is of the twelfth century.[1]

The main political and economic center of Lebanon consists of the narrow coastal plain where ridges of the Lebanon Mountains often reach the sea and separate the coast into a series of small fertile basins. These ridges create a series of hills and valleys that are occupied, and have been occupied, by various religious and ethnic minorities since early history. Lebanon was a home for ocean-going traders such as the Phonecians as well as small tribal groups engaged in farming, herding and specialized crops. What held these groups together was not nationalism but small nuclear families or local religious leaders. Nothing has changed.

To understand the internal politics of Lebanon, one must follow the actions of various major families such as the Gemayels, Jumblatts, Chamouns, Karamehs, etc. One must also try to keep track of the actions and political positions of numerous religious groups and factions, most notably the various Christian sects as well as the Sunni communities and the various Shia factions of the

Moslems. Added to these are the largely non-religious motives of the Palestinians. Finally, there is the role of Lebanon's neighbors Syria and Israel, as well as the involvement of other Islamic states that are not neighbors, but that proclaim militant and religious interest in the existence of Israel, such as Libya, Iran, etc.

Methodologically, trying to unravel the events and circumstances that explain what is going on in Lebanon is something akin to visiting the Mad Hatter's Tea Party in *Alice in Wonderland.* Just as things seem to make sense everyone moves to a new political or geographic position. One solution to making sense of the apparent chaos is to create a chronology of key historical events (found at the end of this paper) and then to determine the primary factor - politics or geography. Complicating matters is the fact that events in Lebanon involve internal and regional as well as international participants. And, these too have changed position, and even the players have changed over time. In this chapter an attempt is made to follow and identify those elements which have been key to various decisions (politics or geography) and finally to draw some lessons as to what went wrong.

THE CREATION LEBANON

In the mid-1800s the area that was to become modern Lebanon was then the autonomous province (sanjaq) of Mount Lebanon within the Ottoman empire. In the mid-nineteenth century (1850-1870), France had gained a dominant political position in the Levant. Great Britain remained dominant in Egypt, Transjordan and on Cyprus. The Ottoman Empire (Turkey) was in decline and many of its peripheral territories were virtually out of control. Under these conditions, there occurred almost continual communal violence as various groups sought autonomy or additional political leverage through the acquistion of more territory. This was especially true in the territory of Greater Syria - which included Palestine, Lebanon and Jordan as well as modern Syria.

Between 1859 and 1860, the Druse, located in what is now Lebanon, began a massacre of Christians living in the area of the Biqa Valley and Shuf Mountains, By the time their activity was stopped (it was not over), it is reported that there were no Christians alive south of the Beirut to Damascus Road. This massacre, and the families/clans involved, was a major factor in the creation of Lebanon as a state, and for the continual internal fighting and turmoil that have characterized Lebanese politics to the present.

To halt the continued killing and to protect the Christians, the French actively entered the scene both politically and militarily. The Christian communities long had been engaged in international trade and had created numerous personal as well as economic ties with various European powers, especially France. To this day, it is common to find the children of Christian Lebanese with French first names and Arab family names. French became a common second language. And, many Lebanese spent their holidays and shopping sprees in Paris and Nice. Meanwhile, Syria objected to continued French rule and sought both independence as well as control of Lebanon.

In 1916 the Sykes-Picot Agreement was signed between Great Britain and France. This effectively divided the non-Turkish portions of the former Ottoman Empire giving France control of the areas north of the city of Acre. This included territory that was to become modern Lebanon and Syria. Palestine, which was under British control, was to remain international or neutral because of its religious significance to the Europeans and Christians.

France thus became the creator and guarantor of a neutral territory referred to as Little Lebanon. This territory extended roughly from a southern border along the ridge associated with Bikfayya (the traditional home and territory of the Christian Gemayel family) north to the present border with Syria. This area was almost wholly Christian in composition. However, it also consisted of numerous separate and warring Christian families and sects. It was only homogeneous in the sense that it was predominantly non-Moslem.

Following the French occupation of Damascus to put down a Syrian rebellion, the League of Nations gave France a Mandate for the entire area (Syria as well as Little Lebanon). In 1920 France linked the largely Moslem south with the Christian north (Little Lebanon) to create Greater Lebanon - resulting in the loss of Syrian authority over these areas. This action remains the basis of current Syrian claims to Lebanon and their hatred of the French (contrasted with the almost adoration of the French by Christian Lebanese).

While many Moslems were now added to the territory under French control, the Christians remained a slight majority. This meant that the Moslem families and sects that had formerly been dominant in their own territory now became a minority - barely. Neither side viewed its decline in power with much grace and both continued to recall earlier massacres. Meanwhile the Syrians continued to fight French occupation. This is an important point to bear in mind when evaluating contemporary Syrian attitudes and behavior relative to Lebanon and its political future.

While Lebanon may have been neutral in terms of regional or European politics, its internal populations and factions were not. In a manner typical of Byzantine politics, tribal warfare linked religion, family, territory and the use of foreign allies in a simple, if primitive, desire to control territory. The result was a kaleidoscope of continually shifting alliances - often involving the use of outsiders to tip the balance. So long as the outsiders had no proprietary interest in Lebanon or any of the neighboring states, Lebanon's neutrality was assured. However, should this condition change . . .

THE GEOGRAPHY BEHIND POLITICS

Lebanon was often referred to as the only democracy in the Middle East. This was pure camouflage. Lebanese politics have always been based upon a tribal, medieval socio-political system of only tenuous political stability. Without a rapidly expanding economy, and the continued presence first of the Ottomans and later of France acting as a final arbitrator of local disputes, Lebanon long ago would have devolved into chaos. And, Syria, which had also been created out of the decline of the Ottoman Empire, and which has never recognized the existence of Lebanon, would have snatched the territory in an instant.

To maintain at least some semblance of political equilibrium, a constitution was developed in 1926. After Independence in 1945, however, the president of Lebanon simply assumed the former powers of the Frence High Commissioner and Ottoman Governors, giving him considerable (and unvoted upon) powers.

However, dating back to the creation of the state under the Ottomans, there always was provision for proportional representation of the various religious communities in the Chamber of Deputies, the Civil Service, the Military and the Cabinet. The result was an unwritten understanding that the President should always be a Maronite (Christian), the Premier a Sunni Moslem, the Speaker a Shiite Moslem and the Foreign Minister an Orthodox (Christian). The Minister of Defense would be a Druse, but the Chief of Staff was to be Maronite (Christian). And so the division was to continue throughout the government. This "arrangement" worked only so long as the various parties played by the rules. However, the rules were more often broken than followed, and internal conflict along family/clan/tribal/territorial lines remained a hallmark of Lebanese politics.

REGIONAL POLITICS AND "NEUTRALITY"

With the creation of Israel in 1948, the neutral role formerly played by Palestine was now lost. Israel clearly was not a neutral state and there was no way it could be supported as such by the United States, France, Great Britain or the Soviet Union - all extra-regional players in Middle East geo-politics. Lebanon was not an Arab state. It remained *de jure* Christian. However, Lebanon's Moslem population was rapidly expanding through both natural birth rates as well as the influx of Palestinian refugees. In contrast with the Christians, the Moslems clearly supported the Arab and Palestinian effort to remove the Jews from the territory they had taken (the former Palestine).

But with only a token army and no natural resources, the only political asset Lebanon could provide was its location, a border contiguous to northern Israel. However, Egypt and Syria, as well as Jordan also had contiguous borders. More importantly, they also had large standing armies. As such, these countries initially assumed the role of Palestinian champion. There was no need for Lebanon to participate. Its size and political un-importance allowed Lebanon to remain neutral.

Meanwhile, internal order was kept, and Lebanon's fragile coalitions preserved, by the continuing interest of Europe and the United States in events in the Middle East. First the French, and later the United States were called upon to provide "neutral" extra-regional troops whose physical as well as political presence were used to restore order and some balance to the bickering and power grabbing endemic to Lebanese politics. But, unlike the French and British, the United States had no economic, political or even social interest in Lebanon *per se.* The American position was that Lebanese should determine Lebanese politics. Someone forgot to tell the Lebanese that they were now responsible to themselves.

The first real American involvement in Lebanon came in 1958 under President Eisenhower. U.S. Marines were landed at Beirut to help restore order after several months of internal fighting and killing. Again, the country and its families and sects had divided Lebanon into a series of hostile territories (Fig. 7.1). Moslems controlled Tripoli, the Biqa Valley and the Moslem quarter of Beirut. The Druse reasserted their independence in the Shuf and the

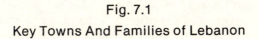

Fig. 7.1
Key Towns And Families of Lebanon

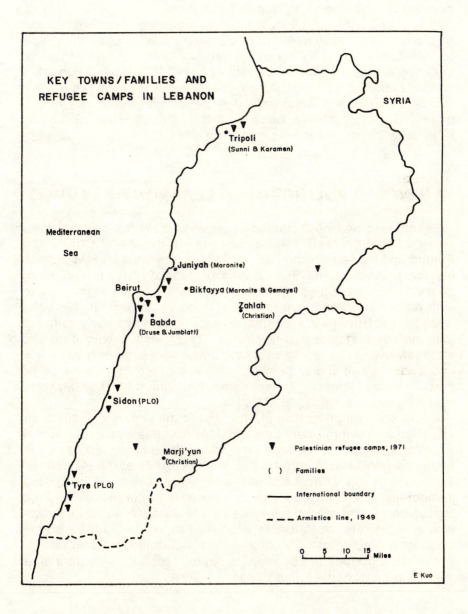

Christians continued to control all the inland transport and commerce and most of the coastal littoral north of Beirut.

However, the American action was tied to events in the entire region more than the situation in Lebanon itself. It was aimed as much at sending a message to Great Britain, France and the U.S.S.R., that the United States would not accept any return to a colonial partitioning of the Middle East.

Americans viewed their action as showing the flag in the Mediterranean and to demonstrate both its ability and willingness to maintain stability in the entire region. It was not just to solve Lebanon's internal problems. The geo-political advantage of a neutral Lebanon was that troops could be put into the region at a location that would not offend the Egyptians, the Arabs or the Israelites. Unfortunately, once American troops were withdrawn from Lebanon, so too was American interest.

A NEW GEO-POLITICS GIVES LEBANON A KEY ROLE

Events leading to the decline of Lebanon's neutral role occurred outside Lebanon itself. First, there was the decline of British and French involvement in the region. Perhaps the date of this demise can be placed on the Suez crises of 1956-1957. With American support of Egypt against Great Britain, France and even Israel, and with American willingness to place troops in Lebanon in 1958, the role of Great Britain as a regional power broker was clearly eclipsed and replaced. However, the United States was a wild card. Its actions were not based upon a long-time knowledge of the politics and sociology of the region, but rather by morality - a sense of "justice" and "right." These same motives had U.S. Marines returning to Lebanon in 1982.[2]

Unlike the French or British, the Americans began to focus their attention and commitments on Israel. At first this was a reaction to Israel's "underdog" position in the region. It also was linked to still fresh images of Nazi Death Camps and the events of the Holocaust. The result was that only Lebanon - a nominally Christian and stable democracy - could provide a neutral territory in the region. So long as its government did not take sides in the Arab/Israeli conflict, this was a viable role. Unfortunately, unlike France, the United States was not willing to play "godfather" to maintain domestic peace. The internal politics of Lebanon began to favor active political and military support of the Palestinians.

THE IMPACT OF ISRAEL

The creation of the State of Israel in 1948 created an entirely new element in regional politics. Its continual defeat of Arab and Egyptian armies forced a shift in both military and political tactics. The use of sophisticated military technology, such as long-range Katuysha rockets, combined with acts of terrorism, both within Israel and on its citizens outside the country, changed the geo-political significance of Lebanon. These changes in turn lead directly to the gradual demise of "neutral" Lebanon. However, they alone did not make Lebanon the military battleground/buffer it was to become.

The creation of Israel not only removed Palestine as the neutral state in the region, it also shifted European and American political emotions and commitment to one state over the others. Israel's historical and emotional significance to both Americans and Europeans had been greatly reinforced by the recent experience of the Jews in Nazi Germany. No one could forget, and Israel would not let anyone forget, the trauma of the Holocaust. In addition, Jewish bankers and influential executives in Europe as well as America created a powerful lobby for support of Israel. This meant that European and American governments saw themselves as dealing with other Europeans (immigrant Jews), not with Arabs. The result was a clear emotional and political partisanship. No longer did the Europeans or Americans act as a neutral factor.

The foundation of Israel created the Palestinian refugee problem (See Fig. 7.1). Care must be taken NOT to identify the Palestinians solely with Moslems. Many Palestinians were Christian. Dr. George Habash, one of the most militant Palestinian leaders, in fact, is a Christian, not a Moslem. Thus the refugees were not merely religious groups. They were a people who had lost their land and who had a definite territory and homeland to which they hoped to return.

Between 1952 and 1954 President Nasser of Egypt, managed to play off the British, the Russians and the Americans as he formed an independent Egypt. In the process, he nationalized the Suez Canal in 1956. This action created a confrontation between Great Britain and France (major users of the Canal) and the United States. It also involved Israeli troops who took part in joint French-British-Israeli operations in the Suez conflict. Because of the United States's support of Egypt and opposition to France and Great Britain's actions, it became clear that President Nasser was calling the shots. Unfortunately, he became overly confident about his abilities. He began both verbal and economic assaults against Israel. Finally, Nasser closed the Suez to all Israeli bound traffic.

As a consequence of Nasser's actions, Israel invaded and occupied Gaza and the Sinai in October 1956. Again, the historic guarantors of peace in the region, Great Britain and France, issued ultimatums to both sides and even bombed and occupied Port Said. At this point, both the United States and the USSR issued warnings and entered the play. Israel did not withdraw until 1957.

In all of this, Lebanon continued to be neutral. Its government and Christian population focused largely on internal politics and economics. However, the Moslem population of Lebanon, goaded on by their pan-Arab nationalism and by the resident Palestinians in the refugee camps, grew increasingly partisan (anti-Israel). The war had again increased the number of refugees and the location of the now semi-permanent camps, and the close associations between the Palestinians and their various Moslem neighbors began to involve the general population of Lebanon. However, there still was no direct Lebanese political, economic, or military participation in the fighting. In fact, because of its international neutrality and stability, Lebanon became a haven for Arab money and families who feared instability in their home countries. Lebanon thrived because of this condition. Non-involvement in regional politics was good business. But Lebanon's neutrality had always been guaranteed by extra-regional powers such as the French and more recently the Americans, not by the neighboring Arab States or any sense of nationalism by the Lebanese population or by a national army.

GEO-POLITICAL CONSEQUENCES OF THE 1967 WAR

The next major event to affect the status and political function of Lebanon was the Israel-initiated War in 1967. One of Israel's first acts was to disable the radar at Beirut International Airport (BIA). This gave the Israelis virtually complete air-superiority in the eastern Mediterranean. Only the American Fleet could monitor their flights and air activities.

Among the consequences of the Six Day War, as the 1967 War became known, was an effort by the military arm of the Palestinian Liberation Organization (PLO), the Palestinian Liberation Army (PLA), to establish political control in Jordan, declaring it a Palestinian state. Thereby the PLO/PLA would gain a territorial base from which to launch continual guerrilla and eventually a formal military attack against Israel, especially the recently Israeli-occupied areas of the West Bank. However, Jordan crushed the effort definitively. The remnants of the PLO and PLA were then forced to leave Jordan to prevent any future occurrence. Their destination? The refugee camps in "neutral" Lebanon. No Arab state would accept the Palestinians, and Lebanon did not have the power (or good sense) to refuse them. This marked the beginning of the end of Lebanon's neutrality, and the emergence of its new role as a buffer - battleground between the Palestinians (PLO and PLA), the Syrians and Israel.

In 1973, the Syrians and Egyptians launched a pre-emptive attack on Israel designed to regain their honor and to once and for all destroy Israel as a presence in the region and to return the land to the Palestinians. Lebanon, with its massive refugee camps and PLO training camps became a crucial geo-political element in the equation.

However, the result of the 1973 War (the Yom Kippur War to Israel, the Ramadan War to Egypt) was another defeat for the Arab forces and a vast increase in the territory of Israel. This time Israel did not return the territory if captured. World opinion favored the underdog and taking advantage of this goodwill, Israel began to consolidate its hold on occupied lands, primarily through colonization by some of the most conservative and aggressive sects and political groups in Israel. This naturally drove more Palestinians into the refugee camps. This in turn increased their hatred and willingness to die in any effort to rid their land and lives of the Israelis. It was now a Holy War - a Jihad for the Moslems and pure hatred for the Christian Palestinians. However, the Syrians and Egyptians were now much more conservative. Not only had the Israelis defeated them several times, but Israel had demonstrated an ability to bomb Egyptian and Syrian territory and cities with impunity. Supporting the Palestinians was one thing. Taking a chance of losing their own cities and territory to the Israelis was quite another.

The Palestinians now received material and verbal support, but actual armed involvement by Arab and Egyptian armies on their behalf was largely a matter of the past. The Palestinians would now have to do their own fighting with only indirect support. This created a new political geography. And its consequences held vast portent for the geo-political position of Lebanon.

By its occupation of the West Bank, Gaza and the Sinai, Israel had created extensive hostile elements within its newly defined territory. The West Bank and all former Arab territories now claimed by Israel de facto represented an insurgent state that required intensive security measures by Israel. The fact that the West Bank and Jordan were contiguous made the PLO and PLA attempt to control Jordan inevitable. The eventual ouster of the Palentinians from Jordan, and their new concentrations in Southern Lebanon made the shift of that area to the status of a war zone equally inevitable. It was not so much a matter of conscious decision as a natural sequence of events. Only Lebanon's refusal to grant asylum to the Palestinians could have changed the future.

POLITICS AND GEOGRAPHY
CREATE A BUFFER/BATTLEGROUND

With the arrival of even more refugees, the various United Nations-sponsored Palestinian refugee camps in Lebanon became a territorial as well as a political base for the PLO/PLA. Initially viewed as only temporary, the actual location of the camps seemed irrelevant at the time. Consequently, the predominantly Christian government of Lebanon located the camps among the poor Shiites populations and on lands claimed by various Moslem factions. To the still dominant Christian leaders, this meant southern Lebanon. However, the Palestinians became increasingly politically organized and militarily active.

Once the PLO and PLA were ousted from Jordan (Black September), the refugee camps became de facto Palestinian mini-states.[3] Not only were they the only territory available to the Palestinians, but the locations of so many camps contiguous to the northern border of Israel as well as to resupply from Syria made them an ideal location for both training as well as the infiltration of terror squads.

While the Palestinians were being ousted from Jordan and moving to Lebanon, there was extensive rioting by Moslem students in Beirut. In their geo-political naivete, the students were supporting the PLO/PLA and demanding that the Arabs and especially Lebanon begin guerrilla actions aginst Israel. Formal wars were now viewed with little favor, especially by those who had been repeatedly defeated. It was now time for the Palestinians to fight on their own, and not attract Israeli reprisals on former host countries. Lebanon was rapidly becoming the universal choice for a buffer-battleground.

For what appear to have been largely personal political reasons, the Moslem premier of Lebanon, Abdullah al-Yafi, offered to arm

Palestinian volunteers for anti-Israeli guerrilla operations using southern Lebanon as their base. Since the removal of France and the benign neglect of the United States, there was no outside power tempering such statements or making it impossible for Lebanon to act on such rhetoric. Lebanon was now responsible for its own actions and comments. This had not occurred before and Lebanon clearly was not ready to defend its own neutrality. In addition, a neutral Lebanon did not seem to be important to the Arabs or Egyptians.

Meeting in December 1968 in Cairo, the Arab League, in early 1969, issued what has become known as the Cairo Agreement. This granted the PLO and the PLA *de facto* control not only of the Palestinian refugee camps but of southern Lebanon as a base from which to launch attacks on Israel. This marked the official end of Lebanon's neutrality. Lebanon had now taken a side in the Arab-Israeli war AND it shared a border with Israel. Israel was given no option but to view southern Lebanon as an area actively threatening to its existence. In the meantime Syria, which had long coveted the territory of Lebanon and had also accepted its share of Palestinian refugees, moved into a favorable geopolitical position.

Most Palestinian refugees in Syria had been incorporated into Palestinian units in the Syrian army. By 1976 Syria was able to send its troops into Lebanon as part of what was called the Arab Deterrent Force. In fact, this became a *de facto* Syrian occupation of Lebanon. In addition, Syria directed its Palestinian units to join the PLA, but they seem to have remained under Syrian direction and control.

The result was that Syria could appear to be a peacekeeper in Lebanon while, in fact, it has virtually absorbed the old Arab portions of Lebanon and the Biqa Valley into Syria. The former Little Lebanon, composed of the Christian north, is only partially under Syrian domination. However, the key city of Tripoli, which is under the control of the Sunni leader, Karameh, and is the terminus of the oil pipeline from Syria, already is under effective Syrian control.

WHAT WENT WRONG?

What the foregoing chronology of events demonstrates very clearly is that Lebanon lost its neutrality, and eventually its sovereignty, through a combination of circumstances that were both internal and external in origin.

First, Lebanon lost its neutrality and viability because it could never develop a sense of national patriotism. Loyalties remained focused on the family/clan. And, as David Knight has so aptly pointed out, this is not the basis of nationalism.[4] Today, states give their name to their citizens. In the past, it was the people or nation that gave their name to a territory (state). Thus, there never emerged such a person as a true Lebanese. There only were people who lived in Lebanon. This meant that even the Army could not be called upon to defend everyone or even all the territory of the state.[5] The Lebanese were not even committed to their own survival.

Second. When a multi-national state has entire regions of its territory occupied by various homogeneous sects or groups who do not share the cultural or political identity of other groups in the state, these regions *de facto* become locally independent. Unless such areas and their populations are integrated by social, economic and transportation features, as well as by a common national ethos, it is unlikely that there ever will emerge more than a loose federation of groups. This is especially true in mountains which physically contribute to social isolation. Afghanistan provides another contemporary example of such divisiveness.

Third. It is clear that most neutral states remain neutral only so long as some extra-regional power or powers are committed to defending their neutrality. Once Lebanon was left on its own, not only did its internal factions begin to fight and divide the country, but neighboring countries and political factions viewed Lebanon as a geographic asset in their fights with each other, and as a geographic base for attacks against Israel.

Fourth. The role of political refugees clearly is crucial. The Palestinian refugee camps, especially their size and locations, made them ideal centers for continued political organization and activity against Israel. Especially crucial was the international support of the camps and their populations. This often meant that the refugees had better food and services than the local people. In addition, the location of the camps along the border with the country to which they were hostile meant the camps inevitably became guerrilla recruiting grounds and safe havens. Similar occurrences are found in the case of the Afghans in Pakistan, the Khmer in Thailand, the Polisario in the Western Sahara and refugee groups in Central America as well as Southern Africa. In short, the geo-political role of refugees in today's world has yet to be adequately appreciated or studied.

Fifth. Directly related to the problem of political refugees is the impact of modern military technology and the new political tactic of terrorism, especially as it is applied to civilian targets and populations. The ability of hand held rockets and of mobile Katuysha rockets to reach over international boundaries and create havoc while the launchers remain in "neutral" territory (or can easily move to neutral territory), thereby creating an international incident should there be a retaliatory strike, is crucial to an understanding of the dynamics of modern "neutrality." This has not only been a problem in Lebanon, but in Afghanistan, South Africa, and Central America as well. With modern military hardware, even a state with no natural resources may find that its geographic location or terrain is an asset to guerrilla operations, And, once guerrilla operations are permitted in some segment of its national territory, the state natually loses its neutral role and becomes a combatant - even if an unwilling combatant. It also gives that territory over to battlefield status - virtually removing it from national sovereignty in a functional sense.

LESSONS IN LOST NEUTRALITY

First, do not allow refugees to remain concentrated and unassimilated, or permit them (or any international organization) to establish a permanent infra-structure.

Two, when refugee populations are kept socially and politically separate AND they are concentrated in territory along the border of their former homes, this area is likely to become a battleground.

Refugee populations should be geographically dispersed or the camps located far from the border. This is especially true when the refugees are political refugees who seek to return home and/or change the government.

Lesson three. Refugees of the same or similar ethnic, linguistic or religious backgrounds, if left concentrated territorially and not dispersed or integrated, may upset a delicate balance of power in the host country.

Fourth, if the refugees remain concentrated and concentrated along the border of a neutral state, that state, at least the border region holding the refugees, will become a battleground. Once the neutral state participates in any way, it *de facto* loses its neutrality and becomes a battleground.

Fifth, if "neutrality" is guaranteed only by outside countries, and it is not a national commitment, as in the case of Switzerland, then it is a fragile condition, subject to rapid change.

Finally, all pretense of non-involvement is lost once a part of the state territory or population becomes a haven for military or political actions against another state, especially if it is a neighboring state.

CHRONOLOGY
KEY EVENTS IN THE HISTORY OF LEBANON

1859-1860	Druse went on rampage killing Christians. Killing started in Shuf at the Gharb and Matted District. Moslems also occupied Zahle.
1860	No Christians existed south of the Damascus Road. Moslems/Druse were held at Bikfayya (Gemayel home).
1860-1861	European Powers held three conferences on the problem. The decision was to create a semi-independent Lebanon dominated by Christians in north.
1916	Sykes-Picot Agreement between Great Britain and France divided the territory of the former Greater Syria. France was to have dominance in the territory north of Acre. Great Britain was to be dominant south of that city. Palestine, due to its religious importance, was to be international (neutral).
1917	Following the Bolshevik Revolution, and a number of diplomatic incidents, Great Britain pledged its support for the Balfour Declaration and support for the creation of a Jewish national home.
1920	LEAGUE OF NATIONS gave France a mandate for authority in Lebanon. France linked the Christian north of the Moslem south to create a Greater Lebanon. This shifted the political balance from 90% Christian to approximately 55%.
1926	Promulgation of a Lebanese Constitution.
1943	Lebanon began the process of independence.
1948	Israel declared its statehood.

1949	The First Arab-Israeli War ended with the signing of a United Nations-sponsored armistice. Over 1000 refugees now inside Lebanon.
1955-1957	Lebanon's neutrality was threatened by Egypt-Syria-USSR alliance and the Suez Crises. Muslim factions pushed for an Arab/Palestinian tilt after Israel joined with Great Britain and France in attack on Suez.
1958	Renewed rioting based upon religion with demands for Lebanese support of Palestinians and Arabs. Country is divided into distinct zones - Muslim concentrations in Tripoli, the Biqa and the Muslim quarter of Beirut. Druse controlled the Shuf. Chamoun was ousted as president, but Christians blockaded all inland transport to force a compromise.
1965	PLO formally created from earlier Palestinian groups.
1967	Six Day War. Israel defeated Arab Armies. In six days Israel occupied Jerusalem and the West Bank. It also controlled Gaza, the Golon and Sinai, but agreed to their return. This created more Palestinian refugees.
1968-1969	To placate student demonstrators, Lebanon's Muslim premier, Abdullah al-Yafi, offered to arm Palestinian volunteers for anti-Israeli guerrilla operations. In December an Arab League conference was held. In 1969 it was agreed to give Southern Lebanon to the PLO as a base. This became known as the Cairo Agreement.
1969-70	200,000 Palestinian refugees in Lebanon. PLO/PLA is finally ousted from Jordan in bloody fighting. This is referred to as "Black September." The PLO/PLA set up a mini-state in Southern Lebanon.
1969	Muamar Qadaffi led a successful coup in Libya and declared war on Israel and his support of the Palestinians.

1973	Ramadan (Yom Kippur) War regained military honor of Egypt, and began the process leading to the Camp David Accords.
1975	Druse (Jumblatts), PLO (Sidon and Tire), Moslems in Tripoli (Karameh) were all stockpiling and receiving continual shipments of arms both through the ports and via Damascus. This forced the Christians (especially the Chamouns) to seek supplies from Israel. Fighting in Lebanon extended from Beirut to Tripoli.
1976	Syrian trained and supplied units of the PLA occupied Christian Damour (south of Beirut) and 6,000 Christians were killed. Memories of the 1860 massacre re-emerged.
	Syria threatened an invasion if Christians continued to arm. Israel threatened repercussions to Syria if they should invade Lebanon.
	July - Syrians occupied Lebanon as a "peace keeping" force known as the Arab Deterrent Force (ADF).
1977-78	Christian factions continued to struggle for titular power. Kamal Jumblatt, Toni Franjieh, Bashir Gemayel were assassinated in power moves by various Christian factions.
1978	February - PLA units occupied the high ground overlooking northern Israel. They began a seige of the local Christian communities led by Lebanese Major, Saad Huddad.
	March - the Israeli Army moved to the Litani River driving out the PLA. Control was then given to the United Nations Forces in Lebanon (UNIFIL). PLO/PLA returned to former positions.
1979	Camp David Agreement was signed between Egypt and Israel (occupied the period 1977-1979). The Agreement returned the Sinai to Egypt, but left the West Bank under Israeli control. The Palestinians were still left out of the process.

1980	Gemayel clan and its supporters occupied the power bases of the Chamoun clan and gained control of Lebanon's government - what was left of it. The Moslem factions continued to largely ignore the Christian political machinations.
1981	Syria launched artillery and airborne attacks on Christian Zahle. Israel responded by shooting down several Syrian heliborne units. Syria countered by installing SAM-6 batteries in the Biqa Valley. These have a range of 180 miles and pose a direct threat to northern Israel. Israel demonstrated its technical abilities by precision long-range attack on the Iraqi nuclear reactor.
1982	Israel launched "Peace for Galilee" invasion of Lebanon and occupation of Beirut. The PLO was forced to leave Lebanon and even lost its base in Tripoli. Syria lost all its Sam batteries to Israeli air strikes. U.S. embassy in Beirut was bombed, killing several Mid-east experts. U.S. Marines' position at Beirut airport was attacked by a car bomb. U.S. launched air strikes on Shuf Mountains and Druze. It lost several planes and some pilots were captured. PLO was finally forced out of Lebanon as a formal force. Palestinans remained in refugee camps and re-infiltration was started.

NOTES

1. This point is a major theme of the book by Jonathan C. Randall, *Going all the Way: Christian Warlords, Israeli Adventurers and the War in Lebanon.* New York: Vintage Press, 1984, passim.

2. Eric Hammel. *The Root: The Marines in Beirut, August 1982-February 1984.* New York: Harcourt, Brace Jovanovich, 1985, passim.

3. I have previously looked at the geopolitical process of creating "insurgent states" and mini state both within and contiguous to the borders of the target country or government. McColl, "The Insurgent State: Territorial Bases of Revolution," Annals of the Association of American Geographers, 59 (1969): 613-631.

4. David Knight. "Identity and Territory: Geographical Perspecatives on Nationalism and Regionalism." *Annals of the Association of American Geographers,* 72 (1982): 514-553.

5. Eric Hammel. *The Root.* op. cit.

CHAPTER 8

ASIA'S PIVOTAL BUFFER STATES

LAWRENCE ZIRING

Buffer states are lesser actors sandwiched between more powerfully endowed, ambitious, and often aggressive entities. The purpose of the buffer state is established by these external competitors. They become sacrificial elements in a larger contest and their particular interests are often ignored by the greater actors who set the dimensions and lay down the guidelines of confrontation. To be designated a buffer state therefore is to witness the diminishing of a State's sovereignty--to acknowledge that its national destiny is influenced from without, and that its territorial integrity is neither fully respected nor legally protected from alien intruders. Buffer states are extensions of balances of power, not international law. As such, they are protected by military-political conditions, not moral-legal procedures. Where their status as buffer states is respected their precarious existence is sustainable. However, in circumstances where the pattern of regional relationships undergoes significant change, buffers are usually the first victims. They pay the price for temporary larger power equilibrium, a cost which oscillates between a loss of national pride on the one side to extinction on the other.

Afghanistan and Iran became buffer states in the latter part of the nineteenth century as a consequence of British and Russian imperial ambitions and rivalries. The Bolshevik Revolution brought a modification in Iran's buffer status after World War One, but Afghanistan continued in that role through World War Two. With the British retreat from India in 1947, Afghanistan came under direct Soviet influence, but its buffer status was sustained until Moscow's decision to invade the country in 1979. This chapter traces these developments to the contemporary period. It also describes how they impacted on neighboring Pakistan. The central purpose of the chapter is to show how the disappearance of Afghanistan as a buffer state affects revolutionary Iran, and transforms Pakistan into the newest buffer state on the rim of Asia.

AFGHANISTAN: CENTRAL ASIAN BUFFER

Afghanistan was perceived a buffer state between British and Russian imperial interests in the nineteenth century. Russia's transcontinental ambitions brought its legions into Central Asia and in due course long-ruling Muslim khanates were defeated and their territories absorbed within the spreading Slavic empire.[1] Britain's power in India was consolidated during this same period and the imperiums eyed one another suspiciously, neither being prepared to accept the other's statements about peaceful coexistence. The British centered their strategy on containing Russian forces in Central Asia on the northern side of the Oxus River (Amu Darya).[2] Afghanistan could not avoid becoming a buffer state given the posturing of its powerful neighbors. Moreover, Britain developed its "Forward Policy" which envisaged the stationing of British-Indian contingents in Afghanistan as well as the subordination of its government to alien influence.

Afghan resistance to this intrusion resulted in the Anglo-Afghan War of 1838-1842. Kabul concluded its primary enemy was Britain and when tsarist emissaries were invited to Kabul following the British withdrawal, London initiated the Second Afghan War (1878). The British were forced to decide on either annexing Afghanistan directly or fashioning a "friendly" government guaranteed to ensure the security of India and the Persian Gulf. After the 1838-1842 war London had assured the Afghans they would not again interfere in their internal affairs. But the 1878 war only added to the fury of the tribal nation. The British realized the permanent garrisoning of Afghanistan against the will of the Afghan nation would bleed their treasury as well as their limited forces, and in time weaken rather than strengthen their hold over India. The British, therefore, opted for Afghanistan as a buffer state, and to ensure its "neutraility" a person loyal to the British Crown, Sardar Abdur Rahman, was placed upon the throne. Kabul was restricted in its relations with other governments, especially imperial Russia.

Given its buffer status, Afghanistan achieved relative stability despite continuing tribal disorders. By 1893 Abdur Rahman was prepared to enter into border discussions with the British Indian government and a legal frontier between British India and

Afghanistan was drawn. Prior to this agreement, Britain entered into another treaty with Russia in 1887 delineating the Oxus River and the southern Pamirs as the northern frontier of the state. The finger of territory in the northeastern corner, Wakhan Corridor, was designed by the British to prevent Russian territory from bordering British India. The buffer state was thus given the sanctity of international law and although the Russians continued to probe for weaknesses in the the agreements they remained intact well into the twentieth century. A history of Afghanistan as a buffer state is more extensively discussed by David Jenkins in the following chapter of this volume.

IRAN AS A BUFFER STATE

Iran's independent status was ignored by Russia as the latter encroached upon and seized Persian territory in the eighteenth and nineteenth centuries. The Treaty of Gulistan (1813) and the Treaty of Turkomanchay (1828) established Russia as the dominant power on the Caspian Sea and the tsar's warm water appetite was whetted by the experience. Britain, however, moved into the breech and established a presence on the Arab side of the Persian Gulf littoral. They also obtained commercial opportunities in Persia (Iran) and signalled their intention to block a Russian advance to the Indian Ocean.

In 1907 an Anglo-Russian Convention divided Iran into Russian and British spheres of influence with a neutral zone between them. The Persian Revolution of 1906 which sought to minimize the role of the monarch and introduce parliamentary government in the country was ignored by the great powers. In fact, the Russians enlisted the deposed Mohammed Ali Shah in an effort to destroy the new consitution. A Persian Cossack Brigade, formed with Russian help in 1883, and led by Russian officers, occupied Tabriz in northwestern Iran. In 1911, the Russians presented an ultimatum to the Persian government demanding the removal of an American financial advisor. Appointed Treasurer General by the Persian majlis (parliament), the American was made responsible for the restoration of the country's financial solvency. Russian pressure, however, produced a coup that terminated the life of the majlis and forced the American to leave the country. Russian influence increased after this incident and did not diminish until World War One and the abdication of the tsar.

The Persian Qajar dynasty also did not survive the war. Its weakness was exploited by Reza Khan, an officer in the Persian

Cossack Brigade who occupied the vacated throne and established his own Pahlavi dynasty. The Persian nationalists were forcefully suppressed by the new shah who presented himself as an Iranian Ataturk and an avid reformer. But Reza Khan was not as successful as the "Father of the Turks."

Given Reza's sympathies with Nazi Germany, Britain and Russia intervened in Iran's affairs once again, forced Reza to abdicate in favor of his son, and sent their troops into the country with the understanding they would be withdrawn within six months from the termination of hostilities. Thus Britain and the Soviet Union again divided Iran into spheres of influence. The Russians, however, also made preparations to transform Iran into a Marxist state. Moscow sponsored the creation of the Iranian Tudeh Party. It also organized separatist governments in the country's northwestern provinces of Azerbaijan and Kurdistan. The British were unable to thwart these actions and the task of convincing the Russians to withdraw their troops from Iran rested with the Americans. Under pressure from Washington, the Russians finally withdrew and the socialist republics which they supported, collapsed. By 1949 United States presence in Iran was assured. Moreover, Iran was drawn into the American--encouraged Baghdad Pact, later called the Central Treaty Organization (CENTO). The Soviets, however, warned Tehran that their 1921 treaty permitted Soviet troops to enter Iran if the latter allowed foreign military forces to operate in the country. Iran was more a client state of the United States, less a buffer. Moreover, under American tutelage Iran loomed large as a pro-western regional power, and the Shah of Iran projected an image of an ever confident and powerful Middle Eastern and Indian Ocean leader.

Iran assumed regional importance after August 1953, when following a brief exile, the Shah was returned to his throne in what has been described as a American organized countercoup.[3] The Shah emphasized his liberal credentials and declared his intention to distribute crown land to peasant farmers. He also sustained the 1950 nationalization of the oil industry but permitted a consortium of foreign companies to exploit the country's petroleum reserves. In return the United States granted Tehran substantial grants and loans to help tide it through an economic crisis and also assisted the government in assembling the Sazman-i-Amniyat va Kishvar (SAVAK) which was concerned with internal as well as foreign security.[4]

The Iranian armed forces also underwent dramatic expansion and modernization. The army was doubled in size and the airforce and navy received similar attention. Pakistan's development paralleled that of Iran in the military field, and both became committed to United States policies opposing the spread of international communism. Iran, however, did not envisage itself in a buffer role but rather as the last line of defense against a Soviet thrust toward the oil lands of the Persian Gulf. Thus CENTO was conceived as a link in a chain of alliances anchored by the North Atlantic Treaty Organization (NATO) in Europe. Pakistan provided the tie to the Southeast Asia Treaty Organization (SEATO) and bilateral arrangements between the United States and Taiwan as well as Japan completed the American sponsored containment network. Iran and Pakistan therefore were significant actors on the rim of Asia. Pakistan's problems, however, were more complex than those of Iran.

THE PAKISTAN DIMENSION

Pakistan was less concerned with the Soviet threat and communist subversion, and more interested in its differneces with India. Iran wanted to champion Pakistani interests but it drew a line where Indo-Pakistani antagonism was a dominant feature. The Shah perceived a Pakistan engaged in self-fulfilling prophecy and swept along by its own rhetoric, especially its allusions to Islam and the need to safeguard the Muslim community of Kashmir. The Iranian monarch wished to avoid such emotional remonstrances, lest he unleash religious forces within his own society. Moreover, the Shah refused to consign New Delhi to the communist camp, and his instincts informed him that the Indians required cultivation. In time, the Shah anticipated mediating the Indo-Pakistani dispute and Islamabad never disabused him of such purpose. By the same token, the Shah endeavored to play the role of honest broker between Kabul and Islamabad, given the fervent belief that local quarrels only played into the hands of their powerful northern neighbor.

Prior to the Iranian revolution of 1978-1979, Pakistan was the more unstable of the two countries. Contrasted with the turmoil that overwhelmed Pakistan, Iran was relatively tranquil. Although the Shah's policies were challenged by aggressive factions, the threat to his pre-eminence appeared minimal. Pakistan, however, suffered from a combination of internal and external disorders. And in 1971 civil war ripped through the country, provided India with an opportunity to settle old scores, and Pakistan was defeated, dismembered, and left in a demoralized condition.[5] Forced to confront the reality of India as the preponderant power in South Asia, Pakistan seemed temporarily content to lick its wounds and repair the damage caused by the war. Moreover, Pakistanis welcomed their first civilian ruler since Mohammed Ayub Khan wrote an end to the country's initial parliamentary experiment in 1958.

· During the same period, Iran loomed large as a regional military power and the Shah began casting glances at the Indian Ocean as well as the Arabian peninsula. Pakistan's Ali Bhutto was impressed with his powerful neighbor and he used some of the Shah's techniques. Most significant was Bhutto's development of the Federal Security Force (FSF). Although he came to power on a wave of popular approval, Bhutto believed it necessary to bolster his authority. Conditioned to anticipate assaults on his leadership and determined to secure the time necessary to recreate Pakistan in his own image, he ordered the FSF to neutralize all potential opposition.

Bhutto took positions which disturbed the Shah. The Pakistani's emphasis on socialist reconstruction, his subtle references to Maoism, and his often overt anti-Americanism were painful reminders that their philosophies were at variance. Bhutto's bilateralism in foreign policy, his desire to become the leading spokesman for Third World causes, his determination to win "friends" in the Soviet Union and North Korea as well as China, troubled the Shah. No less worrisome was Bhutto's Middle East orientation which not only drew Pakistan closer to Saudi Arabia, it also opened the region to Libyan revolutionary doctrine. Despite these problems relations between Tehran and Islamabad remained in place, and the Shah hoped to temper Bhutto's emotional excesses by offering Pakistan large sums of money.

THE SHAH AND THE DAUD

Iran's association with the United States placed the country in the international spotlight. The Shah's regime could not conceal the widespread opposition to his rule, nor could it prevent the dissemination of news concerning the often brutal methods employed in counteracting dissidents. In 1975 the Shah issued a decree establishing Iran as a one-party state, an act which neither won friends nor increased support for his administration at home. In many respects it brought the violent-prone dissidents into coalition with more moderate political opposition. The Shah nevertheless pressed ahead with his *Rastakhiz* (National Resurrection) Party. The monarch apparently believed his police and military establishments were capable of dealing with those refusing to accept his fiat. Criticisms of the one-party state was generally treated with contempt and those rejecting it were summarily judged enemies of Iran and in league with foreign powers.

In March 1975 Iran entered into a $15 billion military and economic package with the United States, which included an American promise to build several nuclear reactors and power stations in Iran. Electronic equipment, telephone systems, and a vast array of modern weapons were at the heart of the arrangement. The Shah shared his riches with friendly governments and Pakistan, Morocco, and Egypt were provided loans. Turkey and Afghanistan were promised aid. It was just at this juncture, when Iran began to loom large as a power with worldwide interests, that the Shah's ambition and belief in his infallibility, caused him to take actions that threw into question his stability as a leader. He ordered harsh action against anti-government demonstrators at Qum. Retaliation by the Marxists and other opponents of the bloodshed at Qum energized more extensive terrorist activities against the state. Law and order in Iran was rapidly disintegrating. The Shah directed his forces to root out the Marxists, but he was equally determined to eliminate his Islamic fundamentalist foes.

The coalition of opposition forces looked to the Shiite religious leaders (fundamentalists) for guidance, and the mullahs ordered their followers to increase the level of violence against the Shah. The mullahs let it be known they wished to rid Iran of both the Shah and his American associates. A total break with the West, with its influence, culture, and physical presence was on the immediate horizon. On January 16, 1979, the Shah left Iran never to return. And on February 1, 1979 Ayatollah Khomeini returned from exile and assumed direct leadership of a revolutionary government. Despite its vaunted military establishment, the Shah's government collapsed before the popular forces led by the ayatollah.

The Afghan monarchy met its denouement several years earlier. King Zahir Shah had eased his cousin, Daud, from the Prime Minister's office in 1963 and had enlisted the support of tribal leaders by getting them to approve a new constitution. The king then made all key appointments to the army, bureaucracy, and judiciary, and in time of emergency could suspend the constitution. Royal family members were prevented from participating in political parties, nor could they hold ministerial office, or obtain a seat in the parliament or supreme court. The king's actions in effect laid the groundwork for the abolition of the monarchy itself. Zahir could not manage the political forces which he himself had spawned. Moreover, given Soviet presence in the country, political organization was destined to follow a radical Marxist course. The formation of the People's Democratic Party of Afghanistan (PDPA), the Khalq, developed from this incubus. Its splinter group, the Parcham, also had its origin in this period.

Both the Khalq and the Parcham had little difficulty in enlisting the support of the educated and professional classes. The monarch insisted upon its own pre-eminence, and despite promises about sharing political power with the larger public, the administration remained frozen in its autocratic form. Economic progress was slow and corruption and inept management prevented genuine development despite efforts by international agencies and foreign governments. The failure of the government was written large in the famine that swept the central and norther regions of the country in 1972.

It was during this period of difficulty that King Zahir Shah attempted to extricate his government from the Soviet web woven by Daud. In December 1971 the king visited London and the two governments agreed to terminate their long lasting enmity. The king also promised the British that his military establishment would not take advantage of Pakistan, given Islamabad's preoccupation with a civil war in its eastern province, and Indian entry into the conflict in December 1971. This new relationship with Britain, combined with increased American efforts at feeding the famine-stricken Afghans (Initiated in "Operation Help" by U.S. Ambassador Robert C. Newmann), disturbed Moscow as well as its supporters in the mountain state. However, it was not until the Shah of Iran pledged joint cooperation between Afghanistan and Iran, and urged Zahir to resolve his differences with Pakistan, that the king's fate was sealed.

The Soviets had invested heavily in Afghanistan. In 1967, Zahir Shah and Aleksei Kosygin entered into an agreement to send Afghan natural gas to the Soviet Union in return for the construction of Afghanistan's airfields and highways. To guarantee their role in the country, the Soviets insisted in 1972 on the signing of a collective security arrangement. The king's hesitation in agreeing to the Soviet demand proved to be his final undoing. Zahir left Afghanistan for medical treatment in July 1973 and during his absence Sardar Mohammad Daud reasserted himself. With assistance from the Afghan armed forces he proclaimed an end to the monarchy, appointed himself president, and described Afghanistan as a republic dedicated to "real democracy" and Islam.

Both the Khalq and Parcham proclaimed their support for the coup. Daud immediately addressed the question of Afghanistan's foreign policy. Among his first public statements was a declaration concerned with liberating the Pushtuns on the Pakistan side of their mutual frontier, which heightened tensions with his Muslim neighbor. The United States and other Western countries followed the Soviet and Indian lead in recognizing the new regime, but the People's Republic of China delayed recognition, citing the influence exerted by the Soviet Union, an argument denied by Daud. He, however, could not avoid intimate entanglement with the Kremlin.

While these developments were moving forward, in Pakistan an insurgency in Baluchistan necessitated the deployment of several of Pakistan's crack army divisions. Pakistan took note of Afghanistan's repeated calls to the Pushtuns and Baluch to demand self-determination. It was also apparent that Baluch dissidents had taken refuge in Afghanistan and a number of leaders had established propaganda offices in Kabul. Bhutto and his government were convinced that Daud and the Soviet Union were behind the turbulence in the frontier region and they publicly accused the former of fomenting revolution and sanctioning terrorist activities that had reached all the way to Islamabad. With the outbreak of hostilities in Baluchistan, the Pakistani government was convinced of Afghan complicity.

The Shah of Iran had cause to worry about the fighting in Pakistani Baluchistan. Iranian Baluch would not be insulated from conflict and its spread to Iran was a predictable outcome of the protracted conflict. The Shah insisted the entire problem was a Kremlin plot aimed at destabilizing the region as a prelude to a Marxist putsch.

By the summer of 1975 Daud was wedded to policies with a socialist orientation. Domestic programs were aimed at eliminating Afghanistan's economic elite. Banks were nationalized, and land reforms broke the back of the privileged landlords. Agricultural cooperatives were established and government bureaucrats placed in charge. The Soviet Union expanded its assistance program and by 1975 was providing the Afghan government with $400 million in aid annually. This figure does not include even higher military expenditures. The Afghan army and airforce came under almost direct Soviet supervision, and their ranks were swelled by broader recruitment.[6] But segments of the Afghan population were unreconciled to the transformation of society, or the Soviet involvement, and violence was a prominent way of signalling dissatisfaction.

The khalg had penetrated the civil service, the military and the professional and student populations. It had also established standing among the tribal Pushtuns, especially among the numerous Ghilzai. Daud could not be oblivious to these activities of the extreme left. Although somewhat constrained by his ties to Moscow, Daud began to re-examine his policies. And when the Shan of Iran offered his good offices in the Afghanistan-Pakistan dispute, Daud displayed greater interest. Moreover, the Pakistani army had suppressed the rebellion in Baluchistan, and Bhutto's military intelligence and FSF had neutralized the more active terrorists. Daud agreed to meet with Bhutto in an effort to normalize Afghanistan's external policies. Conditions within Afghanistan necessitated a consolidation of his authority and a tranquil border with Pakistan was judged essential. The Shan also pledged financial support to Afghanistan in order to provide Kabul with the needed leverage in its dealings with Moscow.

Daud's negotiations with Bhutto, however, were cut short when Pakistan's high ranking generals overthrew their leader and placed the country under material law in July 1977. The leader of the junta, General Mohammed Zia-ul-Haq, declared the coup an internal affair and said the deliberations begun by the Bhutto government with the Afghan leaders would continue uninterrupted. Daud could not ignore the sudden shift in forces in Pakistan. Nor could he avoid the realization that his own army had been infiltrated by elements that were determined to oust him.

On February 20, 1978, Daud revealed a plot to kill him and overthrow the government. Both the Khalq and Parcham, now under orders from Moscow, were implicated in the conspiracy. Daud had been criticized for his new intimacy with the Americans and for his cooperative posture toward the Shah. The Marxists propagandized the view that Daud wanted their assistance in order to impose an absolute dictatorship on the country. The Afghan public was also told the Americans and the Shah had instigated the coup against Bhutto in the hope of thwarting progressive forces in Pakistan. These attacks were similar to those emanating from the Soviet Union. Thus Daud after a protracted flirtation with radical forces, now sought to disassociate himself from these same elements. But the leftists were too deeply entrenched, and given Soviet involvement in the country, Daud's awakening came too late to save him or his regime.

Daud visited Pakistan in March 1978, and both governments publicized the need to sustain communications and to reconcile their differences. Zia spoke optimistically about Pakistan's relations with Kabul and suggested that a peaceful settlement of their dispute might be near. Daud returned to Kabul cognizant of the criticism that was mounting against his rule, but confident he could control the situation.

In April 1978 Mir Akbar Khaibar, a leader of the Parcham was assassinated in the capital. His funeral precipitated a wild demonstration by several thousand leftists. Daud used the occasion of the riots to order the arrest of Khalq and Parcham leaders. He then called for his cabinet to assemble to examine the instability in the country and to decide on action against the Afghan leftists. Before that meeting could be convened, however, disaffected elements of the Afghan armed forces favorably disposed toward the Khalq and Parcham, as well as influenced by Soviet advisors, moved against the government. Daud, his brother Naim, and approximately thirty members of their family and other high placed officials in the government were killed. This was no palace revolution. The military units that perpetrated the coup had no intention of imposing their own rule. The leaders of the Khalq and Parcham were given their immediate release, and Noor Taraki, leader of the Khalq formed the new government. Hafizullah Amin and Babrak Karmal were made deputy prime ministers and Khalq and Parcham members filled positions in the cabinet and government. The political nature of the takeover, and the role played by the Afghan military dramatized the involvement of the Soviet Union in the destruction of Daud. Afghanistan ceased to be a buffer state and seemed destined to assume all the trappings of a Soviet satellite.

Khalq policies, especially those pressed by Amin, however, began to have a telling effect upon the tribal people. Moreover, the more conservative tribes quickly concluded that Islam was in mortal danger in Afghanistan and that the Kabul Marxists had to be resisted. When Karmal sensed the magnitude of this problem he cautioned Amin to slow his reform program, but this only infuriated the Khalqi-Parcham marriage, despite Taraki's efforts, failed and Amin moved ahead with his "modernzing program." Moscow too was disturbed with these developments and with Islamic revolution threatening to destroy the Shah's regime, it was judged necessary to impose other restraints on Amin.

By this time a fundamentalistic Islamic resistance had intensified against the Kabul Marxists. Direct assaults on Afghan army units caused high losses. Tribal guerrillas also killed unprotected foreigners who were taken for Russians, their prime targets. The defection of Afghan army elements also troubled the regime and its Soviet advisors. The Khalq played down resistance to its authority and admitted only to runnng battles with smugglers and conventional malcontents. In the meantime, Kabul remained under curfew, and members of the bureaucracy, the professions, and intelligentsia disappeared from the streets of the capital. The government arrested hundreds of suspects and rumors spread about summary executions in and around Kabul. In an effort to deflect public opinion, Amin renewed the Pushtunistan controversy, arguing that the Pushtun and Baluch people should be given the right to decide their own future.

the Kremlin called Taraki to Moscow in December 1978 and a twenty-year treaty of friendship and cooperation was signed between the two governments. It reaffirmed their treaties of 1921 and 1931, and both agreed that each would respect the sovereignty of the other and would not interfere in the other's internal affairs. Taraki returned from Moscow with orders to reduce Amin's authority and to reinstate Karmal in the government. These efforts failed as Amin assumed the posts of prime minister and foreign minister in March 1979. The Soviets countered by making Taraki president of the Supreme Council for the Defense of the Country, but he was unable to gain the necessary support in the army high command. This contest of wills between Amin and Taraki occurred against a background of tumultuous events in Iran where the Shah had been forced to flee his country and a broad combination of revolutionaries, headed by the Shiite clergy had taken control of Iran. Moreover, the Afghan tribal resistance had multiplied, and fired by religious yearnings, began to assault government positions with more reckless abandon. Given the severity of the fighting, the reluctance to take prisoners, the destruction of the innocents through indiscriminate bombing and shelling, the families of the Afghan rebels, the mujahiddin, were put to flight. Many sought refuge in Iran, but the great majority sought sanctuary in Pakistan. By August 1979 approximately 142,000 refugees had arrived in Pakistan, only a trickle of the tide that was to inundate the country in subsequent years.

Pakistan did not and could not prevent the influx of refugees, the Islamabad government noting that its concern was purely "humanitarian." President Zia publicized his government's intention to remain neutral and he pledged non-interference in the domestic affairs of Afghanistan. At the same time he believed his government could not turn its back on terrified and impoverished people who were seeking shelter from a storm that was ravaging their country.

The Soviets, however, had another view of the Pakistani role. The ratification of the 1978 treaty between Moscow and Kabul was also the occasion for Soviet authorities to condemn the actions of the guerrillas and to infer Pakistani complicity. They also hinted that the Chinese were sending weapons to the insurgents. Some Arab regimes were also accused of aiding the Afghan revolutionaries. Moscow declared Egyptian representatives in Pakistan regularly met with leaders of the Muslim Brotherhood and supplied them with money to purchase weapons. The Afghan government was reassured by its Soviet ally that it could count on its support in crushing the rebellion.

On March 21, 1979, *Pravda* directed its criticism at the United States and West Germany, as well as Egypt, China and Pakistan. All these countries, it stated, were using Islam as a pretext for the reinstitution of the monarchy, and this the Soviet Union would never countenance. The kidnapping and death of American ambassador, Adoph Dubs, in Kabul during this period had all the signs of a Soviet plot. Rumors were rife that Hafizullah Amin and Dubs had developed a close rapport and that the Afghan leader was planning new overtures to the United States. Dubs' death, however, brought the curtain down on American-Afghan cooperation. It also sealed the fate of both Taraki and Amin.

Taraki was summoned to Moscow in August 1979 and ordered to get rid of Amin. When he returned to Kabul, however, Amin had him arrested, tortured, and killed. Amin then sought to consolidate power in anticipation of a renewed Soviet threat. He appealed to his armed forces for support and called upon the Afghan mujahiddin to join with him in the restoration of Afghanistan's equilibrium, but the excesses of the Khalq regime prevented reconciliation.

When Afghan officers sought to regain control of their units, Soviet "advisors" found themselves easy targets. Many died at the hands of their Afghan "colleagues." Moscow rushed more military contingents to Afghanistan when it appeared its grip on the army was being loosened. In December 1979 Viktor Paputin, a high ranking member of the Soviet Committee for State Security (KGB), was dispatched to Kabul to plot the overthrow of Amin and to guarantee the establishment of a government in Kabul favorable to Moscow. The KGB, under Paputin's direction, prepared the groundwork for still another coup and forced Amin to retreat behind the walls of his palace, surrounded by his loyal bodyguard.

The Soviet invasion of Afghanistan was apparently ordered when the Kremlin realized it could no longer trust the Afghan armed forces. On December 27, 1979 approximately 80,000 Soviet troops moved into Afghanistan. Amin was killed, the Kremlin justifying the action by asserting the Afghan government had invited the Soviet forces to assist them in beating back a foreign conspiracy. Moscow wished the world to believe Amin was an usurper and that the only legitimate leader of the Afghan state was Babrak Karmal. Karmal and his Soviet associates were determined to ensure the survival of Marxism in the Muslim country. The mujahiddin were just as determined to continue the struggle, irrespective of the odds against them.

REPERCUSSION

Iran, not Pakistan, was the first country to experience the loss of the Afghan buffer. The Iraqi invasion of Iran may well have been prompted by Baghdad's fear that the Shiite Muslim state, under Khomeini's leadership, was bent on spreading its brand of revolution.[7] Khomeini's link with the Iraqi Al-Dawa and the latter's call to the faithful to assist in the overthrow of the Baathist government of Saddam Hussain has been well publicized. Nevertheless, it can be hypothesized that Iraq struck across the Shatt al-Arab in September 1980 because the Soviets had moved into Afghanistan and appeared to be maneuvering to exploit ethnic as well as sectarian conflict within Iran. Iraq may have believed the time was right for it to make its presence felt in the region. Moreover, given the physical destruction of the Iranian officer corps by the revolution, the desertion of significant army units, Baghdad anticipated only token resistance to its invasion. It also had reason to believe its thrust into oil-rich Khuzistan, what the Iraqis call Arbistan, would be welcomed by the region's inhabitants who would eagerly join in common Arab cause against Iran.[8] But Baghdad set itself limited objectives. It also decided to conserve its weapons and frontline forces. In 1982 the Iraqis were driven back across the Shatt al-Arab and virtually all of Iranian territory was recaptured. When Baghdad indicated its desire to call off the fighting, the Iranian response was both emphatic and determined. The war had become a religious crusade, and the Tehran government declared it would end only after Saddam Hussain had been destroyed and Iraq agreed to rebuild the Iranian cities it had devastated as well as compensate the victims of its aggression. That crusade continued into the winter of 1985, and both countries took a heavy toll of the other's forces.

The Pakistani reaction to the unending war between Iran and Iraq is one of dismay and frustration. As a long-time friend of Iran, Pakistan endeavored to mediate the conflict and President Zia consistently pressed the goal of Muslim unity, but to no avail. The Pakistanis have also failed to pressure the Soviets to leave Afghanistan, and with increased assistance to the mujahiddin from the United States, the war has now, in 1986, intensified. More than 12,000 Soviet troops are in Paktia province along the Pakistan frontier, and Soviet helicopter gunships hunt Afghan mujahiddin on both sides of the frontier. Islamabad has ample cause for concern. For example, the Pakistani border town of Teri Mangal, near Parachinar and deep in tribal territory, has suffered a series of attacks from both Soviet ground and air forces. Despite such cross-border raids, Pakistan practices restraint lest the country become more embroiled with the Soviet Red Army.

Moscow knows the history of the Afghan tribal people. It understands they have never been defeated in protracted conflict in spite of their having lost numerous military campaigns. The Kremlin's strategy, therefore, has been to avoid an all-out drive, but to sustain sufficient pressure in order to maintain the flow of refugees to Pakistan and Iran. Given an estimated 400,000 to 900,000 dead, and the flight from the country of more than four million, Afghanistan is being rapidly depopulated. Soviet comments attributed to statements of Hafizullah Amin that he could rebuild Afghanistan "with one million Afghans," may also describe Moscow's perception of its own policy. The Soviets look scornfully on tribalism and claim "holy mission" as their cause. It is they who are "charged" with bringing civilization to a primitive region, to instill it with new purpose, and to guide its future development. "Mongoliaization" is a term heard in Moscow to describe the current Soviet role in Afghanistan. It can be concluded therefore, that the Soviets anticipate eventual success through a multi-faceted policy that also involves the depopulation of the Central Asian state.

Evidence that the Soviets may have designs on Afghanistan (and Pakistan as well) beyond the destruction of the mujahiddin is found in the formation of the Ministry of Tribes and Nationalities, which has been made an extension of the Khad, the Afghan equivalent of the KGB.[9] The purpose of the ministry is several-fold: (1) to destroy the religious and ethnic character of the different tribes; (2) to alienate the tribes from one another so as to make them more dependent on central government authority; (3) to educate the younger generation to accept a new order of life; and (4) to inculcate Marxist-Leninist values.

If evidence is needed that the Soviets covet Afghan territory it need only be noted that following the Stationing of Forces of Agreement between Moscow and Kabul in 1980, the Soviets and Afghan authorities entered into and signed a treaty (1981) in which the Wakhan Corridor was ceded to the Soviet Union. The Soviets claimed the region was never under Kabul's control. Moscow officials say the local "warlord" fled in advance of Soviet troops and was now residing in Turkey. There was therefore no reason to maintain the fiction that Wakhan had even been an integral part of Afghanistan. Furthermore, Afghanistan was no longer a buffer state and the incorporation of the Wakhan Corridor into the Soviet Union confirmed this fact. In geopolitical terms it is clear by annexing the Wakhan, the Soviets have effectively closed China's border with Afghanistan. No less significant, the Soviet Union now borders directly on Pakistan, is within range of the Karakorum Highway, and in general proximity to the Indus Valley and Kashmir.

The near-presence of the Soviet Union on its western frontier has made it imperative that Pakistan seek a rapproachment with India. The assassination of Indira Gandhi in 1984 brought her son Rajiv to the helm of the Indian state. President Zia's gestures of and meetings with Rajiv have been aimed at reducing tensions between their two countries. It is also in India's interest to understand the Afghan buffer is gone and that Pakistan has assumed that unenviable position. Pakistan does not cherish this role but it does offer some guarantee for its long-term survival. it is necessary for India to recognize, however, that Pakistan can play its role effectively only with India's cooperation. The realities of geopolitics on the rim of Asia in these waning years of the twentieth century require new attention to the "Great Game" that has spread to South and Southwest Asia. But generating cooperation between India, Pakistan and Iran will be a monumental task. Moreover, buffer states are more the instruments of, rather than the bases for, another state's foreign policy.

NOTES

1. Athur Stein, *India and the Soviet Union: The Nehru Era* (Chicago: Chicago University Press, 1969), p. 2.

2. W.K. Fraser-Tytler, *Afghanistan: A Study of Political Developments* (London: Oxford University Press, 1953); and Owen Lattimore, *Pivot of Asia* (Boston: Little, Brown, 1950).

3. Kermit Roosevelt, *Countercoup: The Struggle for Control of Iran* (New York: McGraw-Hill Book Company, 1980)

4. Barry Rubin, *Paved With Good Intentions: Iran and the American Experience* (New York: Oxford University Press), 1980.

5. Lawrence Ziring, "Pakistan: The Yayha Khan Interregnum," *Asian Affairs,*I (July-August, 1974): 402-420.

6. U.S. Department of State, "Soviet Dilemmas in Afghanistan," *Special Report* No. 72, June 1980, p. 3.

7. Godfrey Jansen, "The Gulf War: The Contest Continues," *Third World Quarterly,* 6 (October 1984): 950-952.

8. *Ibid.,* p. 952.

9. Material for this section has been drawn from the research of Azmat Hyat Khan, Research Associate, Area Study Centre, Central Asia, University of Peshawar, Pakistan, 1983-1984.

CHAPTER 9

THE HISTORY OF AFGHANISTAN AS A BUFFER STATE

DAVID B. JENKINS

Of all the people of Central Asia, only the Afghans maintained the vestiges of independence throughout the era of European colonial expansion. Lord Curzon, the British Viceroy of India from 1889 through 1905, once remarked that Afghanistan owes its nationhood solely to its geographic position, for the Afghans, occupying the area of the Hindu Kush - the 600 mile long natural barrier between Central Asia and India - found themselves almost midway between the expanding powers of Britain to the south and Russia to the north. Afghanistan became the classic buffer state, created through diplomacy by the two powers in order to prevent their empires from adjoining physically, and thus theoretically keeping the peace in the region.

EARLY HISTORY

Its distinction as a political buffer state came late in Afghanistan's history. For despite its formidable mountain barriers, the land known today as Afghanistan has historically been a crossroads rather than a buffer. Prior to the fifteenth century, when sea travel supplanted them, the old caravan routes that passed through Afghanistan's strategic valleys were the pathways of the world's ideas, goods and conquerers. Many outsiders,[1] including Cyrus, Alexander, Genghis Khan, Napoleon, Hitler and Brezhnev shaped the destiny of the country. Conversely, as Professor Toynbee points out, a serious student of world history must "always give Afghanistan a central place in his picture."[2]

Afghan history begins sometime during the second half of the second millenium B.C., when a tribe of Aryans passed through Afghanistan from their homeland Eranvej, between the Syr Darya (Jaxartes) and Amu Darya (Oxus) Rivers. Some remained in Afghanistan, while others went on to India to supplant the pre-Aryan Indus Valley civilizations. The Aryans were most probably the first of many peoples who passed through and settled in Afghanistan.

Other nomadic peoples followed, attracted by the rich lands of India. Around the seventh century B.C., Iranian-speaking Bactrians passed through Afghanistan to settle in the Punjab; some remained in the Helmand River Valley and probably became the ancestors of the modern Pushtuns. In the second century B.C., the Sakas came from Iran through southwestern Afghanistan to invade India. The Sakas were followed by the Tukharians, the Ephthalites (White Huns), the Western Turks, the Mongols[3], the Transoxian Turks, the Timurid Turks, and the Uzbeks. There are several theories for these mass migrations. Some maintain that periodic overpopulation forced these wanderers to seek new grazing lands. Semple said that the dry and stimulating air of the steppes induced these peoples to migrate; Holdich claims they did so out of necessity - because it was their very nature to move on.[4] Only in a few cases did the invaders try to subdue the Afghans permanently. More often, the wandering tribes settled and became assimilated into the population.

The civilized empires of the ancient world also expanded through Afghanistan via conquest and annexation. Afghanistan held a key northeastern position in the empires of Cyrus and Alexander. The Sassanid Empire of Iran controlled the land during the third to seventh centuries, and through its own defeat to Arab conquest, allowed Islam to enter Afghanistan. Prior to the eighteenth century, Afghanistan served as the central core of other empires: the Kushan, the Ghaznevid and the Ghori.

Some claim that the area around the Hindu Kush served as a buffer in the days of Alexander. This is not entirely true. The Persians before him found no problem in extending their empire beyond the Syr Darya in the north and to the banks of the Indus in the east. They found the mountain barriers to be only a limited problem, as the passes could be crossed easily enough by a well-supplied force with knowledge of the area's terrain. Alexander was able to push beyond the Hindu Kush to the Syr Darya, and beyond the Indus into the Punjab. He did not get as far into India as he would have wished, but this was not due to a physical or political buffer.

Prior to the introduction of eighteenth century European imperialism, however, there was at least one occasion when the area around the Hindu Kush did serve as a buffer. Between 1558 and 1716, most of what is now Afghanistan was situated as a three-way pivot between the Moguls of India, the Safavids of Persia, and the Uzbeks of Turkestan in which there "was a three-cornered contest in which the Uzbegs (Uzbeks) fought with the Moguls for the possession of Budakhstan (Badakhshan) and with the Persians for Herat, while the Persians and Moguls disputed the ownership of Qandahar."[5] Both the Mogul ruler Akbar and the Safavid ruler realized that Qandahar guarded the only approach to India that outflanked the Hindu Kush. The Hindu Kush was more of a barrier than a buffer, but more often than not corresponded to the area where the frontiers of the three powers met. Basically, it kept the empires separated for 150 years and stayed the Uzbeks from raiding both on a large scale.

By 1721, the two opposing empires had weakened each other enough so that a chief of the Ghilzai tribe, Mahmud, was able to push the Safavids back as far as Isfahan. Mahmud formed the first Afghan empire, which ruled very little of today's Afghanistan. Instead, an Afghan minority ruled a Persian majority from a Persian capital. In the confusion that resulted from the murder of Mahmud in 1725, another Ghilzai - Nadir Shah - proceeded to carve out a sizeable chunk of territory from the Safavid and Mogul empires, conquering as far as Delhi. Nadir Shah also brought under his control the Trans-Oxian lands, and their city-states of Samarkand, Khiva and Bukhara.

As Nadir Shah grew older, he grew paranoid, finally ordering his Afghan officers to kill supposedly disloyal Persian officers within his service. The plot turned against him, and he himself was murdered. Following the murder, Ahmad Shah, leader of Nadir Shah's Afghan troops, fought his way out of the Persian dominated camp and within a year had inherited the Afghan core of Nadir Shah's empire. In this manner, in 1747, Ahmad Shah of the Durrani tribe of the Pushtuns, became the father of modern Afghanistan.

FORESHADOWING OF THE GREAT GAME: 1747-1808

With colonial maneuvering by distant nations, the strategic importance of Afghanistan gradually was realized. Afghanistan had yet to become a true buffer state, but from the late eighteenth century, it served as the center of a large territory separating British India from potential enemies.

The British, initially in India for trading purposes, had become increasingly involved in the political affairs of India following the downfall of the Mogul dynasty in 1707. As they expanded territorially, the British chased the Dutch out of the subcontinent entirely and relegated the French and the Portuguese to small coastal holdings. By the late 1700s, India was the "jewel in the crown of the British empire." Also by this time, certain British statesmen began to realize that India was possibly vulnerable to landward attack. Therefore, during the next century, the British expanded toward the northwest, in search of a defensible frontier. Some claimed this should be the Indus River, while others said the Hindu Kush was better suited. The British also expanded to quell the brigandage of interior tribes, and later, to offset the recognizable increase of Russian influence in the area.

Originally, though, the British considered France as the potential antagonist. In the late 1790s, a sufficient French threat existed that warranted British plans for the defense of India. Most statesmen looked to the sea, but a few visionaries foresaw invasion by land. The Secretary of War for British India, Dundas, with the help of his assistant, Eton, suggested in 1798 a series of buffers, including Afghanistan, Baluchistan, and Sind. Dundas neglected, however, to consider that the three amirs in question had no interest in the French whatsoever. Dundas' ideas foreshadowed later British attitudes toward Afghanistan and neighboring states, for "they tried to negotiate a coalition between three states, mutually hostile and hostile to the British, and all uninterested in the supposed enemy."[6]

As early as 1791, a new aggressor was considered - Russia. Supposing a diplomatic rupture between Russia and England in the offing, the Prince de Nassau presented an invasionary scheme to Empress Catherine II. This called for Russian troops to "march down the plain of the Volga, and cross the Caspian Sea, or move through Bokhara (Bukhara) and Balk (Balkh) to the Indus."[7] Russian military men considered this plan entirely feasible.

Following the 1807 Treaty of Tilsit between France and Russia, and the Treaty of Finkenstein, of the same year, between France and Persia, the British were prompted to make, for the first time, an alliance with the Afghans. This "Treaty of Friendship between the British Government and the King of Cabool (Kabul)," of June 17, 1809, called for the Afghans to war upon the Franco-Persians if they attempted to cross through Afghanistan into British India. It also assured Afghanistan British protection in case of Franco-Persian attack, and provided for eternal friendship and union between the two countries. The Franco-Russian treaty was short-lived, and events soon directed French attention away from Central and South Asia. British and Russian intrigue over the area, however, was just beginning.

THE GREAT GAME

Britain and Russia made Afghanistan a buffer state; the Afghans had little say in the matter. The political, economic, and military maneuverings that occurred at this time because known as "The Great Game" to armchair diplomats.

The Afghan ruling house had collapsed in 1818, and out of the resulting political chaos emerged a trisected state. Dost Mohammed became the most powerful of the three rulers, controlling Kabul and its hinterland. His brother and ally controlled Qandahar, while another ruler sat in Herat. Because of internal dynastic quarrels, it was not until 1836 that Britain again considered major diplomatic relations with the Afghans. In that year, Lord Auckland, the Governor-General of India, sent Captain Alexander Burnes on a mission to Kabul, to "work out (a) policy of opening the river Indus to commerce, and establishing upon its banks, and in the countries beyond it, such relations as should contribute to the desired end."[8] The British, however, wishing to maintain the regional balance of power, were not willing to give all that the Afghans desired.

Events leading up to the first Afghan War soon followed. The Persians and Russians mounted a siege of Herat in 1837. In October of 1838, Russia suggested and supported an alliance between Persia and the Afghan rulers of Kabul and Qandahar. The Russian agent Viktovich went into Kabul to make preliminary arrangements. Dost Mohammed readily accepted Viktovich, for he had fallen out with the British earlier that year. The British could not tolerate any Russian in Kabul, and in retaliation for this political effrontery, seized Karak on the Persian Gulf from Persia. They then moved into Herat in 1839 to prevent the city from falling into Persian hands. Finally, the British decided that Afghanistan would prove a submissive buffer between India and Russia if the old exiled monarch, Shah Shuja, were placed on the throne.

A cause for war was found in Dost Mohammed's "unprovoked aggression against the Sikhs, the 'ancient ally' of the British, and (the British) accused the Amir of unreasonable pretensions, open

Fig. 9.1 Expansion Of Britain and Russia Toward Afghanistan

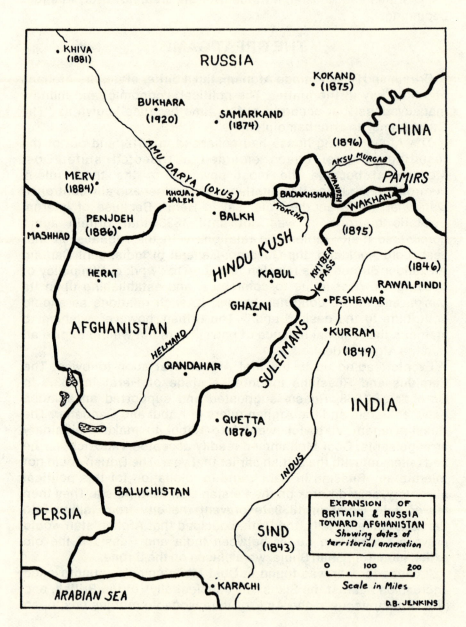

EXPANSION OF
BRITAIN & RUSSIA
TOWARD AFGHANISTAN
*Showing dates of
territorial annexation*

0   100   200

Scale in Miles

D.B. JENKINS

schemes of aggrandizement, and ambitious injurious to the security and peace of the frontiers of India."[9] The British invaded and the First Anglo-Afghan War was on. The essential results of the war were the galvanization of the Afghans into a unified force, the destruction of a British force of 4,500 men, and the death of Shah Shuja.

After the British retreat from Afghanistan, Anglo-Afghan relations cooled until 1855, when Persian threats toward Afghanistan and other areas of British interest forced the British and the Afghans to sign the Treaty of Peshawar, which simply propounded "mutual peace and friendship; respect for each other's territorial integrity; and the friends and enemies of one to be the friends and enemies of the other."[10] This treaty renewed relations and established Kabul as a buffer for India. At this time, both Britain and Russia recognized Persia and Afghanistan as independent states.

The 1860s marked the start of the steady advance southward by the Russians. While other European powers had been colonizing the Americas, Africa and the rest of the world, Russia had been spreading across northern Asia. Its direction of colonization turned southward, as well, in the 1730s. Following the Crimean War, Russia's advance in Central Asia was roughly equivalent in scope and speed to Britain's in India during the first part of the century (see Fig. 9.1). By 1863, the Kirghiz and Kazakh steppes had been subdued. The principalities of Tashkent and Samarkand fell by 1874, Kokand in 1875, and Khiva in 1881.

Russian expansion into Central Asia was based on: need to curb Kazakh raids on Russian caravans and border villages; desire for the agriculturally rich lands of the steppes;[11] greed for the fabled wealth that lay beyond the steppe in Turkestan, India and Persia; the continuing quest for an open, warm water port; and concern about the increasing political and commercial penetration by the British into Central Asia. This latter concern was, of course, mutual; finally, the path of least resistance for Russian expansion was to the south and east, rather than to the west.

By 1869, both the British and the Russians desired a "neutral" Afghanistan under their own influence. The basic concept of Afghanistan as a buffer state had existed as early as 1844, when Russian chancellor Count Neselrode suggested that the two governments should "leave the Khanates of Central Asia as a neutral zone interposed between the two empires, so as to prevent them from dangerous contact."[12] However, this idea was not considered officially until 1869, when Lord Clarendon said, "An aspiring Russian General had only to league with a mal-content prince of India to set the frontiers smouldering. The two should be kept apart by some barrier zone."[13]

That same year, the Russian statesman, Prince Gorchakov, gave positive assurances that Afghanistan was beyond the Russian sphere of influence. He also formally suggested that Afghanistan be considered a possible "neutral zone" between the two empires.[14] Certain British Conservatives in the Indian government, however, believed that Afghanistan should be made a British supervised barrier rather than a true neutral zone. They claimed that the frontiers of Afghanistan were too poorly defined to make an adequate neutral zone, and that the Oxus formed a much more natural boundary between Russia and India.

A neutral zone was established by the Anglo-Russian (Granville-Gorchakov) Agreement of 1873. The agreement, however, defined Afghanistan in terms of "the amir's holdings," leading to confusion over which amir was in question. The British maintained it was Dost Mohammed, whose area of control was much more expansive than the territory of the sitting amir, Sher Ali, which was accepted by the Russians. A compromise was made, but the boundaries were left ill-defined. For this reason, Badakhshan and Wakhan, which had never been under Sher Ali's control, became a part of Afghanistan. The Russians cried "territorial annexation," but conceded this issue to the British.

When the Conservatives came to power in 1874, however, the British "forward policy" - territorial expansion toward a defensible border - was re-established. In 1876, Disraeli appointed Lord Lytton as Viceroy of India, with clear instructions to "secure points necessary for the safety of India, and to do this with the least possible danger, disturbance or expense."[15] In Lytton's opinion, both Afghanistan's existing frontiers were unnatural - the Oxus made a poor boundary, and the boundary with India was archaic, having been inherited from the Sikhs. Therefore, Lytton sought a "scientific frontier" - "a Frontier which unites natural and strategic strength, and by placing both the entrance and exits of the passes in the hands of the defending Power, compels the enemy to conquer the approach before he can use the passage."[16] Only one such scientific frontier was apparent: the Hindu Kush, historically, the great natural barrier between India and Central Asia. Lytton found himself with three courses of action: (1) Establish British influence within Afghanistan to the exclusion of the Russians; (2) Reach a mutually satisfactory agreement with Russia; and (3) Try to stop the Russian advance in Central Asia by setting up a line, which when crossed by the Russians could be taken as a *casus belli*. Lytton reasoned that since his third choice was impractical, and his second would take too long, his only option was the first.

Sher Ali noted the change in British policy, and turned to the Russians for help against the supposed British aggressor. In November of 1878, bonds of friendship were drawn up between the visiting Russian mission, headed by General Stoletoff, and the amir of Afghanistan, who at this time told his people to "go home and sharpen your knives and lances, and saddle your horses, so that you may be ready to fight the enemies of our country (Britain)."[17] The Russian mission withdrew in December but soon the Russophobes in Parliament had further cause for anxiety in the actions of the Russian General Kauffman, whose army, sent to quell unrest in Russian Central Asia, was camped a short distance from the Afghan border. Finally, a cause for war was established when Lytton sent General Neville Chamberlain (with a large armed party) to the Khyber Pass to meet with Sher Ali. Chamberlain was attacked, as both he and Lytton suspected would occur. The Second Anglo-Afghan War followed.

The British fared better in this war than in the first, and, in the resulting Treaty of Gandamuk (May 26, 1879), the amir was forced to cede several strategic mountain passes in the Suleiman Range, lying between Afghanistan and northwest India. The treaty also provided for British construction of a telegraph line from Kurram to Kabul, and the improvement of roads to India by the Afghan government. Most important, the amir agreed to conduct no foreign relations without first seeking Britain's approval. Such measures were designed to focus Afghan attention upon the British and away from Russia. Lord Lytton said, "we shall never again altogether withdraw from Afghanistan,"[18] and Disraeli, although forced to substitute the Suleiman Range for the "scientific frontier" of the Hindu Kush, was satisfied that his forward policy had made India safe from invasion.

With a new amir, Abdur Rahman Khan, taking the throne in 1880, the "buffer state became a buffer in more than name; it began to represent something stable, which owed its strength primarily to the Amir's determination to keep all foreigners at arm's length, and secondly to the remote but solid support of Britain. It was a boundary lightly to be infringed."[19] However, buffers may be outflanked, as the Russians soon attempted to demonstrate.

In 1884, the Russians moved on Merve (now Mary in the Turkmen SSR), claiming it beyond the bounds of Afghanistan. The British said that any Russian advance on Herat would mean war. The

Russians continued their advance, but stopped at Penjdeh. The crisis dissipated through careful arbitration in mid-1885, following the return to power by the Liberals. The resulting agreement finally called for the demarcation of Afghanistan's boundaries.

DELINEATION OF THE BUFFER'S BORDERS

An effective buffer state should be delineated accurately so no question exists as to its bounds. As other colonialist powers were doing elsewhere in the world, Britain and Russia plotted the country's border lines, often with little regard to tribal frontiers. The boundaries established in the late nineteenth century remain the same today, and, since World War Two, have served as the root of many of Afghanistan's problems.

Perhaps the most important area which figured into the initial boundary formulation was northwestern Afghanistan near where the borders of Iran, Afghanistan and Soviet Central Asia meet. The regional center of this area, Herat, has long been considered the "Key to India," for the city controls the valleys which lead to the subcontinent. This valley corridor from Herat to the Indus is protected to the east by mountains, and to the west by empty desert. Tamerlane, among others, used Herat as the base for his march on India in the fourteenth century.

The British recognized the strategic importance of Herat:[20]

> A body of European troops, established at Herat, and standing with its front to the southeast, would draw upon it the attention of the whole population of India. In that lies the significance of a military occupation of Herat; and it is not without reason that a number of English experts, knowing India well, have expressed their belief that were an enemy to occupy Herat with a powerful force, the English army, without firing a shot, would consider itself half beaten.

The British insisted upon Herat's inclusion within the bounds of Afghanistan in order to stay the momentum of expansion that had led Russia to Penjdeh. The Russians initially proposed a "no-man's land" between Mashhad and Herat, but the British claimed: "The attempt to force a recognition of a 'no-man's land' between Meshed (Mashhad) and Herat is, in reality, nothing more than an effort to extend the Turcoman region wedge fashion between Persia and Afghanistan. Russia, in occupying Merv, will inevitably claim the right to extend her power along this wedge also."[21]

The northern boundary was redrawn to allow for the newly created Russian bulge. When the boundary reached the Amu Darya, there was less disagreement as to the actual line. Long recognized as the boundary between Russia and Afghanistan, the Amu Darya between the junction of the Kokcha River and the post of Khoja Saleh was designated the official boundary in a joint protocol in 1887.

The upper Amu Darya provided some difficulties in border delineation, however. Here, near the Pamirs, where many tributaries flow into the main river, Russian geographers claimed that the Pyandzh was the main stream, and thus, the border. The Afghans maintained that the Aksu Murgab - further to the north - was the parent trunk.[22] The Afghan claims did not hold up, however, and the British thought the issue not worth pursuing further.

This definition of the course of the Amu Darya created, in 1895, the narrow Wakhan Corridor. Sir Thomas Holdich, who helped demarcate the boundary, says that such a strip of land was established solely to keep apart two powers whose contact might prove disastrous:[23]

> It is not an imposing buffer - this long attenuated arm of Afghanistan reaching out to touch China with the tips of its fingers. It is only eight miles wide at one point, and could be ridden across in a mornings ride. It presents no vast physical obstacle to an advance of any sort; physical obstacles, however are not wanting, but difficult enough to answer all possible purposes. It is a political intervention - a hedge, as it were - over which Russia cannot step without violating Afghanistan, and the violation of Afghanistan may (or may not) be regarded as a "casus belli."

Holdich pointed out that the Wakhan as a buffer could only survive as long as the Amir of Afghanistan, to whom it was literally given, "fulfills his undertaking to maintain order (there)."[24] Today, the Wakhan has been annexed by the Soviet Union.

Afghans claim that the Afghan-Indian border has historically been the Indus River. This was true from the founding of the Durrani Empire by Ahmad Shah Durrani until 1818. At this time, the Sikhs conquered Peshawar, and pushed Afghanistan back to near its present southern border. When the Sikhs fell to the British in 1849, the British inherited these trans-Indus territories. At this stage, some British statemen felt it wise to return these lands to Afghanistan. "My proposal in 1849," said Sir G. Campbell, "was to give these extra-Indian districts back to the Afghans, the original and rightful owners, establishing our scientific military frontier upon the Upper Indus."[25] But Parliament opted for a boundary along the Suleiman Mountains.

In 1893, Sir Mortimer Durand projected the boundary through these mountains, and gave the border its nickname - the Durand Line. Abdur Rahman Khan was dissatisifed with the line, even though it gave him some additional territory. But:[26]

> He was desirous that the frontier tribes, having same blood, religion and language should be left to him. He offered to make them loyal subjects to himself and friendly to the British. He also pointed out that if they were severed from the parent-stock, the British Government, would never be in a position to assimilate them into British India. The tribes would never accept the threat to their independence and therefore this attempt of anxieties and difficulties to the British Indian Government.

The British, on the other hand, declared that:[27]

> The relation of the Afghan boundary to that actual hill barrier of the frontier is important . . . it is, on the whole, a conventional line laid down with careful recognition of ethnical requirements, separating Baluch from Afghan, and Afghan from the frontier tribes who, however much affiliated to the Afghan, have never been under Afghan (or any other) domination.

The new boundary severed one third of the Pushtun tribe - Afghanistan's dominant ethnic group - from their Afghan homeland. Border struggles continued beyond 1947, to become the central problem dominating Afghan-Pakistani relations.

RECENT HISTORY

Afghanistan remained a buffer until a few years after World War Two. Then, events occurred that started the country on the road to Soviet domination, culminating in the 1979 invasion.

Habibullah Khan succeeded his father Abdur Rahman upon the latter's death in 1901. British and Russian rivalry increased during the first few years of the century, but the isolationist tendencies of Afghanistan averted any frontal clashes. In addition, Russia was soon humiliated by the outcome of the Russo-Japanese War of

1904-05, and Russia and Britain soon found themselves on the same side of the political fence in opposing the growing German influence in Europe. The 1907 Anglo-Russian Convention of St. Petersburg thus settled four points: (1) Persia was divided into zones of Russian and British influence; (2) Both countries recognized Chinese control of Tibet and pledged noninterference there; (3) Russia agreed that Afghanistan was outside its sphere of influence; and (4) Britain agreed not to interfere in the internal affairs of Afghanistan.

By the start of World War One, other European powers - notably Germany - began taking interest in Afghanistan. Pan-Islamic agents sponsored by the Turkish government and secretly supported by the Germans infiltrated Afghanistan, as well as India, Persia, and Arabia, in order to incite the Muslim populations to rise up against Britain and Russia.

Indeed, many Afghans saw World War One as a chance to join forces with Turkey and liberate all Muslim lands from the Europeans. But despite the pro-Central Power feelings among the people, Habibullah Khan never entered the war. He feared something that no Afghan amir of the past century ever had cause to fear - a joint Anglo-Russian attack on Afghanistan. By 1916, Britain's advances in southern Persia, Russian victories in the Caucasus, and perceived secularism in modern Turkey, dampened any Afghan desire to join the war.

Following the Russian Revolution, Anglo-Russian relations again deteriorated. Afghan nationalism was now on the rise, and the Third Anglo-Afghan War was the result. The Afghans call this their War of Independence, for they fought for the right to make their own foreign policy and other decisions. With artillery provided by the Bolsheviks, the Afghans attacked first this time, in May of 1919. The British blamed the Soviets for inciting the rebellion; they said that behind it was a Soviet-Afghan push for India.[28]

Within three months, the war was over. Neither side actually won, although both acquired territory at the expense of the other. The treaty, signed in August, called for peace, prohibited the import of arms into Afghanistan through India, and reset the boundary as it was before the war. Lastly, it called for talks in six months, which finally granted Afghanistan its own foreign policy making power. The buffer state was at last fully neutral.

Despite Afghan delegations to the Soviet sponsored Pan-Oriental Congress at Baku in 1919, Afghan-Soviet relations became strained. Afghanistan secretly supported anti-Soviet Muslim revolt in Soviet Central Asia. But following the Red Army's major 1922 victory in Bukhara, the amir adopted a more pragmatic position, reviving a 1921 treaty that established diplomatic relations and promised Soviet technical and material aid to Afghanistan.[29]

In 1924, tribesmen of the Soviet Central Asian republics began circulating Communist propaganda to their kin across the Afghan border - especially to the Turkomans of Herat. In 1925, a near-war resulted from the Russian takeover of the island of Urta Tagai in the Amu Darya. But, despite these incidents, the amir remained pro-Soviet. Therefore, when the Afghans revolted against the westernizing reforms of Amanullah, the Soviets accused the British of inciting the rebellion, in order to place a pro-British amir on the throne and re-orient the buffer state once more toward Britain.[30]

A political moderate, Nadir Shah, assumed the throne in 1929. Upon his assassination in 1933, his son - Zahir Shah - succeeded. Nadir Shah dismissed the Russian advisors hired by Amanullah, and still mistrusting the British, replaced them with Germans, Italians, Japanese, and some Indians. At the time of World War Two, the Afghans hoped for a joint German/Japanese attack on the Soviet Union, leading to the liberation of Khiva, Samarkand, Merv, and Bukhara, and thence a great Central Asian Empire under Afghan rule. But, when the Soviet Union joined the Allies in 1941, it also joined Britain in calling for all Axis non-diplomatic personnel to leave Afghanistan. In order to preserve its expressed neutrality, the Afghan assembly responded by ordering non-diplomatic nationals of all belligerents out of the country.

In 1947, Britain pulled out of the subcontinent. To the south of the Durand Line, Pushtun-inhabited lands that many Afghans had assumed would revert to Afghan control, instead became part of the new nation of Pakistan. Afghanistan rationalized that if these Pushtuns could not be a part of Afghanistan, they should be organized into a separate and independent Pushtunistan. They insisted that a free Pushtun election be held under United Nations guidance, in order to determine their own fate. This policy "flavors all Afghan foreign relations, and is directly responsible for Afghan acceptance of Soviet aid in 1950, date of the first Pakistani retaliatory "blockade" of goods in transit to Afghanistan."[31]

To counterbalance the Soviets, the United States made an attempt to take the place of Britain. But Afghanistan refused to join western treaty organizations; it could not ignore its 1250 mile common border with the U.S.S.R. When Pakistan received U.S. arms after joining SEATO and CENTO, Afghanistan turned further toward the Soviets.

Mohammed Daud, Prime Minister for Zahir Shah from 1953 to 1963, made Pushtunistan the major driving force of his foreign policy. Because of the inflammatory issue, the border with Pakistan was closed by both sides a number of times. The Afghans, with no other trade outlet, increasingly turned to the Soviets. The Soviet Union became the only country to side with Afghanistan on the Pushtunistan issue. Afghanistan became the model of a country which could receive aid from the U.S.S.R. without being dominated by the Soviets, or turning Communist.

In his latter years, however, Zahir Shah seemed to gravitate toward the United States. In response, U.S. aid rose to rival Soviet aid. This, coupled with a claim of growing government corruption, precipitated the Afghan coup of 1973, which established Daud as head of republican government. Citing Pakistan as the only country with which Afghanistan would have a political dispute, Daud continued his gamble of accepting Soviet aid. Within a year, however, the wary Daud realized he must attempt to decrease Afghanistan's dependence on the Soviet Union, in order to preserve the country's neutrality. In 1974, he began by imprisoning 260 Afghan Communists and making pacts with the U.S. and China.

But the Afghans disliked Daud; three counter-coups were attempted within his first year alone. He maintained power only through the military's support. By 1976, he realized that the loyalty of the armed forces was itself in doubt, for the army had been sending its officers to the U.S.S.R. for training, and was now honeycombed with Soviet agents. Daud's gamble had failed; within a few years, the Communists, and eventually the Soviets themselves, would take over the government. Because of his relations with Pakistan, western preventive assistance at this late stage was out of the question.

On April 17, 1978, the communists staged a successful coup under the leadership of Nur Mohammed Taraki. On December 23, 1979 *Pravda* announced that "Western, and particularly American mass media have recently been disseminating deliberately inspired rumors about some sort of Soviet 'Interference' in Afghanistan's internal affairs. Things have even gotten as far as allegations that Soviet 'combat units' have been introduced in Afghan territory."[32] The next day saw Soviet divisions airlifted into Kabul. Other Soviet troops followed, some utilizing the natural transportation corridor through Herat. Amin was executed, and Babrak Karmal was returned from exile and installed as puppet president. The Soviets justified the invasion by citing the Soviet-Afghan Treaty of 1978, and by alleging imperialist agitation (the populist uprisings). They have remained in Afghanistan ever since, bogged down in a costly conflict with the same tribes that have fought all invaders since Cyrus. Many Soviet lives and even more Afghan lives have been lost, and today, more than one third of the preinvasion population are refugees (See Lawrence Ziring in the preceding chapter for a more detailed analysis of Afghanistan's recent history).

When the British pulled out of India, Afghanistan maintained some of its buffer functions, for Pakistan and Iran remained pro-West. Up until the 1978 Taraki coup, the leaders of Afghanistan had tried to maintain a careful balance of right and left, and thus keep the basic neutrality necessary for a buffer state. But, with the Soviet invasion, any such neutrality ceased to exist.

EFFECTIVENESS OF AFGHANISTAN AS A BUFFER STATE

Afghanistan's establishment as a buffer state was assisted by its physical geography. Such barriers as the Hindu Kush do not necessarily dictate buffers, however, nor are all buffers barriers. The Pyrenees, Andes, and Caucasus have all served as relatively efficient barriers, yet no buffer state in recent history arose in their midst. On the other hand, such classic buffer states as Belgium and Poland are in no way barriers to the passing of powers from either side, as historical invasions of France and Russia by Germany have demonstrated. A buffer state is a political rather than a physical creation, arising out of political necessity.

It was only through the efforts of British and Russian diplomacy that Afghanistan became a buffer state. Without these two relatively equivalent powers on either side, Afghanistan would be very different today, perhaps nonexistent. If the Russians had not subdued Central Asia, but rather had directed their efforts of conquest in the Caucasus and Balkans, Afghanistan possibly would have been annexed by Great Britain as an outlying province of India. Based on this scenario, any buffer state created between Britain and Russia would have been placed further north; perhaps an independent Kokand or Khiva would be the result. Similarly, if Britain hadn't moved into northwest India in the 1840s, Afghanistan perhaps would have been conquered by the Russians in the 1880s as the last in the string of their Central Asian victories. Finally, if neither European power had expanded beyond its territorial limits of around 1825, either a large, independent Afghan Empire, or several small Khanates possibly would have resulted.

Historical events such as the fall of the Moguls and the Crimean War, however, made it almost inevitable that British and Russian expansionism would meet around the Hindu Kush. It was the mutual distrust that one held for the other that demanded the creation of a buffer state. Even when Britain and Russia were on friendly terms, as they were from 1907 until 1917, the buffer state endured, rather than face division into zones of influence, as Persia was.[33] After 1947 Afghanistan remained as a sort of buffer between the Soviet Union and pro-western Pakistan and Iran, yet following the British withdrawal from India, there was no power to the south of Afghanistan to balance the strength of the colossus to the north. An allusion could be made to two vacuum cleaners applying equal suction upon a ping pong ball. When one vacuum cleaner is removed, the ball is sucked into the other. Pakistan was a weak replacement for Britain, and the United States was too far away to ever fully counter Soviet influence. Political developments including the sporadic closings of the Afghan-Pakistan border, and Indian pro-Soviet policy under Mrs. Gandhi, naturally directed Afghanistan toward the Soviet Union.

Hannah points out that there are two conditions which must be met in order to establish a viable, landlocked, neutral buffer. The first is a mutual agreement of the bordering powers to sustain the buffer, and the second is willingness on the part of the buffer to accept its role by maintaining a balance of relations with its neighbors.[34] In the case of Afghanistan, these conditions were essentially met for almost one hundred years, despite disagreements over the extent and boundaries of the state, and despite Afghan leanings toward one side or another. Since 1947, however, both conditions have failed. If the word "buffer" is to be applied to Afghanistan today, it is only in the sense of a Soviet satellite selected to further distance the Muslim peoples of Soviet Central Asia from the Islamic fundamentalism to the south.

During the Great Game, however, Afghanistan was an effective buffer. For, despite mistrust and misunderstandings, Britain and Russia never fought each other in Central Asia. The buffer state had served its desired purpose.

NOTES

1. Abdul Qadir Khan, "Afghanistan in 1934." *Journal of the Royal Central Asian Society*, 22 (April 1935).

2. Arnold Toynbee, "Afghanistan as a Meeting Place in History," *Afghanistan,* 25 (April-June 1960): 59.

3. Afghanistan suffered particularly under the Mongols of the thirteenth century. In retribution for executing its Mongol governor, Genghis Khan ordered the complete destruction of Herat. Reportedly, only 40 of the city's 600,000 inhabitants survived the Mongols' wrath. Other Afghan cities suffered similar fates. Travelling close to a century later, Ibn Battuta found formerly thriving cities such as Ghazni and Balkh still in ruins. Many Afghan cities even today have not recovered their pre-Mongol populations. See John A. Hermann and Cecil Robert Borg, *Retracing Genghis Khan: A Record of a Journey Through Afghanistan and Persia* (Boston: Lothrop, Lee and Shepherd Co., 1937).

4. K. D. Codrington, "Geographical Introduction to the History of Central Asia." *The Geographical Journal,* 104 (September, 1944): 90.

5. W. K. Fraser-Tytleer, *Afghanistan: A Study of Political Developments in Central and Southern Asia* (London: Oxford University Press, 1960), p. 38.

6. Edward Ingram, "A Preview of the Great Game in Asia-II: The Proposal of an Alliance with Afghanistan, 1798-1800," *Middle East Studies,* 9 (May 1973): 160.

7. Lt. Col.DeLacy Evans, *The Designs of Russia* (London: John Murrary, 1828), p. 15.

8. Lt. Col. Sir Alexander Burnes, *Cabool: Being a Personal Narrative of a Journey to, and Residence in that City in the Years 1836, 7 and 8* (London: John Murray, 1842), p. 1.

9. Vartan Gregorian, *The Emergence of Modern Afghanistan: Politics of Reform and Modernization, 1880-1946* (Stanford, California: Stanford University Press, 1969), p. 101.

10. Great Britain, *British and Foreign State Papers,* Vol. 63 (1872-1873), (London: William Ridgeway, 1979), p. 1296.

11. Among other things, the Russians sought new lands on which to grow cotton, for the American Civil War had produced a worldwide cotton shortage. Owen Lattimore, *Pivot of Asia* (Boston: Little, Brown and Co., 1950), p. 28.

12. A.P. Thornton, "The Re-Opening of the Central Asian Question, 1865-1869," *History,* 16 (October 1956): 122.

13. A.P. Thornton, "Afghanistan in Anglo-Russian Diplomacy, 1869-1873," *Cambridge Historical Journal,* 11 (1954): 211.

14. Great Britain, 1879, p. 658.

15. James G. Allen, "Strategic Principles of Lord Lytton's Afghan Policy," *Journal of The Royal Central Asian Society,* 24 (July 1937): 432.

16. George N. Curzon, *Frontiers* (London: Oxford University Press, 1907), p. 19.

17. Great Britain, *British and Foreign State Papers,* Vol. 69 (1877-1878), London: William Ridgeway, 1885), p. 340.

18. Gregorian, p. 115.

19. Fraser-Tytler, p. 173.

20. Charles T. Marvin, *The Russians at the Gates of Herat* (New York: Charles Scribner's Sons, 1885), p. 96.

21. Marvin, p. 51.

22. The Afghans sited toponymic evidence for the assertion, stating that the name "Oxus" was a Greek corruption of the Turkish "Aksu" - meaning "white water."

23. Sir Thomas H. Holdich, *The Indian Borderland: 1880-1900* (London: Methuen and Co., Ltd., 1901), pp. 284-285.

24. Curzon, p. 29.

25. Mohammed Ali, "The Durand Line," *Afghanistan,* 10 (October-December 1955):6.

26. Ali, p. 11.

27. Sir Thomas H. Holdich, *Political Frontiers and Boundary Making* (London: MacMillan and Co., 1916), pp. 276-277.

28. In fact, the Bolshevik Blue Book read, "Without the liberation of India, there can be no social catastrophe in the West." See Mustapha Chokaiev, "The Bolsheviks and Afghanistan,"*The Asiatic Review,* 25 (July 1929):497-516.

29. This aid included the twelve biplanes of Afghanistan's first air force.

30. Many Soviets, British anti-imperialists, and American newspapers were convinced that Col. T.E. Lawrence (of Arabia) - then translating Homer in an isolated camp along the border - helped incite the rebellion.

31. Louis Dupree, "The Durand Line of 1893: A Case Study in Artificial Political Boundaries and Culture Areas," *Current Problems in Afghanistan,* a Princeton University Conference, Princeton, N.J., 1961, p. 87. See also Dupree's definitive work on the country,*Afghanistan* (Princeton, N.J.: Princeton University Press, 1973).

32. Alvin Z. Rubinstein, "Soviet Imperialism in Afghanistan," *Current History,* 79 (1980):83.

33. Holdich, 1916, p. 117.

34. Norman B. Hannah, "Afghanistan: The Great Gamble," *Asian Affairs, an American Review,* 6 (January-February 1979): 188.

CHAPTER 10

KOREA, A BUFFER STATE

JOHN CHAY

"From a political point of view," William Elliot Griffis wrote of Korea at the turn of the century, "the geographical position of this country is most unfortunate. Placed between two rival nations, aliens in blood, temper, and policy, Chosen has been the grist between the upper and nether millstones of China and Japan."[1] Although Griffis, a specialist on Japan, lacked a profound understanding of Korea, breadth of his knowledge of the Far East enabled him to make this perceptive statement. His words, which accurately described the difficult position of Korea at the time of his writing, still summarize the Korean predicament. Although modern technology has transformed considerably the geographical factor in international relations, the locational factor, as the case of Korea in Asia well illustrates, still is important and may remain so for a long time in the future. The geographical position of Korea can best be defined with reference to the concept of a "buffer state," an idea that provides a most useful framework to help explain the situation in which Korea and a number of other nations find themselves.

In order to explore the position of Korea as a buffer state, this chapter will raise a number of questions. What are the definitions and the definitional characteristics of the buffer state? What are its functions? And, what would be its future? In the process of exploring these questions, an examination will be made of Korea's history as a buffer state.

The idea of a buffer state is relatively uncontroversial. Nicholas J. Spykman has defined buffer states as "small political units located between large states."[2] Pitman B. Potter spoke of them in similar words: "A weak state, small in size, probably without a positive foreign policy of its own, which lies between two or more

191

powerful states and thus serves to inhibit international aggression."[3] Most simply stated, then, a buffer state is a small state situated between or among two or more large powers. Beyond these dictionary definitions, a buffer state appears as a relatively complex entity, with at least nine significant characteristics: (1) location, topography, and other geographical factors, (2) strategic position, (3) size and strength, (4) historical factor, (5) neutrality, (6) balance of power, (7) independence, (8) foreign policy pattern, and (9) the functions. Korea as a buffer state will be examined in terms of these nine definitional characteristics.

Korea is a small power squeezed between two large powers - China and Japan, and thus is one of the best examples of a buffer state. Keen observers have long noted the nation's special geographical position. Shannon McCune, one of the most prominent geographers of Korea, wrote: "The buffer position of Korea in the Far East dominates the political geography of the peninsula."[4] Some even exaggerated her geographical position by describing her as a "dagger" pointed at the heart of Japan and as a "forward base" for the invasion of the island empire or as a "hammer" ready to strike at the head of China or as a "springboard" for the Japanese jump to the Asian mainland.[5] These colorful phrases underline the importance of Korea as a buffer state.

Undoubtedly the most important characteristic of the buffer state is its geographical location. A weak or small state which is located between two or more states iis in a perilous position. Border, terrain, and other geographical factors are also important, although not as much as the location factor.[6] Korea is located among three major Far Eastern powers: Japan is to the south and east, separated from Korea by the Sea of Japan and the 120-mile wide Korea Strait; China is to the north and northwest, with the Yalu and Tuman Rivers and Paektusan functioning as the border; and Russia is to the northeast, with the border running 11 miles along the Tuman River. Korea's location has been the most important determinant factor in the creation of the international system surrounding the peninsula. In the north the Yalu and Tuman Rivers and Paektusan, the highest mountain in Korea, form a natural border and, to a certain extent, have in the past created a physical barrier.

The waters surrounding the three sides of the peninsula have long been used more to improve contact and interaction than as a barrier between Korea and both Japan and China.[7] The peninsula is characterized mostly by rugged mountains, and they have always impeded would-be invaders, even in recent years; they were not, however, rugged enough to deter any potential aggressor.

Closely related to the location factor is that of strategic position. A weak or a small nation located on the periphery of the international system is in a much better position than ones in the central position of the system.[8] Unfortunately for Korea, she occupies one of the most strategic positions in the Far East.[9] It should be pointed out, nevertheless, that nations in these strategic positions are not without compensation. Politically and militarily centrally located nations also occupy the same position for cultural and commercial activities, and, as will be illustrated in the following pages, greatly benefit from their strategic position.

Size is a very important element in the concept of the buffer state. It is always characterized as small or weak. If it were large or strong, it would not be a buffer state; it would be equal with the two other large powers and there would be three large powers instead of two large powers and a buffer state, or a "middle kingdom" and two powers as China boasted for many centuries. The buffer state is definitely a subset or a part of a group of countries called "small powers." The measurement criteria can be a subject of debate; recent studies have been cautious in this matter, and Michael Handel and others have used not only population and territorial size but also other standards of measurement, including the GNP, the GNP per capita, the armed forces, defense expenditues, petroleum and other energy resources and their consumption, crude steel output, the size of the merchant marine as factors.[10] Korea (North and South), with a current total population of about 60 million and an area of 83,717 square miles, would not be a small nation. Were Korea located in Western Europe, it would, in terms of population, rival Italy and the United Kingdom. In area, a unified Korea would be about the same size as Austria and slightly smaller than West Germany and the United Kingdom. But, unfortunately squeezed between two large powers, her "border pressure," or, more appropriately, her buffer pressure is great. If China and Japan are combined, the area ratio is about 47 to 1 and the population ratio is 17 to 1. When Russia is included, the pressure is even greater.[11]

Along with the above three geographical factors, historical factors, or the psycho-cultural dimension, cannot be neglected in the study of border states. Every nation has a peculiar historical past in dealing with its neighbors; Korea is no exception. To the Japanese, the Koreans contributed more in the cultural domain than they received, and the Koreans, until the late nineteenth century, received little cultural pressure from Japan. The Koreans, however, had a long tradition of receiving much from Chinese culture, and this influence created a certain traditional weight or pressure in Korean minds. The tributary relationship which existed for a long time between these two nations was more cultural than anything else. Overawed by the glory of Chinese culture, the Koreans were content to live within the sphere of Chinese cultural influence.

Neutrality is another important factor for the buffer state. Trygve Mathisen pointed out in his study that a buffer state might be fully neutral or might be allied to and controlled by one of its large neighbors.[12] Annette Baker Fox created different categories for neutral states: a neutral ally and an unneutral neutrality.[13] Different shades of neutrality may be allowed and a neutral nation may deviate toward an alliance with one of its neighbors, but, to play its genuine role a buffer state may want to adhere strictly to its neutral position.[14] Although Korea has never been neutralized by the guarantees of large powers, the nation remained in a neutral or a semi-neutral position throughout most of its history.

In a real sense, a buffer state is more a system itself. What large neighboring states do or not do is much more important than what the buffer state itself does or does not do. Further, the existence of a balance of power seems to be very important for the successful existence of a buffer state. Not only a balance of power, but also a balance of interest and intention of the neighboring large powers should go with it. Only as long as a balance of power, interest, and intention exist between the large neighboring powers, will the buffer system survive; when it disappears, the buffer state will also disappear. Spykman put the matter in the following words: "In an area of contending forces, the continued existence of buffer, as well as the stability of a frontier, is an indication of a system of approximate balanced force."[15] In the Korean peninsula, the state of a balance of power remained most of the time when the two neighboring powers came together, and when it disappeared, the state itself disappeared.[16]

Another important characterisitic of the border state is its independence. It may be true that independence and sovereignty can be compromised, especially in the modern context when the line between independence and dependence is often blurred. However, if too much compromise is made and if the state becomes too dependent on one of the large powers, its role as a buffer state obviously disappears. While it is true that Korea maintained tributary relations with China for almost two thousand years beginning in the early second century B.C., it is also true that, except for a short period during the domination of the Mongols and the Manchus, the dependency relationship was more cultural and Korea remained independent until 1910, when Japan annexed her. Since neither of the two large neighbors would permit the other to take over the buffer state, both powers recognized the importance of Korean independence. Only aggressive leaders of the two powers used the "dagger" and the "hammer" as excuses for their territorial aggrandizement.

Measure of military might is another necessary characteristic of the buffer state. Without adequate military strength, a buffer state cannot maintain its independence, and its status as a buffer will sooner or later disappear. Throughout her whole history, Korea never had sufficient strength to stop invasions by her two neighbors, especially from the mid-Koryo period, about 1200 A.D. on, and this was the weakest point for the buffer system in Korea. Japanese leaders in the nineteenth and twentieth centuries took much pleasure in pointing out that Korea was too weak to maintain her independence and that a qualified neighbor would have to absorb her.

The preceding seven characteristics belong to the structural side of the buffer state; and the following two definitional characteristics are more functional. One concerns foreign policy behavior, while the other involves the roles played by the buffer state. Because a buffer state is one of the small states, the former shares many characteristics with the latter. Maurice A. East and Ronald P. Barston, who studied small states, point out that small states lacked both a wide range of means and machinery for their foreign policies and had consequently limited their involvement in international affairs. East pointed out further that, because of the limited resources for the conduct of foreign policies, the small powers could not have the luxury of playing at ambiguous and verbal diplomacy and resorted more to conflictual and non-verbal actions in international affairs.[17] Since no systematic study of the buffer state's foreign policy behavior has been made, generalizations of a hypothetical nature will be attempted. Like other small powers, the buffer state's resources for the conduct of foreign policy are limited, thus restricting the range and scope of policy options. On the other hand, the buffer state may have to be much more cautious than other small states in resorting to conflictual behavior, simply because its situation makes a much more dangerous game for the buffer state. The buffer state may also play a role cautiously counterbalancing one side's pressure with that of the other side or playing one off against the other. Like other small powers, the buffer state may be actively involved in regional and universal collective security systems and in small power organizations. Youngnok Koo has characterized Korean foreign policy behavior until recent years as passive.[18] This is an accurate description of Korean foreign policy for most of its history; the only qualification is that, up to mid-seventh century, the Koreans were often active in dealing with both the Chinese and the people in Manchuria. For the post-World War II period, especially in the past two decades, the North and South Korean governments have followed a characteristic behavior pattern of a small power in matters of foreign policy: active in the third world, regional, and universal international organizations; active expansion of the diplomatic bases but still limited in scope, range, and means of diplomacy; and cautious or almost timid in taking advantage of the international environment surrounding the peninsula.

Lastly, the buffer state had definite roles to play. There are two major roles for the buffer state: sometimes it serves as a barrier to prevent conflict between its two large neighbors and sometimes it acts as a highway or facilitator of war between these powers. There is much temptation to consider these roles as qualitatively different and to call one positive and the other negative. It can easily be discerned that these two seemingly contradictory roles really belong to the same dimension, and when the positive force becomes excessive it becomes negative. When the pressure coming from large neighbors is relatively small, it can be stopped or absorbed, often with considerable pain, by the buffer state. But when it is too great, it either may simply pass through the buffer state and explode in the other large power or it may be met within the buffer state by a certain amount of counter-pressure from the other large neighbor. Whether military action occurs within the buffer state or outside of it, when the major issue of contention concerns the buffer state, the fate of this unfortunate country will be decided at the end of the war. It should be pointed out that this pressure is not just confined to political and military spheres; cultural and commercial forces may also become excessive and disruptive, even destructive to the culture and society of the buffer state. With these points in mind, it now may be asked: What roles did Korea play as a buffer state over the past two thousand years of history?[19]

Looking back over the long history of Korea, we find that until the latter part of the nineteenth century her relations with external powers were confined to her two large neighbors, China and Japan, especially the former. Throughout the two millennia, Korea was much more than the mere object of other powers' action. She was very much an independent nation, and what she did or did not do was certainly important for the buffer system in the peninsula. But, she was a pigmy between two giants, and what happened in those two countries was equally, and probably even more, important to what occurred in Korea. When these two nations were busy with their own affairs and thus did not have the excessive energy needed to be involved beyond their borders, Korea was ignored to develop her life. However, when these neighbors became vigorous and filled with excessive energy they almost always became expansionistic and their overflowing energy found an outlet in the neighboring small kingdom. When the pressure was not excessive, Korea absorbed it successfully for her own development; when the pressure increased she would still have to absorb it, but with considerable pain; when the pressure became excessive, the buffer state of Korea became a military highway for a neighbor to invade the other. The most destructive and the worst case for her was the situation in which the great pressure of one large power was met violently by the other power in the peninsula, with the result that the buffer state became a battle ground. This kind of showdown was followed by elimination of the influence of one large power from the scene and by the disappearance of the buffer state of Korea. This pattern will be explained in the following pages. For the sake of convenience, the more than two thousand years will be divided into eight periods: 1. Ancient Korea, 2. the Three Kingdoms, 3. the Silla Dynasty, 4. the Koryo Dynasty, 5. the Yi Dynasty before 1860, 6. the Yi Dynasty from 1860 to 1910, 7. the vacuum between 1910 and 1945, and 8. the post-World War II period.

During the period of Ancient Korea, which ended in the first century B.C. after at least 800 years of existence, the Koreans went through, as also happened in the Ancient Middle East, Ancient Greece, and many other places, the process of the formulation of an early political system. Tribal states, or castle-town states in Ki-Paik Lee's terms, emerged all over the Korean peninsula, especially along the major rivers and the seacoast, and were gradually transformed into petty kingdoms. Then, a consolidation process began about 400 B.C. that involved alliances and conquests and, by the middle of the first century B.C., three kingdoms occupied the main part of the peninsula.[20] In China, which had gone through the process much earlier, the Chou Dynasty ruled for most of this period and the Han Dynasty had just appeared in the early second century B.C., just before the end of this period. In Japan, a similar process of transformation took place.

In these early years, because the largely feudal, decentralized society in China did not produce much energy, and because the Japanese were occupied with their own problems, Korea did not feel any political and military pressure, In the cultural domain, however a very significant transaction took place during this period. Through the emigration of Kija and Wiman and their followers to Korea from China and through a gradual diffusion process, metal technology - first bronze through the fourth century B.C. then iron technology - came to Korea from China. Fortunately for the Koreans, the coming of these technologies was gradual, and they did not confront a great degree of pressure, as happened in the Ancient Middle East. The Koreans were good cultural transmitters, and they exported what they had imported to the Japanese during this period, thus influencing the development of the Yayoi culture on the island.[21] Korea acted during this period as both a cultural absorber and cultural transmitter.

Seven hundred years of Korea's second period were lively with the formation of three kingdoms. The Koreans acquired organizational techniques from the Chinese during this period and, together with the vigor of the newly united Kingdoms (allied kingdoms in Ki-Paik Lee's words), produced the most active period in their history. The strongest of the three kingdoms was the Koguryo, which at its peak occupied the northern and central parts of the peninsula and about the same amount of land in Manchuria, with the center of the Kingdom being more in Manchuria than on the Korean peninsula. Silla and Paekche occupied the southeastern and the southwestern parts of the peninsula, and they were equally healthy and dynamic. At the same time, China was also moving forward under the Han dynasty which had unified the nation, sometime before the Three Kingdoms emerged on the Korean peninsula, and was dynamic both in its internal and external policies; the T'ang rulers established complete control of China immediately before the end of the Three Kingdoms period in Korea. A parallel situation took place in Japan: the nation was unified for the first time in her history, and the energetic Yamato period overlapped with the last three hundred years of Korea's Three Kingdom period. Thus the East Asian world witnessed during this period the emergence of three rapidly changing and growing nations, a situation somewhat similar to that of Europe in the early modern period when the nation-state system began to emerge.

The expanding power and influence of Han China reached the northwestern part of the Korean peninsula in the late second century B.C. and established the so-called Han Commanderies, replacing the Wiman's rule in Ancient Korea, which was then consolidated and lasted for about 400 years until the early fourth century after Christ. This was the only time when direct rule by the Chinese people was maintained on Korean soil, and Chinese military and political dominance over the Koreans reached its highest peak in the history of the relationship between these two nations. The cultural influence of Han China over the Koreans was considerable, and the Koreans learned much from the Chinese in both the material and the spiritual realms. Both Confucianism and Buddhism, along with organizational skills, iron technology, and other cultural traits, came from China to Korea during this period; some of these were later exported to Japan.[22] From the other direction, Japanese influence reached the southern coast of Korea during this period and, under the leadership of Empress Jinggu, avenues of cultural importation from Korea were opened.[23] Thus, during the period of the Three Kingdoms, Korea quietly absorbed great military and political influences from both China and Japan and at the same time absorbed cultural influences from China and transferred it to Japan, thus serving as cultural transmitter.

A phenomenon occurred during this period and which deserves special attention was the particular mode of diplomacy of the divided buffer state with two large neighboring powers. Three was certainly not a stable number in international relations, and all three Korean Kingdoms were trying to unify the peninsula at the expense of the two others. In this common struggle, each of the three kingdoms employed the same policy of using one or even both neighboring powers for the purpose of conquering the two adversaries.[24] This was certainly a risky game. All three tried to woo the favor of powerful T'ang China and also of Japan. The Silla Dynasty, with the help of China, was able to unify the peninsula. As will be discussed in the following pages, Silla was rather fortunate to succeed in her unification efforts without being subjugated by the strong former ally.

Another phenomenon surrounding the buffer state of Korea during this period (and it is not necessarily confined to this period) was that of the existence of a sub-buffer system or a satellite buffer system. Just as Korea was the buffer state between China and Japan, especially during this period, so Korea also acted as the buffer state between China and the semi-nomadic states in Manchuria. Or, sometimes, Korea played the role of a large state along with China for the states in Manchuria, which then became buffer states.[25]

The little more than three centuries of the Silla period were, in cultural terms, the most glorious epoch in Korean history. For the first time the nation was unified under autocratic monarchs and enjoyed an Age of Enlightenment. This cultural prosperity was not confined to Korea; China and Japan also enjoyed a high degree of cultural prosperity. Actually, the golden age of culture originated in China and spread to Korea and Japan. The dynamic nature of the Dynasty was not just in culture; it also found expression in the arena of politics and other areas of national life. The characteristics of Japanese culture were about the same as in China and Korea. During the Nara and Heian periods, the Japanese people enjoyed cultural prosperity and peace. The Koreans most actively learned from the Chinese in every aspect of life during this period, more so than in any other period.[26] The Japanese borrowed from both the Chinese and the Koreans, and Korea remained a cultural highway throughout the 300 years period.[27]

As has already been indicated, the energy of T'ang China was expressed also in the military and political arena, and the Chinese undertook a most ambitious policy toward the Koreans in the mid-seventh century. T'ang China, in alliance with Silla, fought the long-time enemy Koguryo in the northern part of Korean peninsula; then, still allied with Silla, it turned to Paekche. Or, as seen from Silla's viewpoint, she unified the Korean peninsula with the assistance of T'ang China. But, to the surprise of the Silla people, as soon as the war was over, the Chinese began to treat their former ally, Silla, much like a defeated state and openly showed their intentions of permanently ruling the whole peninsula. The Silla people courageously opposed the Chinese and defeated their army in Korea and expelled them from the Peninsula. In this effort, Silla skillfully played her diplomacy and enlisted the support of her former enemies - Koguryo and Paekche. This was one of the most successful cases of the Koreans bravely defending their nation against a neighboring giant. One reason for Silla's success was that T'ang China was quite different from both the Mongolians and the Manchus in that the Chinese were probably too civilized to be long involved in this muddy imperial struggle far away from the homeland.[28]

The five hundred-year Koryŏ period, between the early tenth and the late fourteenth centuries, was, in political terms, a continuation of the bureaucratic monarchial system of the Silla period. In both Korea and China, the cultures had some refinement but, in general, it was a time of decline. Exept for the Koryŏ both blue pottery and the development of skill in printing, Korea lacked any new innovations. In the latter part of the thirteenth century, Mongolian domination came to Korea. In Japan, the peaceful but decadent Heian period gave way in the late twelveth century to the Kamakura Bakufu, and the samurais in this decentralized feudal society dissipated their energy by continually quarrelling among themselves.

Under the Sung Dynasty, China was most amicable, and the Koreans felt the least pressure from her. The relationship between Korea and China continued mainly through friendly diplomacy and commercial transactions. To China the Koreans exported gold, silver, and bronze, along with ginseng and some other minor consumer goods; from China she imported linen, books, pottery, medicine and many luxury items.[29] Korea did not feel any military or political pressure from either the Heian or the Kamakura regimes in Japan.

The most dangerous threat to the Koreans came from the Mongolians toward the end of the Koryŏ period. The Mongolian highland and the Manchurian plain were similar to the Arabian peninsula in Ancient Middle Eastern history, in that they sent wave after wave of wild invading forces to the south. No matter what the pretexts for the invasion were, the real reason behind these invasions was the desire of a semi-nomadic people for agricultural land in the south. Korea absorbed a great amount of pressure in six invasions in the 30 years that began in 1231. The king and his royal family first took refuge on Kanghwa Island, which the Mongolians were not able to reach. Soon, however, the king decided to leave the island and to submit to the Mongolians, and Korea entered a century of humiliating subjugation that lasted until 1356. Within a dozen years of their surrender, the Koreans had to cooperate with the Mongolians on their invasion of the Japanese Islands.

At first, the Koreans advised against the Mongolian plan for the invasion, but being unable to persuade them to change their mind, the Koreans had no choice but to cooperate with them by providing ships, supplies, and a part of the invasion force. The two Mongolian expeditions to Japan of 1271 and 1281 ended in disaster. This is the only case in which the buffer state of Korea tried to prevent pressure by one large power against the other, and failing to do so, it acted as a transport route for the invasion.[30]

The Yi Dynasty, the last ruling house in Korea, began at the end of the fourteenth century and lasted for five hundred years until 1910. It was in general a continuation of the Koryo Dynasty, as the Koryŏ Dynasty had been a continuation of the previous dynasty: all had served a bureaucratic monarchial system and, to a large extent, controlled by the Confucian scholar officials. This same system had already existed for 800 years, and stagnation was inevitable; Yi Korea lacked from the beginning the vigor of the Three Kingdoms or the Silla Dynasty. Fortunately, China was under the rule of the Ming Dynasty, which also lacked the vigor of the Han and T'ang Dynasties. In 1644, the semi-nomadic Manchus took over China but before long they were conquered by the mighty Chinese culture and were tamed and corrupted. On the Japanese Island, a feudal society continued. But, in the latter part of the sixteenth century, centripetal force won out and the resulting unification of the nation produced some restless energy, and Korea had its impact.

Korea felt a little more pressure from China under Ming control than the nation had felt from China under the previous Sung Dynasty. Additionally, the founder of the Yi Dynasty, Yi Sŏngke, wanted to strengthen his position by receiving the sanction of the great neighbor, and an extensive tributary system began at the very outset of the new dynasty. Three to four regular missions and additional special missions traveled every year from Seoul to Beijing. As usual, trade went on with the tributary missions; Korea exported to China ginseng, animal skins, and other similar consumer goods, and imported linen, medicine, books, pottery and other refined goods.[31] The Yi rulers maintained a general policy of friendly relations with Japan, even though there was a continuing problem with Japanese piracy, which began in the early thirteenth century and continued throughout this period. The Japanese government itself was unable to control the piracy, and it caused much trouble for the Koreans in coastal areas. Cautious in dealing with the Japanese, the Korean government allowed only limited trade to the residents of Tsushima, the Japanese island in the Korea Strait. The Japanese continued to benefit from cultural imports from Korea as well as from commercial transactions. They took from Korea rice, cotton goods, pottery, books, bells, and other similar goods and sent to Korea bronze, tin, and medicine.[32] The peaceful years of the "Sadae kyorin" (Serve the great and maintain a friendly relationship with the neighbors) policy did not last forever; the storms came in the late fifteenth and sixteenth centuries.

The first storm came from Japan under the leadership of Toyotomi Hideyoshi, who had just succeeded in unifying Japan and had to find an outlet for the excessive energy of the samurai class.[33] Hideyoshi's intention of conquering the Asiatic continent was definite, and he expressed it well in his own words: "I will make a leap and land in China and lay my laws upon her. I shall go by way of Korea and if your soldiers will join me in this invasion you will have shown your neighboring spirit. I am determined that my name shall pervade the three kingdoms."[34] Korea, under the leadership of the Confucian scholars, was almost defenseless, and Hideyoshi's troops, 150,000 in his first invasion of 1592 and 140,000 in his second invasion of 1597, swept through the peninsula like a hurricane. However, the Japanese forces overran but could not conquer Korea, and the invasion failed to leave any long-lasting mark on Korean culture. The Chinese originally dispatched 5,000 and then an additional 40,000 troops to help their vassal nation but these troops could not control the Japanese forces and more damage was done to the Koreans. Some cultural changes were brought about by the two Japanese expeditions: the first Christian missionary came to Korea with one of the Hideyoshi's generals, even though no impact from this visit was recorded; further, the Japanese culturally benefited from the items they took from Korea.[35] During these violent years, Korea absorbed a tremendous amount of pressure coming from a large neighbor, absorbed it with great pain, and successfully prevented it from going to the other side; at the same time, Korea acted as a cultural highway.

Within three decades of the Japanese invasion, the Koreans had to face another storm, this one coming from the north. The seminomadic Manchus were different from both the Chinese and the Mongolians, who had come and gone quickly. The Manchus came and their influence remained in the Korean peninsula. In the early seventeenth century, they struggled to conquer the vast land of China and, under these somewhat uncertain circumstances, the Yi government decided to remain loyal to Ming China. The Manchus probably feared Korean aid for the Ming Chinese, which has been given as the reason for the Manchurian invasion of Korea; however, the real reason seems to have been very similar to the one for their invasion of China and for the Mongolian invasion of China and Korea -- the lure of agricultural land for a seminomadic people. Whatever the reason, the Manchus invaded Korea in 1627 and 1737, first with 40,000 and then with 100,000 men. Although the pressure level was somewhat lower than that of the Japanese, which the Koreans had just experienced, the Manchus were much cruder and more harmful to the Koreans. After ten years of struggle, the Korean court decided to surrender, and the nation fell into the postion of a vassal. The pressure the Koreans received from the Manchus was much greater than that they had received from the Chinese and almost as great as that from the Mongolians. The cultural and commercial impact of Ch'ing China was also considerable. Again, Korea absorbed the shocks.[36]

The half century prior to 1910 in Korea was the most dramatic period in her history. Literally bombarded from all directions, she was not able to absorb the pressure successfully; hence, Korea finally broke down and the buffer state disappeared at the end of the period. This process resulted largely from conditions in East Asia surrounding the Korean peninsula. The single most important factor for this condition was the beginning of the Western impact upon the three countries in the region. Modern Western culture had come first to China and Japan, and by 1860 these two nations had fully opened to Western culture. Unfortunately, mainly because of her geographical location, the opening of Korea was delayed by over two decades and this delay of twenty years in the late nineteenth century, when changes were taking place at such a high speed in the region, made a great difference for the Koreans. Another important factor for the situation in Korea was the way the Koreans responded to Western Culture. Under the burden of traditional culture-- even more so than was the case in China--the Koreans responded too slowly and too little. To make matters more difficult and complicated, the European powers began to be involved in Korean affairs. The United States played a special role in Korean history by opening the nation to the Western world in 1882 and it remained as a special nation. Russia, as will be soon explained, was heavily involved in Korea, especially during the ten-year period of the 1890s and the early 1900s. England had to be involved since Russia was involved in Korean affairs; other European powers played tangential roles. Against this background, Korea played the difficult role of a buffer state in this critical period of fifty years.

The first increase in pressure on Korea came from Japan in 1876. In this year, 22 years after Commodore Perry had opened Japan and only eight years after the Meiji Restoration, two Japanese gunboats came to the Kanghwa Island outside of Inchŏn, and opened Korea to Japan, in a style similar to Perry's opening of Japan to the West. Korea did not have any choice and reacted as Japan had in 1854. This was certainly a challenge to China, who had by this time greatly relaxed the tributary system for Korea. She responded immediately to counterbalance Japanese ascendancy in Korea by helping the Koreans to open their doors to the Western powers, a process that began in 1882 and was complete within a few years. The Japanese tested their strength in Korea in 1882 and 1885 by involving their small military forces and, realizing that they needed more time, they decided to wait for a decade before making a further attempt. When the showdown came ten years later, the large but traditional Chinese force could not match the small but effective Japanese military force which had been trained in the Western style. When, in 1895, China was eliminated from Korea as a factor in the buffer system, the system itself was supposed to cease to exist. But, in the fall of 1895 and the spring of 1896, when Russia emerged as a new antagonist against Japan, the buffer system was immediately restored. However, history in Korea repeated itself in the following decade, and, after waiting for a decade, Japan for the first time defeated a European giant- Russia. Korean independence disappeared along with the balance of power in 1905, and five years later Japan formally annexed Korea. Thus Korea twice became a battleground within a ten-year period, in 1894-5 and in 1904. This is a typical case in which when one of the two large powers determined to decide the issue on the battlefield and the other power is not willing or fails to concede, a confrontation is inevitable. Unfortunately for the Koreans, most of the battles in the two wars took place in their country. Korea's role as a buffer state seemed to be ended forever, but thirty-five years later, when the Second World War was over in the Far East, she returned to the map as a separate, if not entirely independent, entity and a sort of buffer state role also returned to the peninsula.

Because the United States and the Soviet Union were on opposite sides of Japan, they began to be involved in Korea at the end of the Second World War, and, because of the division of the peninsula between the two by the 38th parallel and the Cold War which soon began, the two powers became the two large states in the new buffer state system in Korea. The division, which was created as procedural expediency to receive the surrender of the Japanese army in Korea, was critical for later developments in Korea. It was an artificial division for the Koreans, who had maintained a coherent political unity for over two thousand years, and an unification effort was inevitable, as it was elsewhere under similar circumstances. Korea in a sense went back to the period of the Three Kingdoms, where every kingdom tried to unify the nation at the expense of the other two. History repeats itself in a very similar way under very similar circumstances.

The artificial division of the territory has already brought one war to the Korean people. Within two years after the birth of the two Koreas in 1948, North Korea made an attempt to achieve unification by force, which resulted in a three-year war which ended in an armistice in 1953. A significant development throughout this period was that China and Japan - the two old rival powers - returned to the peninsula; one in a dramatic way in 1950 and the other gradually and almost unnoticed through an economic avenue, as had happened a century ago. Now, the two Koreas are placed between two groups of large powers: the United States and Japan on one side and the Soviet Union and China on the other. During the past three decades, the two Koreas have strenuously widened the scope of their diplomacy: they have expanded their economic and cultural relationship with all "non-hostile" nations; they have expanded their diplomacy with the third world powers; they have made a continuous effort to conduct their diplomacy through regional and universal international organizations; and they have maintained a close relationship with their ideological allies.[37] These policies were very much in keeping with the typical foreign policy of two small powers. The biggest question in the two Koreas' foreign policy is that of unification. What would be the future of the two half-Koreas? This is a real question in the coming years not only for the Koreans but also for all nations who are involved in this buffer system.

Before turning to what the future holds, a brief summary of the multiple roles of Korea as a buffer state is in order. Of the two roles of the buffer state - positive and negative, the role played by Korea was mostly positive. Throughout over two thousand years of history, she silently absorbed all pressure coming from both directions. The only exception to this before the late nineteenth century was the Mongolian invasion of the thirteenth century. Korea was an "effective" buffer state, if the "effective" and "ineffective" categorization can be used, as it is in the case of borders. The history of the buffer state also shows that once a large neighboring power had decided on a showdown on the battlefield and the other power refused to back down, as had happened in other buffer states, war was inevitable, and Korea became either a military highway or a battleground; this was the case in the Mongolian invasion of Japan and the two wars at the turn of the century.

To explore the future possibilities of the buffer state Korea, it seems to be necessary to answer first, a question: Under what conditions is a buffer state most likely to survive? To answer this question, we have to return to the definitional characteristics which were listed at the beginning of this discussion. Of the nine characteristics at least five may be deemed to be essential for the survival of the buffer state: geographic location, independence, neutrality, native strength, and the balance of power. For obvious reasons, the locational factor is essential for a buffer state; unless a nation is located between two large powers, it cannot be a buffer state. Korea has no problem with regard to the locational factor; unfortunately, she will always be between two large neighbors - China and Japan. Independence and sovereignty in the modern world are no longer considered to be absolute, but a concession is a concession, and it undermines the basis of the buffer state. The two half Koreas are too dependent upon their allies and this will remain a problem in the future. Closely related to independence is neutrality; deviation again will lessen the value of the buffer state. Neutrality is a touchy issue for both Koreas, and this is another problem area for the future of Korea. A certain amount of the buffer state's own strength is as important as its independence, because without it, independence cannot be maintained. For Korea, the real problem for their strength is the division; a unified Korea would be strong enough to be a good buffer state, but as long as she remains split, it will be hard for her to play the role of even a half buffer state. As was stated earlier, the environmental factor is extremely important for the buffer state; only where there is a balance of power will the buffer state continue to exist. There seems to be a built-in tendency to maintain a balance of power within any international system, but there is no guarantee that the four large powers will maintain forever the balance of power and interests in the Korean peninsula.

In addition to these five factors, there are two more very important issues for the future of Korea as a buffer state. One is technological change and the other is unification. Modern technology in transportation, communication, and military affairs seems to have almost completely wiped out the distance and space factor in our lifetime. An important question is whether the buffer state as such will still have a meaningful role in the future. An important general question is whether any technological revolution can completely change the whole pattern of human life. Along with space ships, we still see people traveling by airplane, train, and automobile and there are still small weapons and tanks, along with ICBMs. Probably distance and space are not completely irrelevant and may exist as factors for a long time in the future. Trygve Mathisen's view on the issue is that, while technological progress has reduced or changed the importance of buffer states, they are not unimportant. Nicholas J. Spyman holds a similar view: "Fortunately, buffer states have endured not merely because of the recognition of their positive protective value but also because it has always seemed better to a nation to have the territory beyond its border in the hands of a small state than to have it become an integral part of a large military unit."[38]

The unification issue is the most serious one for the future of the two half Koreas. Because of both the inherent desire of the Korean people for unification and the ideological differences between the two Koreas, the Korean peninsula is one of the most unstable and dangerous spots in the world. Already there has been one war into which were drawn a large number of nations, and the danger of another conflict remains a real one. The world is still entrapped by ideology, whether it is political or religious, and this ideological trap is most severe on the Korean peninsula. Getting out of the ideology trap is not easy, but unless this is done, unification is impossible, and unless unification is achieved, independence, neutrality, self-strengthening, and even the balance of power - all necessary conditions for the survival of the buffer state - are not possible.

Events in China in the post-Mao years will have an impact upon the world; the impact of these changes upon the Korean peninsula will be especially great. China is now trying to find her way in a changing world; in a sense, her present situation is about the same as what she faced in the latter part of the nineteenth century. She may fail again, but China in the late twentieth century is quite different from the China in the late nineteenth century: she is much more serious about her modernization efforts this time and, moreover, her one billion population is totally mobilized and fully awakened due to the revolutionary moves of the post-World War Two era. The long-range impact of a successfully modernized China will be significant upon the Korean peninsula. Busy with her internal problems, China is taking presently a mild posture toward Korea, but how long her present posture will last is a good question. History tells us that whenever China became strong and vigorous, Korea was not able to escape from her expansionist pressure. Another important factor for the future of Korea is the situation in Japan. Although presently occupying a secondary role to the United States, she is already a giant in the world economy and it is also a good question to ask how long she will maintain her present posture toward Korea. If China changes her attitude toward Korea, the Japanese will have to react immediately, as has happened in the past; should such events occur, the buffer system surrounding the Korean peninsula will again become active. An important warning to the Koreans is the time factor; if the Koreans read correctly the present and the future of the situation surrounding their country and make the necessary political adjustment successfully and work out the difficult task of unification, the nation will be ready to play the role of a buffer state in the new situation.

NOTES

1. William Elliot Griffis, *Korea, the Hermit Nation*, 9th ed. *(New York: AMS, 1971), p. 9.*

2. N.J. Spykman, "Frontier, Security, and International Organization,"*Geographical Review*, 32 (1942):440.

3. Pitman B. Potter, "Buffer State," *Encyclopedia of Social Sciences*, 3: 45.

4. Shanon McCune, "Korea," in G. Etzel Percy and Associates, eds., *World Politics*, 2nd ed. (New York: Crowell, 1957), p. 592. See also Kyung Cho Chung, *Korea Tomorrow: Land of the Morning Calm* (New York: Macmillan, 1956), p. 5; Youngnok Koo, "The Conduct of Foreign Affairs," in Edward R. Wright, ed., *Korean Politics in Transition* (Seattle: University of Washington Press, 1975), p. 208; Japanese Foreign Minister Komura Jutaro's proposal, *Nihon Gaikobunsho (Japanese Diplomatic Documents)*, 39 vols. (Toykyo: Nihon Kokusairenggyo Kyokai, 1936-59), 36, 1: 1, *New York Times*, 21 March 1892, 9:3.

5. McCune, "Korea," p. 597; Chung, *Korea Tomorrow*, p. 5; Koo, "Conduct of Foreign Affairs," p. 208. Also see T. F. Tsiang, Sino-Japanese Relations, 1870-1894," *Chinese Social and Political Science Review*, 17 (1933):53.

6. For location and other geographical factors in international relations see Michael Handel, *Weak States in the International System* (London:Cass, 1981), pp. 70-4; Annette Baker Fox, *The Power of Small States; Diplomacy in World War II* (Chicago: Chicago University Press, 1959), p. 8.

7. For a discussion of the Korean boundary see Shanon McCune, "Physical Basis for Boundaries in Korea," *Far Eastern Quarterly*, 5 (1946):272-4, 280-1.

8. Ronald P. Barston, *The Other Powers; Studies in the Foreign Policies of Small States* (London: Allen and Unwin, 1973), p. 22; Handel, *Weak States in the International System*, p. 72.

9. Chung, *Korea Tomorrow*, p. 5; *London Times*, 1 February 1885, 5: 1.

10. Handel, *Weak States*, pp. 31-3; Barston, "External Relations for Small States," pp. 39-43, 50-5; Maurice A. East, "Size and Foreign Policy Behavior; A Test of Two Models," *World Politics*, 25 (1973):557.

11. Both Hendel and Barston put Korea in a small state category: Handel, *Weak States*, pp. 32-3; Barston, "The External Relations of the Small States," pp. 52-3.

12. Mathisen, *The Functions of Small States*, p. 109.

13. Fox, *the Power of Small States*.

14. Spykman, "Frontier, Security and International Organization," p. 441. Spykman points out that neutrality is one of the two most important characteristics of the border state.

15. Spykman, "Frontier, Security, and International Organization," p. 441.

16. Hans J. Morgenthau treats Korea as one of the classical cases of balance of power system: Hans J. Morgenthau, *Politics Among Nations; the Struggle for Power and Peace,* 4th ed. (New York:Knopf, 1956), pp. 171, 282, 405-7.

17. East, "Size and Foreign Policy," p. 576; Barston, *The Other Powers,* p. 19.

18. Koo, The Conduct of Foreign Policy," p. 208.

19. For discussions on the roles of the buffer state see Spykman, "Frontier, Security, and International Organization," pp. 440-1; Mathisen, *The Functions of Small States,* p. 598; Chung, *Korea tomorrow,* p. 5.

20. Ki-paik Lee, *Hankuksa Shinron (New Introduction to a Korean History),* revised ed. (Seoul:Ilchogak, 1983), p. 27.

21. Lee, *Hankuksa Shinron,* p. 27. See Also Woo-Keun Han, *The History of Korea* (Honolulu: University Press of Hawaii, 1970), pp. 12, 15; Takashi Hadata, *A History of Korea* (Santa Barbara: Clio, 1969) pp. 2-5.

22. Lee, *Hankuksa Shinron,* pp. 32-4, 60-2; Pyung-Do Yi, *Kuksa Taekwan (Survey of a National History)* (Seoul:Paikyungsa, 1954), pp. 35, 60-1; Han, *The History of Korea,* pp. 18, 22; Hadata, *A History of Korea,* pp. 4-5; William E. Henthorn, *A History of Korea* (New York: Free Press, 1971) pp. 17, 23, 35; Ralph Clinton, *Tree of Culture* (New York:Knopf, 1961), p. 582.

23. Clinton, *Tree of Culture,* pp. 581-2; Hadata, *A History of Korea,* p. 23.

24. Yi, *Kuksa Taekwan,* pp. 75, 98; Henthorn, *A History of Korea,* p. 33; Clarence Norwood Weems, ed., *Hulbert's History of Korea,* 2 vols. (New York: Hillary, 1962), 1:72.

25. Lee, *Kuksa Shinron,* p. 31; Han, *The History of Korea,* p. 222; Hadata, *A History of Korea,* p. 3.

26. Lee, *Hankuksa Shinron,* p. 91; Yi, *Kuksa Taekwan,* p. 121; Han, *The Korean History,* pp. 102-6; Hadata, *A History of Korea,* p. 31.

27. Henthorn, *A History of Korea,* p. 59.

28. Lee, *Hankuksa Shinron,* pp. 86-7; *Kuksa Taekwan,* pp. 75-7, 81-2, 113-4; Han, *The History of Korea,* pp. 75-83; Henthron, *A History of Korea,* pp. 51-3; Hadata, *A History of Korea,* p. 24. Also see Hadata, Ibid., p. 25

29. Henthorn, *A History of Korea,* p. 101; Hadata, *A History of Korea,* p. 52; Han, *The History of Korea,* p. 153; Lee, *Hankuksa Shinron,* p. 156.

30. Lee, *Hankuksa Shinron,* pp. 179-80, 187-90; Yi, *Kuksa Taekwan,* pp. 220, 242-5; Henthorn, *A History of Korea,* pp. 117-9, 122, 128; Hadata, *A History of Korea,* pp. 52-4; Han, *The History of Korea,* pp. 167-71, 175; McCune, "Korea," p. 603; Nicholas J. Spykman and Abbie A. Rollins, "Geographic Objectives in Foreign Policy I," *American Political Science Review,* 33 (1939):397.

31. Lee, *Hankuksa Shinron,* p. 228.

32. Yi, *Kuksa Taekwan,* pp. 259-61, 295, 336-8; Lee, *Hankuksa Shinron,* pp. 230-1; Hadata, *A History of Korea,* pp. 54-5, 75; Henthron, *A History of Korea,* pp. 155-8; Han, *The History of Korea,* pp. 224-6.

33. Lee, *Hankuksa Shinron,* p. 250; McCune, "Korea," p. 603; Clinton, *Tree of Culture,* p. 584.

34. Weems,*Hulbert's History of Korea,* 1:347.

35. Yi, *Kuksa Taekwan,* pp. 359-77; Hadata, *A History of Korea,* pp. 75-8; Griffis, *Korea, the Hermit Nation,* p. 88; *Weems, Hulbert's History of Korea,* 1:343; Henthorn, *A History of Korea,* pp. 178-85; Han, *The History of Korea,* pp. 268-72. On the cultural inpact see Lee,*Hankuksa Shinron,* pp. 254-5; Yi,*Kuksa Taekwan,* pp. 378, 395.

36. For the motivation of the invasion see Lee, *Hankuksa Shinron,* p. 256; McCune, "Korea," p. 603. For the process of the invasion see Han, *The History of Korea,* pp. 277-8; Yi, *Kuksa Taekwan,* pp. 385-6. And for the consequences of the invasion; Henthorn,*A History of Korea,* p. 199; Yi,*Kuksa Taekwan,* pp. 402-4; Han,*The History of Korea,* p. 229.

37. For discussion on the diplomacy of the two Koreas see Koo, "Conduct of Foreign Affairs," p. 237; Chalmers Johnson, "East Asia: Another Year of Living Dangerously," Foreign Affairs, 62 (1983):739-40; Byung Chul Koh, *The Foreign Policy of North Korea* (New York: Praeger, 1969), p. 166; John Chay, "North Korea: Relations with the Third World," in Jae Kyu Park and Jung Gun Kim, eds *The Politics of North Korea* (Seoul:Kyungnam University Press, 1979) pp. 269, 273.

38. Mathisen, *The Functions of Small States,* p. 126; Spykman, "Frontier, Security and International Organization," p. 441.

CHAPTER 11
URUGUAY: THE QUINTESSENTIAL BUFFER STATE

JOSEPH S. TULCHIN

No matter what the theoretical perspective or definition employed, Uruguay fits the description of a buffer state. The territory now included within the modern nation-state was a contested frontier between European empires as early as the seventeenth century and actually changed hands more than once during the colonial era. The modern nation itself was created deliberately, through outside intervention, as a buffer between two larger, warring states, both of which claimed the territory as theirs. This condition is part of the nation's historical tradition and has become an integral part of its national consciousness. The nation's identity is built around the inescapable fact that it is virtually surrounded by two vastly larger and more powerful neighbors, both of which have stated and reiterated their concern over their internal affairs within Uruguay, and both of which have shown themselves eager, on more than one occasion, to intervene directly in those internal affairs or to exercise influence over them in less direct ways. It is hardly surprising, therefore, that so much of Uruguay's national energy has been spent in establishing a national identity that is separate from those neighbors and in assuming international postures independent of them, nor is it surprising that those efforts have been only partially successful.

Being a buffer state and being conscious of that condition do not always go together, either among decision making elites or among the broader public. In the case of Uruguay, however, everyone is acutely sensitive to the reality of the nation's condition, but it has been a source of considerable disagreement for more than two centuries as to what the appropriate response to the condition should be. It is obvious that the condition of being a buffer state

213

has affected the geopolitical position of Uruguay since independence and has been the most importance determinant of the nation's foreign policy. Less obvious, but fully as important in the nation's development, the buffer condition also has had a profound impact on the nature and functioning of the political system, on the economy, the nation's cultural life, and even on its language. That said, however, it is extremely difficult to measure systematically in what manner or to what degree the buffer condition affects any particular dimension of national life. Without such systematic measurement, coherent analysis is difficult and prediction of Uruguay's international behavior or of the stability of the subsystem of which it is a part would be an exercise in speculation.

This chapter is an experimental effort to define the critical variables or dimensions that comprise the condition of being a buffer state for Uruguay, as well as an effort to suggest how the Uruguayan case helps us to understand the phenomenon of the buffer state within the international state system. Even the most cursory review of Uruguayan history indicates that the conditions of buffer state have varied over time for Uruguay. Therefore, the study will begin with an historical section, in order to get a clearer idea of how the dimensions of the buffer condition have changed over time and how their interaction or interrelationship may have changed under different historical conditions. On the basis of this empirical description, we will attempt to combine the variables and suggest what their interrelationship might be - a sort of informal model - so that we can evaluate the consequences of being a buffer for Uruguay at particular points in time and under certain conditions. Ultimately, we are concerned with understanding how being a buffer state affects Uruguay's chances for national development and its continued success as a modern nation state.[1]

BUFFER ROLE AND NATIONAL DEVELOPMENT

The territory on the eastern bank of the Uruguay River and north of the broad estuary known as the River Plate did not attract attention from the earliest Portuguese and Spanish *conquistadores.* Sparse populations of semi-nomadic Indians were a sufficient deterrent to all but the most intrepid gauchos from Buenos Aires who forayed into the area from time to time to collect hides from the herds of wild cattle that roamed over the plains and the rolling hills near the river bank. In 1680, the Portuguese established a settlement directly across the river from the Spanish center at Buenos Aires, at Novo Colonia do Sacramento. Local Spanish forces ousted the Portuguese from Colonia no fewer than four times in the next century, only to have the settlement restored to Portuguese control by political considerations in Europe.

While the Spanish were willing to allow the Portuguese their outpost on the River Plate, they certainly were not prepared to cede control over the entire area. By 1726, there was a permanent settlement at the natural harbor of Montevideo, from which the Spanish pretended to exert administrative control over the hinterland and to inhibit Portuguese pretensions in the area. This curious administrative division was complicated further by the fact that officials in Montevideo made little effort to exercise any control over the land to the northeast, lying between their settlements and the southern outposts of the Portuguese colony of Brazil. That area remained a kind of no-man's land until the last quarter of the eighteenth century, when, as a result of the so-called Bourbon Reforms, the Banda Oriental became a province within the newly created Viceroyalty of the River Plate, and the Portuguese were forced to give up Colonia.

Throughout the colonial era, Uruguay was a stage on which vast imperial forces manipulated the figures.[2] This area, in other words, was defined as an insignificant colonial frontier by two rival European empires whose own independence of action was influenced by another power, Great Britain. The local populations had little or no say over their own destiny. Of course, as the eighteenth century drew to a close, France challenged British imperial pretensions, further complicating the rivalries between Spain and Portugal.

Uruguay's colonial heritage, therefore, was as an expendable pawn between rival empires, rivals whose colonial policies, as often as not, were affected by pressures of politics in Europe, and, particularly in the eighteenth century, by the influence of Great Britain over Portuguese actions. This confusion or ambiguity of control appeared to suit most of the inhabitants of the area. Even after 1776, when they were unequivocally under Spanish rule, the inhabitants of the regions struggled to distance themselves administratively from the control of the city of Buenos Aires. While in the seventeenth century, most of the settlers had come from Buenos Aires or were linked directly to ranching interests in the hinterland of that city, by the middle of the eighteenth century, backed by British commercial interest, the ranchers of the Banda

Oriental had come to have economic and commercial interests of their own quite separate from those of the *portenos* across the river delta. They would not willingly give up the independence of action they had enjoyed before they became part of the new viceroyalty.

As if to foretell coming events, Montevideo became independent of Buenos Aires when it fell temporarily under British control in 1807. British troops seized the city in February and held it for eight months while they waited for the opportunity to recapture Buenos Aires. While they waited, British merchants turned the city into a free port and the Orientals were introduced to a level of prosperity they had never known. Thus it was that when Napoleon Bonaparte forcibly ousted the Spanish monarchs and replaced them with his disreputable cousin, Joseph, thereby precipitating a crisis of legitimacy throughout the Spanish empire, the citizens of Montevideo and the Banda Oriental consistently and deliberately opposed the positions proposed by the porteno leadership. Out of this very fluid situation, there emerged several factions among the Orientales, each with its external allies, a characteristic of Uruguayan politics for the next century.

The hero of the Uruguayan struggle for independence was Jose Gervasio Artigas, a quixotic figure who struggled fruitlessly to link the Banda Oriental to a federation of states in the River Plate. But the federalist option never succeeded in dominating Argentine politics during the early years of the nineteenth century, so that external support for the Artigas position was weak. Newly independent Argentina and the Portuguese, later the Brazilians, fought in Uruguay through their proxies for several years until, in 1825, they declared war on one another to gain control of the oriental province. That war ground to a standstill, with rather dire results for Argentine stability and for the commercial situation in the entire River Plate delta. At this point, the British, who were the power behind the Brazilian throne and who had the most to lose commercially from continued intranquility in the region, interposed themselves between the combatants and brought them to sign a treaty in 1828 in which both recognized the independence of the Republica Oriental del Uruguay.[3]

That recognition was no bar to their continuing interference in Uruguay's factional politics. Very soon after the treaty, Juan Manuel de Rosas emerged as the most powerful figure in Argentina, and gradually put an end to the debilitating internecine conflict on the west bank of the river. As he consolidated his power, he began to meddle in affairs on the east bank, and threw in his lot with Manuel Oribe, leader of the Blanco party. Oribe's rival, Fructuoso Rivera, leader of the Colorado party, countered by joining the coalition of Rosas' opponents, even joining the French and the province of Corrientes in declaring war on the governor of Buenos Aires province. The French combined with the British to prevent Rosas from establishing a naval blockade of Montevideo. Rivera ultimately played a supporting role in the overthrow of Rosas in 1851 by J.J. Urquiza, the caudillo of Entre Rios province, who benefitted significantly from the aid of Brazil.

Saved from Argentine pressure, the Uruguayans almost fell into the hands of the Brazilians. The treaty of alliance which preceded the campaign against Rosas included a clause in which Brazil committed itself to defend the legal order in Uruguay, a standard, none-too-subtle invitation to intervene in Uruguayan affairs. This produced a harsh reaction from factions in both the Colorado and Blanco parties, which began to see that defeating one of the two threatening neighbors did not necessarily guarantee independence and protection from the other. Thus, while political groups in Uruguay took the external forces as a given in their struggles for power and would turn to whichever of the neighbors was not predominant at that moment to help them in their effort to gain power, they consciously avoided actions that might tip the balace of power between them too much in either direction.

Despite this clear, repeated pattern and the equally clear, self-conscious assumption by Uruguayan governments of the role of buffer between two larger neighbors, there were some significant differences between Uruguay's relations with these neighbors during the nineteenth century. These differences helped shape the dimensions of the buffer role that Uruguay would continue to play in the twentieth century, despite important changes in the Atlantic world. Most significant was the nature of the frontier between Uruguay and its neighbors. The frontier with Argentina was clear, it was settled and it was dynamic. There were only minor disputes with Argentina over the waters of the river delta, disputes that would drag on until the definitive treaty was signed in 1973. But these disputes did not affect the internal cohesion of either society or its population.[4] The river system which was the boundary between the two nations was a bridge as much as it was a dividing line. Furthermore, the Argentine territories on the other side of the boundary were populated and constituted that nation's dynamic center of economic and political activity. To round out the idea of a dynamic frontier, Montevideo, the capital of Uruguay and the macrocephalic center of the nation's population, its government, and its economy, was much closer to Argentina than to Brazil. As if to emphasize that proximity and the intimate relationship between the two communities, Montevideo was the traditional haven for Argentine exiles, who gathered in friendly territory to plan their return and the overthrow of their opponent in Buenos Aires.

By contrast, the frontier with Brazil was ill-defined geographically, administratively, and culturally. The region was sparsely populated and on neither side of the boundary was the immediate hinterland a dynamic region critical to the nation's well-being. Linguistically, culturally, ethnically, commercially, and even politically, the area on both sides of the boundary was a kind of third republic, semi-independent of the central authorities in Montevideo and Rio de Janeiro. This situation would change in the twentieth century, principally as a function of the consolidation of the Uruguayan national state and the economic development of the southern states of Brazil. But, to this day, the departments along the river delta are more effectively integrated into the Uruguayan nation than are the departments along the northeastern frontier.[5]

Through the remainder of the nineteenth century, Uruguayan politics were dominated by the internecine conflict between the two major parties, with the "outs" using external pressure or the threat of such pressure whenever they could to improve their domestic leverage. The process of national consolidation in Argentina and the gradual decline of regional conflicts there made it harder for Uruguayan politicians to use those conflicts as weapons in their own political struggles. Almost as a response to the national consolidation in Argentina, the Uruguayans put an end to their own seemingly interminable civil strife and, under the leadership of the Colorado caudillo Jose Batlley Ordonez, organized a national state that could claim legitimately to respond to the needs of all groups and factions and that could pretend to control effectively the entire territory of the nation. While it would be only a slight exaggeration to say that the nation was held together during the nineteenth century by external pressures, not internal cohesion, by the beginning of the twentieth century, the conditions were established for the creation of a national state that was capable of functioning on its own.[6]

Although it is certainly true that events in Argentina influenced the nature and timing of national consolidation in Uruguay, it is also true that events in the Atlantic world had considerable influence over that process. The expansion of the international capitalist economy, especially Great Britain's capacity to export capital and the ravenous seemingly insatiable need of Britain and the other European nations for primary products to supply their industries and foodstuffs to feed their increasingly urban populations, presented an opportunity that no one sensitive to it would reject. Uruguay, like Argentina, already was producing meat and cereals for export by 1850. How much more could they produce if they only could ensure tranquility in the areas of fertile land, extend a transportation infrastructure onto these lands, apply new, available technology to the preservation of the meat, and attract the labor and capital necessary to exploit these un- or under-exploited areas.[7] Gradually, a national elite coalesced around this opportunity and became an oligarchy determined to end the internecine political strife and to provide a climate conducive to foreign investment and immigration. That oligarchy focused on the establishment of a vibrant economy dedicated to the export of agricultural and pastoral commodities.[8] The large central city, Montevideo, was designed as the administrative center of the nation and the commercial entrepot of the burgeoning commercial trade with Europe. That function would affect the nation's relations with its larger neighbors.[9]

The most dominant figure in the process of national consolidation was Batlle. He served as president from 1903 to 1907 and again from 1911 to 1915. Under his powerful leadership, Uruguay established the first welfare state in the hemisphere. Batlle imposed on the country a collegial executive, which he dominated, and pushed through the legislature the first measures that came to characterize the central government's willingness to shoulder the burden of its citizens' welfare. This commitment depended upon the constantly expanding revenues from the nation's exports, and the strong confidence that those revenues would continue to expand. It depended, too, upon a sense of international security. Uruguay could afford to build an elaborate state welfare apparatus because it did not see itself threatened from outside. The nation saw itself as in a secure, privileged position.

While, during the Batlle administrations, Uruguay continued to be careful to maintain a balanced, neutral position in its relations with Argentina and Brazil, by the second Batlle administration, it was aggressive and assertive on the broad stage of international affairs. Under the leadership of Batlle's foreign minister, Baltasar Brum, Uruguay began to play a special role in various international forums as the spokesman for democratic and humane government and the peaceful settlement of disputes through multilateral accords. Within the hemispheric community, Uruguay soon distinguished itself as a consistent defender of pan-americanism and of the leadership of the United States within the Pan American Union. That position was more or less congruent with the line followed by Brazil, but it was totally contrary to the stance assumed by Argentina. Indeed, some commentators have suggested that the Uruguayan position in the Pan American Union and the policy supporting the Allies during World War I was the result of Brazilian influence over Uruguayan policy.[10] However logical that argument may appear, there is no concrete evidence to support it. On the other hand, there is ample evidence to suggest that Batlle and Brum and other leaders of the Colorado party were deeply impressed with Woodrow Wilson's policies and with his defense of democracy. Furthermore, like other nations in South America, Uruguay considered itself sufficiently far away from the Caribbean and sufficiently more advanced than the nations in that zone that it never would consider itself subject to United States intervention. Finally, it is also true that Uruguay was totally dependent upon the U.S. during World War I for fuel, shipping and major imports, so that a policy other than the one actually adopted undoubtedly would have carried greater risk. It is at least probable, therefore, that such a policy struck the mildly nationalistic leadership as the most likely through which a small, relatively unprotected country could defend itself against larger neighbors by projecting its influence in international affairs with minimum risk. The war provided Uruguay the context within which to elaborate a role or position as a spokesman for international law and the peaceful adjudication of disputes, as well as an ardent supporter of multilateral agreements and organizations.

For half a century, Uruguay maintained the international role of a privileged spokesman for democracy and a loyal friend of the U.S. in hemispheric affairs. The policy brought notable benefits to Uruguay. It was among the original members of the League of Nations, thanks to its rapid, unquestioning acceptance of the peace terms offered by the Allies, and it retained its position in the new organization even after the U.S. refused to join. During the 1930s Uruguay was a warm supporter of the Good Neighbor Policy and enjoyed President Franklin D. Roosevelt's protection during the depression and in the years leading up to the Second World War. During the war, Uruguay continued its unequivocal support for U.S. policies, even though such support ran directly counter to Argentine policies and, for a time, embarrassed the independent line adopted by Brazilian dictator Getulio Vargas. This policy received its most extreme expression in the declaration of Foreign Minister Enrique Rodriguez Larreta, in 1945, when, referring to the military regime in Argentina, he called for collective intervention by the nations of the hemisphere in any nation of the hemisphere whose government violated human rights and the political freedoms of its citizens. None of the other Latin American nations seconded this proposal, because most of them were deeply hostile to any policy or plan that opened the way for any nation or nations to interfere in the internal affairs of any other nation. That reminded them too much of U.S. interventions earlier in the century. Only the U.S. government commented favorably on Rodriguez Larreta's declaration, and some critics within Uruguay implied that the proposal had been formulated at the behest of the government's U.S. "masters."[11]

Argentina's aggressive contrariness during World War II had made it difficult for Uruguay to use traditional balance of power methods to preserve tis independence of action, and so it fell back upon an external patron, as it had fallen back upon Great Britain for protection during the nineteenth century, to maintain its independence. The Uruguayan policy of friendship with the U.S. constantly created tension with Argentina, whose foreign policy always seemed to run counter to the objectives of the United States.[12] In the early years of the twentieth century, Brazil had followed a foreign policy that emphasized friendship with the U.S. but Vargas, who ruled from 1930 to 1945, studiously played down that friendship, thinking to maximize his benefits by playing off the Axis against the Allies. Argentine did not. In these circumstances, Uruguay resumed its traditional role as safe haven for political opponents of the Argentine regime. Now, during the war, it did so while publicly criticizing that regime. Thanks to technological advances in communication, the Argentine exiles could use Uruguayan soil to beam radio broadcasts back to Argentina. Those broadcasts denounced the regime of Juan D. Peron, who emerged out of the military junta that seized power in 1943 to become the nation's strongman from 1945 to 1955, when his own military forced him to flee.

As it had during World War I, Uruguay used its position to gain founding membership in the postwar international organization of the United Nations. Uruguay was rewarded with positions on the Security Council and other important committees, while Argentina had to be squeezed in at the last minute. Uruguay maintained its position of loyalty to the U.S. as the postwar peace deteriorated into the Cold War. Through the 1950s, there was a constant stream of public complaints by Uruguayan leaders about U.S.S.R. influence in the region. Given the feeble condition of the Communist Party in Uruguay and the docile nature of the labor movement, it is probable that such statements were references to international leftists movements and not to the U.S.S.R. itself, although the rhetoric must have been pleasing to official ears in Washington.[13]

The special role of Uruguay in international affairs, based on its democratic government, its strong support for the U.S., and its aggressive criticism of non-democratic regimes, began to erode in the 1960s as the government became bogged down in inter-institutional haggling between the executive and the legislature over how to do deal with the deteriorating economy, and the growing guerrilla movement known as the Tupamaros. As early as 1968, Jorge Pacheco Areco, who, as vice president, had succeeded to the presidency upon the death of Oscar Gestido, began to restrict civil liberties. This process culminated in June 1973, when President Juan Maria Bordaberry joined with the military in a presidential *autogolpe.* He was himself replaced, by Dr. Aparicio Mendez, in 1976.

Throughout this period, Uruguay bent and swayed to pressures from its larger neighbors. In 1964, it had once again offered safe haven to a political exile, this time to former president Joao Goulart, who had been ousted by the military, with the connivance or, it was alleged, with the support of the United States. In 1966, the Argentine military removed the civilian president, Arturo Illia. A few months later, the Argentine newsweekly, *Confirmado* remarked, (February 16, 1967):

> ?Puede el Uruguay, pais de estrategica ubicacion en la Cuenca del Plata, dar la espalda a Paraguay, Bolivia, Brasil, y Argentina? Los amantes de la democracia representativa oiensan que si, los de la geopolitica no.

Rather than stand resolutely in favor of democracy, without regard to the changes in regime occurring in any of its neighbors, Uruguay now seemed to follow the turns of political fashion. Not only did it follow Brazil, Argentina, and Chile into military dictatorship, it also adopted the monetarist economic model or policies asserted by those regimes, as the appropriate way to deal with Uruguay's economic problems, although Uruguay's economic malaise differed markedly from the situation in Brazil or Argentina.

Again, Uruguay seemed to follow Brazil and Argentina by returning to democratic government in 1985. While it is clear that the pattern of events reflects the influence of Uruguay's neighbors, and several interviews with members of Uruguay's military and the government under military control emphasized the attention to events in neighboring countries paid by Uruguay's leadership, there have been sufficient differences to lead some observers to insist that the transition to democracy has been peculiarly Uruguayan.[14] This is an argument that cannot be won. Suffice it to say that Uruguay has shown itself to be a penetrated political system and that its historical role as buffer between large, more powerful neighbors now includes a marked sensitivity to the type of regime in power in those neighbors.

During the past fifteen years, when Uruguay abandoned the foreign policy it had maintained since the First World War, its foreign policy has been characterized by extreme caution. Not only has it been careful to tread softly between its two larger neighbors, but it also has been reluctant to assume a prominent position on any issue of significance in the United Nations or other international forum. The patronage of the U.S. seems also to have been lost. Since the Cuban revolution, the defense of democracy has been subordinated in U.S. foreign policy to the struggle against communism. In economic matters, U.S. efforts to defend its markets against aggressive international competition has wounded Uruguay severely. To compound the hurt, the U.S. government has been unwilling to make an exception for Uruguay's principal exports - leather, wool, and cereals - even though officials in the congress and the executive admit that the amount of goods coming from Uruguay would be insignificant and that they did not have Uruguay in mind when they enacted the trade restrictions causing so much damage to Uruguay's foreign sales. This lack of concern by the U.S. and the understanding that economic support from that direction is highly unlikely, has led to a resurgence of economic and political nationalism, a nationalism that re-emphasizes Uruguay's historical role as a buffer in the southern cone power system. But the nature of the buffer role has changed since the nineteenth century, and to understand how it will function in the future, it is necessary to summarize the elements or dimensions that characterize it. These dimensions can be studied empirically, over time, and can be used to estimate the most likely posture or policy that Uruguay will assumed in a specific situation.

URUGUAY'S BUFFER DIMENSIONS

The principal dimensions of the role of buffer that Uruguay will play in the power subsystem known as the Southern Cone include: (1) the balance of power between Argentina and Brazil; (2) the type of regime in those nations; (3) the permeability of the Uruguayan political system and Uruguayan society; and, (4) the broader context of international affairs, especially the disposition of the hegemonic power to play the role of Uruguay's patron. The first factor determines the role Agrentina and Brazil want to play in Uruguayan affairs. In turn, their capacity to act or to project their influence outside their borders is a function of *their* stability, the nature of their political systems, and *their* economic well being. These will determine the geopolitical space within which Uruguay can act and the extent of its independence of international action. The more stable each is politically and the stronger each is economically, the greater their capacity to act internationally. However, that capacity might be useless in the hands of a regime that was isolated politically from the international community, as was the Argentine military after 1980. Similarly, the extraordinary legitimacy accorded the democratic regime of President Raul Alfonsin has enhanced the leverage of his government in international affairs, despite the weakness displayed by the lagging Argentine economy.

The impact of the type of regime on Uruguay's international position already has been discussed. This dimension operates only when Uruguay is out of step with both of its larger neighbors, and it does not enjoy the protection of a powerful, distant patron, such as the United States. In other words, it is not the type of regime, *per se* that will have an effect on the buffer role of Uruguay, but, rather, whether the type of regime in Uruguay differs from the type in its two larger neighbors. Thus, in the two cases discussed previously, Uruguay followed its neighbors into a military dictatorship and then followed them out of the dictatorship and back to democratic rule. It is likely, therefore, that so long as both neighbors remain democratic and civilian, Uruguay will also, despite increasing economic difficulties and social tension. On the other hand, it is not likely that regime changes in neighboring countries will determine regime changes in Uruguay; rather, they will have the effect of strongly reinforcing tendencies within Uruguayan politics.

The permeability of the regime and society is a complex concept and is, itself, composed of several elements. It has to do with the ease with which outside influences are felt within the society and how those influences are transmitted into the foreign policy of the nation. In the case of Uruguay and its relationship with Argentina and Brazil, the permeability of the society is affected by such diverse factors as language, transportation facilities, exchange rate policy, tourism, and the media of communication.

Uruguay not only serves as a geopolitical buffer between two larger countries, it also serves as their principal vacation spot. Punta del Este, perhaps the most famous beach south of Copacabana, and by far the cleanest, is the goal of thousands of Brazilian and Argentine tourists each year, although most of those who stay for prolonged periods are Argentines. Most of the Brazilians come for the shopping. They stay only a few days and go home. During the summer months, a sleepy town of no more than 20,000 people is transformed into a booming, bustling resort with nearly half a million people looking for ways to spend money and get a sunburn. The homes, chalets and condominiums in the area, mostly owned by foreigners, are estimated to be worth nearly five billion dollars, more than the nation's Gross National Product. A depression in Argentina or in Brazil might mean a drop in the tourist influx and a loss to Uruguay of millions of dollars in income from the tourist trade. Further north, along the country's eastern shore, the smaller beach communities are dominated by Brazilian money and Brazilian tourists. To the west of Montevideo, the dominance of Argentine capital is clear. During the Argentine boom years of Economics Minister Jose Martinez de Hoz, Argentine investors stirred the real estate market in the sleepy town of Colonia, just across the broad river from Buenos Aires. Hydrafoils brought stressed-out *portenos* to Colonia in 45 minutes where they could sit calmly on the patios of their remodeled colonial houses and watch the lights of Buenos Aires while they enjoyed a drink and *asado.* The strength of the Argentine peso led to serious discussions of building a bridge across the river in order to improve trade and relations between the two nations, a project that had been discussed off and on since the beginning of the twentieth century. When the Argentine peso collapsed in 1982 and the real estate market in Colonia went into a decline, discussion of the bridge became desultory.

In terms of tourism, Uruguay is a land bridge between Argentina and Brazil. If the currency of one is markedly weaker than the other, literally hoards of tourists from the stronger currency country drive across Uruguay to the weaker currency nation to spend their leisure time. In 1974, when the Argentine peso went into a tailspin, there were articles in Brazilian newspapers on "How to buy Argentina." As if to return the favor, similar articles about Brazil appeared in Argentine newspapers in 1979 and 1980, when the peso was relatively strong against the cruzeiro. In both instances, Uruguay's tourist trade benefitted. The ferry stations in Colonia and Montevideo were busy around the clock, and bus companies offered packaged tours suitable for all income levels. Today, when both Argentina and Brazil are trying to figure out ways to repay their staggering foreign debts, tourism has fallen to more modest levels, and Uruguay has had to turn to other forms of economic activity to finance its own economic recovery.

Given the size of the Uruguayan economy and the ease with which goods can be moved from Brazil or Argentina, it is clear that exchange rates and tariffs are highly sensitive instruments of policy. From the Uruguayan point of view, completely free trade would be suicidal to their industries. On the other hand, an excessively protectionist trade policy would be economically regressive and an exchange policy that discriminated against one of the two neighbors would be a source of international tension. During the 1970s, Uruguay experimented with an open financial market, and benefitted handsomely from a situation in which it assumed the role of a South American Panama. However, in the transition to democracy, the corruption within the military leadership that came with the creation of such a financial haven was exposed and exploited by the new civilian regime. It remains to be seen whether the new regime will allow the continuation of such an open financial market within an economy that is being closed partially to protect local industry, jobs, and currency markets from the influence of international organizations such as the International Monetary Fund.

Whatever the economic policies of the civilian regime, it will have to contend with complementary structural changes in the international environment. These changes involve a palpable shift in the relative geopolitical weight of Uruguay's larger neighbors. Brazil's economic capacity and its influence in all of South America has increased dramatically in the past few decades, and now exceeds Argentina's by a wide margin. Correlated closely with this shift in relative influence, it is now much more important to Argentina than it is to Brazil to project is influence across the River Plate into Uruguay. Trade with and investment in Uruguay are much more important to Argentina now than they are to Brazil. In geopolitical terms, it is now more significant to a more modest Argentina to exert influence over its smaller neighbor than it is for

Brazil, which now enjoys predominant influence in Bolivia and Paraguay. As Brazil's power in the continent grows, it can afford to allow Argentina to achieve and maintain preponderance in Uruguay. Uruguayan leaders will have to take this into account as they formulate their foreign policies. It will effect their options especially at times like the present when the U.S. refuses to play a constructive role in the area.

In cultural terms, so long as there is relative freedom of the press, Uruguay is far more vulnerable to Argentine penetration than it is to a Brazilian presence. The simple reason for this is the proximity of Montevideo to Buenos Aires. Montevideo is the population center of the nation. The overwhelming majority of newspapers are published there, most of the movies are shown there, and virtually all of the radio and television transmission is done there. And, Montevideo is definitely a Spanish city, not a Portuguese city. It is well within earshot of Buenos Aires radio and, with a little electronic help, television sets in Montevideo can pick up Argentine programs. All other things being equal, Uruguay will be more permeable to Argentine cultural influences than to Brazilian. The only exception to this, of course, is the northern boundary, which is a cultural and linguistic extension of Brazil.

The concept of Uruguay serving as a land bridge between two powerful neighbors has become central to the geopolitical thinking of many Uruguayans. From the far left to the far right, authors concerned with Uruguay's place in international affairs are convinced that the nation's future security and any future influence it might have in world affairs lies in serving as a bridge between Argentina and Brazil, and not as a buffer in the sense that the term was used in balance of power politics in the nineteenth century.[15] The key to Uruguay's success in playing such a role is its capacity to integrate its national territory in economic terms and to create an infrastructure of communication and transportation that unifies the space within the nation's boundaries.[16] In such a manner, there would be a unified national market, for the first time, so that it would be economically and politically feasible to talk about protecting national industries and national markets, and it would be possible to evaluate the costs and benefits to the entire nation of policies affecting the linkages between it and its neighbors. Under such conditions, Uruguay could contemplate joining with Argentina and Brazil in formulating development policies, rather than to watch, fearful, hoping only to play off one neighbor against the other. Such conditions would allow Uruguay to develop economically and to play a constructive role in regional affairs, without having to worry about becoming subordinated to one neighbor or the other, or without having to sacrifice its independence of action to dependence upon a distant hegemonic power, such as the United States, in order to preserve its international integrity. While such a situation may still be more a policy goal than a realty, it does represent a viable option for a nation that has served as a buffer in international politics for more than two centuries.

NOTES

1. For a general summary of Uruguayan history, see Russell H. Fitzgibbon, *Uruguay: Portrait of a Democracy* (New Brunswick, N.J: Rutgers University Press, 1954); George Pendle, *Uruguay,* 3rd ed. (New York: Oxford University Press, 1965); and Philip B. Taylor, Jr., *Government and Politics of Uruguay* (New Orleans: Tulane University Studies in Political Science, 1960). For greater detail, see Juan E. and Alcira Pivel Devoto, *Historia de la republica oriental del Uruguary 1830-1930* (Montevideo: Editorial Medina, 1945), and Alberto Zum Felde, *Proceso historico del Uruguay,* (Montevideo: Arca, 1967).

2. Fitzgibbon, *op.cit.,* p. 10.

3. The most accessible treatment of these events is John Street, *Artigas and the Emancipation of Uruguay* (New York: Cambridge University Press, 1959). For a geopolitical interpretation of the period, see Anibal Abadie Aicardi and Oscar Abadie Aicardi, *Portugueses and Brasilenos. Hacia el Rio de la Plata; un informe geopolitico (1816)* (Recife: Pool Editorial, 1977).

4. Calixto Armas Barea, et. al., *El Rio de la Plata: Analisis del Tratado Sobre Limites Fluviales y Frente Maritimo en la Perspectiva de Argentina y Uruguay* (Santiago: Instituto de Estudios Internacionales, Universidad de Chile, Serie de publicaciones especiales, no. 18, 1976).

5. Bernado Quagliotti de Bellis and Victor Chamorro, *Uruguay y su espacio. Antecedentes y una propuesta* (Montevideo: Geosur, 1979).

6. On the life and times of Batille, see Milton I. Vanger, *Jose Batlle y Ordonez of Uruguay: The Creator of His Times* (Cambridge, MA: Harvard University Press, 1963); and his *The Model Country: Jose Batlle y Ordonez of Uruguay, 1907-1915* (Hanover, NH: The University Press of New England, 1980). Also, see G.G. Lindahl, *Uruguay's New Path: A Study in Politics During the First Colegiado, 1919-1933* (Stockholm: Library and Institute of Ibero-American Studies, 1962).

7. Peter E. Winn, "Uruguay and British Economic Expansion, 1880-1893," Unpublished Ph.D Thesis, Cambridge University, 1972; J.P. Baran and B. Nahum, *La historia rural del Uruguay moderno* 7 vols (Montevideo: Ediciones de la Banda Oriental, 1967-78); and, on the consolidation of the state around an economic and political plan, Oscar Oszlak, *La formacion del estado argentino* (Buenos Aires: Editorial de Belgrano, 1982).

8. Raul Jacob, *El Frigorifico Macional en el Mercado de Carnes* (Montevideo: Fundacion de Cultura Universitaria, 1979): Simon G. Hanson, *Utopia in Uruguay* (New York: Oxford University Press, 1938); and M.H. J. Finch, *A Political Economy of Uruguay Since 1870* (New York: St. Martin's Press, 1981).

9. Jaime Klaczko and Juan Rial, *Uruguay, el pais urbano* (Montevideo: Ediciones de la Banda Oriental, 1981).

10. Arthur P. Whitaker, *The United States and the Southern Cone* (Cambridge, MA: Harvard University Press, 1976). See, also, Oscar Abadie Aicardi, *El Uruguay, Los EE. UU, y la Union Panamericana* (Montevideo: Impresora Cordon, 1969).

11. Eduardo Victor Haedo, *El Uruguay y la political internacional del rio de la Plata* (Buenos Aires: EUDEBA 1973), pp. 42-48.

12. Joseph S. Tulchin, "Two To Tango: From Independence to the Falklands/Malvinas Crisis, Argentina and U.S. Foreign Policies Have Been Out Of Step," *Foreign Service Journal,* vol. 59, no. 9 (October 1982).

13. Edy Kaufman, *Uruguay in Transition: From Civilian Military Rule* (New Brunswick, N.J.: Transition Books, (1979), pp. 11-12.

14. Interviews by the author with members of the Uruguayan Defense College and members of the School of Diplomatic Studies, Montevideo, October 10-13, 1983; Liliana De Riz, "Uruguay: la transicion desde una perspectiva comparada," Paper presented at the *Seminar on Democracy and Uruguay* (Washington, D.C.: The Woodrow Wilson Center, 1984); and Leonardo Molino, *Come campiano i regimi politici* (Milan: Franco Angeli Editore, 1980).

15. For a sample across the political spectrum, see, among others, Vivian Trias, *Uruguay y sus claves geopoliticas* (Montevideo: Ediciones de la Banda Oriental, 1972); Alberto Methol Ferre, *Geopolitica de la cuenca del Plata. El Uruguay como problema.* (Buenos Aires: A. Pena Lillo editor, 1973); Roberto Area Pons, *Uruguay: ?Provincia o nacion?;* (Montevideo: Ediciones del nuevo mundo, 1967); and Israel Wonsewer and Juan Young Casaravilla, *Uruguay en la Economia Mundial* (Montevideo, Centro Latinoamericano de Economia Humana, 1976).

16. See Bernardo Quagliotti de Bellis and Victor Chamorro, *Uruguay y su espacio. Antecedentes y una propuesta.* (Montevideo: Geosur, 1979)

CHAPTER 12
BUFFER STATES: OUTLINING
AND EXPANDING EXISTING THEORY

GERALD L. INGALLS

Technological change and the massive social, economic and political upheavals of independence and liberation movements of the past four decades have given rise to an extremely dynamic system of nation states. While many of the major players in the international system have remained relatively constant, a number of new, regional and international powers have emerged. In fact, one of the more significant changes in the international system has been in the number of total players involved. While a relatively small number of global and regional superpowers still dominates the international system, in terms of the sheer numbers of nation states alone, the system is markedly different from that which existed in the decades before 1945. This climate of change in the number and character of the players has demanded fresh appraisals of the models and concepts used to analyze, probe and explain the workings of the international system of nation states. In the chapters of this book the authors have addressed the need for reshaping and redefining one such concept - the buffer state.

There has been relatively little recent effort to augment the general body of knowledge on the buffer state. The dearth of research on buffer systems is linked to the advent of the nuclear age and space shortening technologies, particularly ICBM's and high speed, high-tech weaponry which brought in to question the need for buffer systems. Without doubt modern weapons systems and technologies and new political, economic and cultural alignments have drastically altered the international political system. In the vacuum surrounding the withdrawal of classic international power brokers, particularly colonial powers, from some theaters of international drama, many of the classic, traditional buffers have undergone significant changes or even disappeared altogether. In the face of recent economic and political unification movements in Western Europe the need for traditional buffer states such as Belgium, the Netherlands and Luxembourg has been drastically reduced. In other situations buffers have undergone or are currently experiencing significant change; consider the examples of Korea, Eastern Europe and Afghanistan. Still other buffer states and systems have recently emerged; consider the examples developed in this book - South Africa, the Caribbean and Lebanon. However, as is made very clear by the examples offered in these essays, buffers remain important tools of international relations. Equally clear is the need, in the face of sweeping changes in the international system, to approach the issue of buffers from fresh, innovative directions.

To this end the authors of chapters in this text addressed four key objectives: a definition of what is meant by buffers; an analysis of the structure and functions of buffer states/systems; an elaboration of existing theory of buffer states/systems; and a demonstration of the directions in which it is possible to move with new elements of the theory of buffer states. The essays in this text demonstrate that if the concept of buffer states is to remain a viable tool for the analysis of international politics and international relations it is essential that the definition of buffers be clearly elucidated and expanded. Just as the relationship between states is dynamic so must be the concepts with which we consider these relationships. While in practice buffer states may remain viable and functional elements of international relations, without the type of redefinition offered in these essays the concept of buffer systems could well be relegated to the exclusive use of historians.

This chapter outlines the major elements of the definition of buffers which has emerged in the articles and case studies presented in this book. This definition has been predicated on the collective restatement of the classic concept of buffer states offered in the chapters of this book. However, these authors have not simply offered case studies to demonstrate the continuing viability of the buffer state concept in the 1980s; they have also demonstrated the need for careful reappraisal and expansion of certain dimensions of the classic definition of buffers. Hence this chapter attempts to address both the changes in the classic theory of buffer states and the new directions for future research on buffer states the authors have advocated or implied.

A CLASSIC DEFINITION OF A BUFFER STATE

The basic definitions of a buffer state offered by Potter (1930), Spykman (1942), Mathisen (1971), Partem (1983), or any of the authors in this text were posited over a period of five decades yet there is remarkably little difference among them.[1] A general, basic definition of a buffer state with which each of these individuals might agree would likely begin with the proposition that a buffer state is a small political or administrative unit located between and separating two larger opposing powers.

Clearly, for any systematic and functional evaluation of the character of specific buffer states or of the relationship among the buffer and the two opposing powers it buffers, much greater operational detail is required. Such an operational definition involves elaborating on several parts of the basic definition. First, recognizing that the buffer does not exist as an independent entity, it is necessary to define the major components of the system of which the buffer is a part. Second, it is necessary to specify more completely the characteristics of the two larger opposing powers. Third, it is necessary to specify the characteristics of the buffer state. Finally, it is necessary to address the relationship which exists among the parts of the system.

THE BUFFER SYSTEM

In the chapter on Eastern Europe, Olav Knudsen summarizes the terminology which can be used to address the components of a buffer system. He distinguishes among buffer zones or areas, buffer systems and buffer states. Buffer areas or zones are controlled by one or more small states and located between two opposing and much greater powers. The latter, the opposing powers, are in actual or eminent danger of conflict and, by virtue of their overwhelming political, military or economic size relative to a small contiguous state, these powers subsume a small nation state lying between them as a buffer to potential conflict. The complete collection of larger, opposing, but roughly equal powers and the smaller, contiguous buffer state is the buffer system. The relationship among the three elements of the buffer system determines the strength of the buffer effect or the degree to which the buffer state is resistant to "outside encroachments."

One consistently repeated characteristic of a buffer system involves the location of the two powers and the buffer state.

Thomas Ross emphasizes the importance of vicinal location or location with reference to the neighbors. Ross, in this volume, suggests that this location need not necessarily be contiguous but goes on to note that "the buffer state owes its existence to the location of two or more politically or militarily powerful spheres of influence with close proximity to one another." The importance of location is echoed in the articles by Chay, Jenkins and Maila. Each of these authors notes that in the classic definition of the buffer system the interpretation of this locational variable most often assumed the three major elements of the system were contiguous. The buffer state was literally assumed to lie "between" the two powers.

CHARACTERISTICS OF THE OPPOSING POWERS

Within the buffer system the opposing powers - those being buffered from one another - have certain characteristics in common and have a certain relationship to one another and to the buffer state. There is general agreement among the authors of this text that larger powers will, indeed must, have considerable size advantage over the buffer state, both in economic and military strength. As is noted in this book by Chay, if the buffer is sufficiently large and powerful it is an equal partner in the system, not a buffer. The two larger opposing states must be sufficiently more powerful than the buffer to impose their will upon it. The greater the relative power disparity between the small buffer state and the two larger powers, and the greater the degree of power parity between the larger powers, the stronger will be the buffer effect and the greater will be the stability of the buffer system. As long as there is relatively equal and constant pressure from both sides the buffer system will be maintained. Thus the two larger powers must be in contention one with the other and must each be committed to the maintenance of the buffer system. As is demonstrated in the essay by Jenkins, the British withdrawal from India eliminated the pressure from one side of the buffer system centered on Afghanistan. With no effective power to counter the Soviet influence, Afghanistan was pulled into the Soviet sphere. Under most circumstances the classic buffer system operates under the premise that there will be reasonable resistance to the absorbtion of the buffer by either of the powers. This resistance could, and as most of the chapters in this book suggest, come as a consequence of relative power parity between the larger powers.

CHARACTERISTICS OF THE BUFFER STATE

As is the case with the other elements of the buffer system, there seems to be general agreement on many of the overall characteristics which most buffer states hold in common. The variables which describe the buffer state appear to fall into several general categories. The characteristics of a buffer system seem to describe: 1) size, measured in economic, political or military strength and which is often summarized in terms of the degree of power disparity relative to the larger powers; 2) location, measured in terms of strategic position, physical or environmental features, strategic transportation routes or geopolitical position; and, 3) sovereignty, measured in terms of degree of autonomy and commitment to continued independence.

Size is one of the more critical elements of the buffer state concept. As Chay suggests in the article on Korea, size can be measured along a number of dimensions including various social, psycho-cultural, economic, political or military characteristics. In so far as the buffer state itself is concerned, the overriding issue is size relative to the two larger powers which are assumed to be disproportionately larger, or at least enough so that the buffer state must acquiesce to the creation and maintenance of the buffer system.

The relative size of the large powers and the buffer state becomes an issue in the level of dominance of one or both of the larger powers. There must be sufficient balance within the buffer system to maintain the buffer state. As Maila suggests, the issue of sovereignty is paramount; the buffer state must maintain its national sovereignty or its very existence as a state is threatened. Often, the buffer state seeks to maintain its sovereignty by maintaining a neutral position *vis-a-vis* the interplay between the two opposing powers within the buffer system. It seeks to maintain its independence and autonomy and, as Knudsen points out, the leadership of the buffer state must have a strong commitment to continuing and fostering the independence and autonomy of their state. Ultimately the success or failure of the buffer system depends in large measure on the balance of power between the two opposing states, their continued acceptance of the buffer state, the strength of the buffer state and its continued commitment to national autonomy and independence.

Another critical characteristic of the buffer state has to do with its location which is defined in several ways. As previously stated, location of the buffer state with reference to the two opposing powers can be a primary variable in the strength and durability of the buffer system. As Chay indicates, location can also be interpreted in a strategic sense not only in reference to the opposing powers but also to the other nations within the international system. In addition to external location factors Ross specifies a set of internal characteristics such as physical features - in particular difficult terrain or topography - and the presence of major transportation routes which may well contribute to the foundation and maintenance of a buffer state.

Location has historically been a vital characteristic of the buffer system. As is indicated time and time again with the examples introduced in the chapters of this book, conventional warfare of decades past often required two opposing powers to gain military access to one another directly across intervening territory. Hence, buffer states could literally separate opposing states. The argument some now have with the buffer state concept is often focused on the impact of space reducing technologies. While modern technology has eliminated the effectiveness of the physical, or spatial barrier, it has not reduced the need for the buffer state. To the contrary, the need may be even more acute. Without question, however, the way in which we view the buffer system must be modified to fit the political, economic and military circumstances of the 1980s.

NEW DIRECTIONS IN DEFINING THE BUFFER STATE

Just as the authors provide definition, restatement and elaboration of the classical concept of the buffer system, so do they open new vistas for buffer state research. Several of the most intriguing possibilities have to do with the most basic elements of the concept of the buffer state - the definition of what constitutes an opposing power, the relationship among the elements of the buffer system and the locational characteristics of the buffer state and the buffer system.

One of the overriding issues of the buffer system is its purpose or the reason for its existence. In the classic interpretation the buffer state is viewed as a national entity which separates the conflicting national interest of two relatively equal powers each of whom is considerably more powerful than the buffer state. Some of issues raised in the chapters of this book appear to challenge the classic view that buffer systems exist solely to mitigate conflicts in national aims. It is possible that a buffer might exist: to separate conflicting ideological aims (Albania); to separate conflicting cultural, ethnic, or racial groups (South Africa); to serve as a defensive zone (Lebanon); or even to act as economic bridge between nations (Uruguay).

In most of the classic works on buffer states it is assumed that the larger, more powerful states surrounding the buffer are indeed nation states possessing - as Ross describes them - all the characteristics of nations: people, territory, a distinctive homogeneous core which has organized an independent government to exercise sovereignty over the territory. Indeed from a historical perspective buffer systems have been composed of nation states. However, one of the most dynamic elements of international systems in recent decades has been the emergence of "states" which have most if not all of the characteristics of a nation state except perhaps a stable and permanent territorial base. In most instances these are "states" created by revolutionary, independence, liberation or resistance movements. Such revolutionary "states" most often operate in open hostility to the legally constituted government of a large power. As such these "states" function as the one of the opposing powers of the buffer system. In such cases the government of the nation against which the revolutionary or liberation movement is directed might well attempt to create a buffer state to blunt or eliminate the effect of the movement. The non-conventional buffer system of southern Africa described by Sheridan Johns is an intriguing glimpse of a complex buffer system created by South Africa to combat black nationalism in southern Africa. Another example of a non-conventional buffer system comes from the Israeli-Palestinian conflict described by Robert McColl. The Palestinian efforts to gain territory to accompany the other vestiges of statehood led to loss of neutrality, and, eventually, the sovereignty of Lebanon. In addition, efforts of the P.L.O. have led Israel to create a buffer zone along its border with Lebanon designed to protect areas of north Israel from Palestinian attacks. This buffer exists in an area of Lebanon controlled by the Southern Lebanese Army.

In each of these examples one of the large powers in the buffer system is a non-traditional state with no permanent territorial base. Nonetheless the buffer system which emerges plays the same role as that of a classic buffer system in which each of the elements is a traditional nation state. The major differences come in the expected life of the buffer system. One element of a non-conventional buffer system - the liberation, revolutionary or resistance movement - is committed to undermining not only the buffer area, zone or state created by the other, but also the opposing larger power itself. While the buffer system functions, the buffer is maintained by one of the powers and undermined by the other. Thus, unlike the classic buffer system in which both larger powers and the buffer state itself are committed to the maintenance of the system, this type of non-conventional buffer system has both larger powers committed to the destruction of the system. The liberation movement is committed to the destruction of the state it opposes; the state is committed to eliminating the need for the buffer by defeating the liberation movement.

A variation on the classic interpretation of the locational variable is outlined in the papers by Johns, Kelly and Tosches. Johns argues that the white majority in South Africa has developed not only a classic buffer system consisting of buffer states lying in a belt north of South Africa but also a set of internal buffers - black homelands. In this instance these buffers are intended not as a counter to a second powerful nation state lying outside and contiguous to the border of South Africa, but rather are intended to buffer South Africa from a political movement - black nationalism - which exists both within South Africa and also in the nation states contiguous to it.

In the chapter on Middle America, Kelly suggests that a hierarchical buffer system has emerged in Central America and the Caribbean and for at least one level of the hierarchy the locational - contiguity - criteria seems less critical to the functioning of the system. Kelly outlines the dimensions of a buffer zone consisting of Caribbean and Central American states which lies sandwiched between the non-contiguous states of the Soviet Union and the United States. Nested within this regional buffer system is a second zone of buffer states lying within Central America which separates the regional powers of Nicaragua and Guatemala. Of course, even in this second level of buffer states the United States and the Soviet Union are the primary powers.

Tosches cites an example of a buffer system in which the buffer, Albania, separates the states of China and the Soviet Union. In this instance the buffer system has an ideological, rather than a nationalistic base. The physical location of the powers is not as much of a factor as is the ideological location.

The South African, Middle American and Albanian examples serve notice of the need for flexibility in addressing the locational component of buffer systems. As is demonstrated by the examples of Lebanon, Afghanistan before 1945, and Uruguay, contiguity can be a critical component of strong buffer systems. However, space shortening technologies, the struggles of one ideology against another or the actions of liberation and revolutionary movements against national governments may produce buffer systems in which physical location in general and contiguity in particular is not necessarily a critical element in understanding the functioning of the buffer system. Given the frequency with which such ideological or revolutionary conflicts have occurred in recent times there exists a bountiful supply of examples on which to base a careful reappraisal of the locational variable in buffer systems.

SUMMARY AND CONCLUSIONS

The definition of buffer states which emerges from the essays of this book is multi-dimensional, broad-based and well founded in the classic dimension of what constitutes a buffer state. Clearly, most elements of the classic definition of what constitutes a buffer state remain as viable, even critical components around which to build a conceptual foundation for analyzing buffer systems. The classic definition of a buffer system and a buffer state fit well the role played by many states in the community of nations today. However, as the authors of these chapters suggest, it may well be necessary to broaden the context under which buffer systems emerge and are maintained.

The two primary areas in which the concept of buffer states and systems must be broadened and redefined have to do with the locational criteria for buffer systems and the question of non-traditional buffer states and opposing powers. Clearly, in the context of buffer systems, location can no longer be confined to physical or environmental characteristics. Location must be broadened to encompass economic, geopolitical and ideological dimension as well. Furthermore, if the concept of the buffer state is to remain a functional tool in the analysis of international systems, it must be redefined to meet the circumstances of current methods of international conflict resolution. Certainly, ideological conflict, wars of liberation, revolution or independence and movements to establish cultural, racial or ethnic autonomy or identity are critical elements of the current international system. As is indicated by the research presented in several chapters of this book, buffer systems emerge to mitigate such non-conventional conflicts as well as those induced by conflicting national aims. Since it is possible to argue that such conflicts are the exception and more the rule of the current international system, there are many examples on which modifications of existing concepts of buffer systems may be based. Continued research is necessary to gauge the components of such non-conventional buffer systems and to effectively meld these to classic concepts of the buffer state.

NOTES

1. Trygve Mathisen, *The Functions of Small States in the Strategies of the Great Powers.* Oslo, Universitetsforlaget, 1971; Michael Partem, "The Buffer System in International Relations, *Journal of Conflict Resolution,* 27 (1983):3-26; Pitman B. Potter, "Buffer State", *Encyclopedia of Social Science,* 1930; and Nicholas J. Spykman, "Frontier, Security, and International Organization," *Geographical Review,* 32 (1942):436-447.

ABOUT THE CONTRIBUTORS

John Chay was educated at Yunsei University (Seoul, Korea), and earned his B.A., M.A., and Ph.D. from the University of Michigan. He has studied and conducted postdoctoral research at Stanford University. He is professor of history and serves as Chairman of the Department of History at Pembroke State University. Much of his current research is concerned with Korean-United States relations and he has published *The Problems and Prospects of American-East Asian Relations,* Westview Press, 1977. He has written chapters in several books dealing with Korean/Asian - United States relations and has published in professional journals.

David B. Jenkins is presently a geographer with the United States Government. He was educated at Indiana University of Pennsylvania and the Pennsylvania State University. This chapter is based on his master's thesis at the Pennsylvania State University. His professional interests include political geography, toponymy, and paleontology.

Gerald L. Ingalls, is associate professor of geography at the University of North Carolina, Charlotte. Educated at the University of Southwestern Louisiana, University of Florida, and Michigan State University (PH.D.), his research interests include political geography, Middle East and North Africa, and electoral geography.

Sheridan Johns is a political scientist specializing in African politics. He completed his undergraduate educate at Amherst College and received his doctorate from Harvard University. Presently an associate professor of political science at Duke University, he also taught at Northwestern and Brandeis University as well as the University of Zambia. He is the co-editor of *Mining for Development in the Third World* and is the author of *From Protest to Hope, 1882-1934* (Volume 1 of *From Protest to Challenge: A Documentary Survey of African Politics in South Africa.* He has authored journal articles and book chapters dealing with politics in central and southern Africa.

Philip Kelly, associate professor of political science at Emporia State University (Kansas), received his graduate degrees from the University of Florida and the University of Nebraska. His primary research interests include general geopolitical theory and geopolitics of Latin America. He presently serves as secretary-treasurer of the Midwest Association of Latin America Studies and co-authors the Fitzgibbon-Johnson Image-Index survey of Latin America democracy. He has published numerous articles in professional journals.

Olav Knudsen since 1971 has been affiliated with the Department of Political Science, University of Oslo and since 1984 has been visiting professor, University of Kentucky. He was educated at the University of Oslo and the University of Denver. He has conducted research on transnational relations and his publications include *The Politics of International Shipping,* Lexington Books, 1973.

Joseph Maila is professor of political sciences and political philosophy at the Faculte' des Sciences Humaines (Social Sciences) of the Universite' Joseph of Beyrouth (Lebanon) where he is also the Vice-Dean. He has been several times visiting professor in Paris (France) and in Laval (Canada) and has given conferences in many countries of Europe and North America. He is mainly interested in politics of the Middle East and has been writing extensively on the Lebanese issue, violence and political regimes in the area.

Robert W. McColl is professor of geography and East Asian Studies at the University of Kansas (Lawrence). His Ph.D. was awarded by the University of Washington. He has field experience in approximately two dozen countries of Asia, Southeast Asia, Southwest Asia and Europe. His book *Coping with Natural Environments,* with Glen Marotz, was published in 1982 by Kendall-Hunt Publishing Company. Professor McColl is the author of several journal articles and book chapters dealing with political geography and has research interests and the definitions and applications of military geography.

Thomas E. Ross is professor of geography and Chairman of the Department of Geology and Geography at Pembroke State University. He served in various overseas posts while a member of the United States Air Force (1960-1964). Educated at Marshall University and the University of Tennessee (Ph.D., 1977), Ross has research interests in cultural and regional geography. He is the author of a regional atlas and has published journal articles dealing with historical, economic, and environmental geography. He is currently editing a book focusing on the cultural geography of North American Indians.

Albert M. Tosches is assistant professor of geography at Salem (Massachusetts) State College. He has doctoral work at the University of Washington and received his master's from Boston University. His undergraduate degree was granted by the University of Chicago. Most of his research has emphasized Albania and Yugoslavia.

Joseph S. Tulchin is professor of history and Director of the International Studies Program at the University of North Carolina, Chapel Hill. Prior to assuming his present position, he was on the faculty at Yale University. His undergraduate education was taken at Amherst. He studied at Harvard and Cambridge for his M.A. and Ph.D. degrees. A student of Latin American international relations and Latin America - United States relations, he is the author of *Aftermath of War: The Latin American Policy of the United States, 1918-1925* (New York University Press, 1971) and co-author of *Latin American Nations and World Politics* (Westview Press, 1984).

Lawrence Ziring is Director of the Institute of Government and Politics and professor of political science at Western Michigan University. The research for this chapter was conducted during his tenure as Fellow and Senior Research Office, Oxford University, in 1984. His research interests are in the area of international politics and foreign policy with special focus on Asia and the Middle East. He is the author/editor of ten books, the most recent being *The Asian Political Dictionary,* with C.I.E. Kim in 1985. Professor Ziring's Ph.D. was earned at Columbia University in Political Science.

INDEX